JAPAN IDEABOOK

BELVEDERE

JAPAN

DESIGNS FROM KIMONO MOTIFS · GRAPHIC – FLORAL – GEOMETRIC

IDEABOOK

ARRANGED AND EDITED BY WOLFGANG HAGENEY

BELVEDERE

EDITION BELVEDERE CO. LTD., ROME - MILAN (ITALY)

BELVEDERE DESIGNBOOK

FASHION
TEXTILES
GRAPHIC
DESIGNS
VOLUME 25

JAPAN IDEABOOK

PUBLISHED BY
EDITION BELVEDERE CO. LTD.
ROME-MILAN (ITALY)

© COPYRIGHT 1987
BY EDITION BELVEDERE SRL

PRINTED IN ITALY BY
STUDIO TIPOGRAFICO, ROME
PHOTOLITHOGRAPHY BY
COLOR SEPARATIONS BY
BELVEDERE LABORATORIES, ROME
LAYOUT, GRAPHIC DESIGN
& TYPE SETTING BY
STUDIO BELVEDERE, ROME
ART DIRECTOR: HWH & BVR

PRINT PRODUCTION: MARCELLO CARMELLINI
STUDIO PRODUCTION: ROSA LENGSFELD
EDITOR & PUBLISHER: WOLFGANG H. HAGENEY

EDITION BELVEDERE CO. LTD.
00196 ROME/ITALY, PIAZZALE FLAMINIO, 19
TEL. (06) 360.44.88/360.29.60

ISBN 88-7070-075-5

Are you on the search for the land of the rising sun, in which geishas celebrate...

...the art of Zen in little tea-houses in the midst of charmingly laid-out ornamental gardens, or deferentially entertain by traditional performances, dressed in richly colored and ornamented silk kimonos; the land in which fiercely determined samurais, full of pride and dignity, sacrificially take their own life at the slightest glimmering of personal defeat? Are you on the search for the land of the eternal cherry-blossom which seems to enchant everything with its scent? If you are, you will experience disappointment: for even in Japan these are realities which have long ceased to exist. Only in films or in books can such long-vanished times be brought back to life once again.

Yet if you want to feel at least a breath of that exciting and bewitching cherry-blossom fragrance, and penetrate the pictorial and conceptual world of that Far-Eastern island empire which is still so firmly rooted in traditions and above all in our imagination, at least in part, like the fairy-tales of early childhood, then you will have to immerse yourself in a multiplicity of details, in those important details in which the Japanese were always such consummate masters. Perhaps it is just here that lies the key by which we can gain access to that piece of legend that we Europeans now and again so urgently need in order to enliven and enrich our imaginative powers with new illusions, and with exotic and alluring images.

And even though the patterns and motifs illustrated here form only background material for this Japanese tradition, a few little fragments of it do nonetheless come into play. Those so important decorative gems of craftsmanship which first gave rise to the fame for consummate perfection, for the attention to even the smallest detail.

The ornament, the decorative, the world of motifs, the arrangement, the nuances of colors: all these were elementary prerequisites which played so essen-

tial a role in the formal process of creating Japanese art products. Whether in the art of gardening, in the tea ceremony, in Zen meditation, in the Kabuki theatre, in the manufacture of kimonos or also in the field of the arts and crafts: it is the tendency towards perfection in craftsmanship, towards the autonomous mastery over material and matter, that yields the sum of what we marvel at in astonishment as the result, as perfect harmony and inner balance. And not infrequently do we ask ourselves in wonder whether the result was really worth all the effort and expenditure put into it. Yet this tiresome question does not trouble the Japanese. For them, it is the means that constitutes the result, and not the end product.

What so immensely impresses is often, besides, on closer inspection, only a multiplicity of small details which operate perfectly and are executed in a masterly way. And the mastery over the material is nearly always based on an enormous skill in craftsmanship. What often seems to form a sophisticated "work of art", and to leave on us so astonishing a total impression, is not so much stamped by an universal genius, as by the use or combination of tiny individual procedures which are mainly very simple in nature. It is part of their mentality and conception, moreover, that they are endowed with an almost natural tendency to survive, as if no problems of changing times and tastes, no trends or fashion phenomena existed.

The world of pictures and motifs that springs from the imagination of Japanese masters or craftsmen, is a world of stoic composure and inner peace. It is a world that knows no artifice, no ideological superstructure, no metamorphoses and no dialectical leaps. It is deeply rooted in the world of everyday objects, in the preoccupation with earning one's daily bread, or is inspired by nature and its seasons. Continuously recurring themes are bamboos and pines, which with their evergreen forces of life have provided a rich treasury of motifs since time immemorial. Flora and fauna have been a boundless source of inspiration in representational art. The pattern of the tortoise shell has thus always exerted a quite particular fascination on the Japanese artist, just as have fans or umbrellas, straw hats or similar motifs. Japanese landscapes, rivers and above all the ocean are favourite subjects which constantly recur on the utilitarian objects of daily life. Fish and seafood are in this respect just as much of central importance as the holy mountain Fujiyama.

Cut off from other cultures and essentially turned in on itself as a result of its island-character, a correspondingly simple, almost peasant-like kind of ornament developed in Japan. In innumerable small black and white patterns it still continues to be used for everyday kimono fabrics today.

Although the stream of ideas seems to be almost limitless and the often simple motifs sometimes appear poetic, even at times recalling the fairytale-like, the mode of representation nonetheless remains rather repetitive. The fascination it has is undoubtedly not based on the inspirational force of the Japanese spirit alone, but far rather on a closed world of ideas which with almost religious zeal, like a prayer-wheel, continuously suggests anew to the beholder a form of security, inner peace, constancy and endurance.

Sei alla ricerca del paese del sol levante, dove le geisha, in piccole case da té immerse in giardini di fiori, sistemati con amore, celebrano l'arte dello zen? Oppure le vuoi vedere nei loro kimono di seta dai colori sgargianti che dispensano, con reverente ossequio, trattenimenti con spettacoli dalle ricche tradizioni in cui fieri e dignitosi samurai si tolgono solennemente la vita con selvaggia determinazione al minimo sospetto di una personale sconfitta, anche se soltanto apparente? Sei alla ricerca del paese dagli eterni fiori di ciliegio, la cui fragranza sembra stregare ogni cosa? Allora rimarrai deluso, poichè persino in Giappone queste cose ormai non esistono più. Semmai i "tempi passati" rivivono nei film o nella letteratura.

Se vuoi comunque captare almeno un effluvio di quell'eccitante ed accattivante profumo di ciliegio in fiore e penetrare nel mondo di immagini e di idee di quell'impero insulare dell'Estremo Oriente, ancora così saldamente ancorato, almeno in parte, nelle tradizioni e specialmente nella nostra fantasia come le favole della prima infanzia, allora dovrai immergerti in una miriade di piccole cose, entrare in quei dettagli essenziali dei quali i Giapponesi sono sempre stati eminenti maestri. Forse è questa la chiave che dà accesso a quello scorcio di leggenda di cui noi Europei abbiamo urgente bisogno per stimolare ed arricchire la nostra immaginazione con nuove illusioni, con esotiche ed ammalianti raffigurazioni.

Sebbene i modelli e i motivi rappresentati in questo volume sono solo lo sfondo di quelle tradizioni giapponesi, occorre dare risalto ad alcuni campioni, rimarchevoli gioielli decorativi dell'artigianato artistico, che hanno prima di tutto dato origine alla fama di compiuta perfezione, di scrupolosa cura anche del più piccolo particolare.

Ornamento, decorazione, mondo dei motivi, disposizione, sfumature dei colori: ecco le premesse essenziali che hanno avuto un'importanza primaria nel processo di creazione della produzione artistica giapponese. Sia nell'arte di sistemare i giardini che nella cerimonia del tè o nella meditazione zen, sia nel teatro kabuki che nella confezione dei kimono o anche nell'arte applicata, la propensione a raggiungere la perfezione nel lavoro artigianale e l'autonoma padronanza del materiale e della materia, producono un insieme, una concordanza perfetta, un equilibrio interiore che ammiriamo con grande stupore. Non di rado ci chiediamo meravigliati se il risultato giustifica il dispendio e gli sforzi consentiti. Ma questo fastidioso interrogativo non tormenta affatto i Giapponesi, ai loro occhi il risultato non è il prodotto finito ma il cammino percorso.

Ciò che desta un'enorme impressione, osservando più da vicino, è spesso semplicemente una moltitudine di minuti dettagli che legano alla perfezione perchè sono stati eseguiti con arte. La padronanza dei mezzi è quasi sempre frutto di una straordinaria prestazione artigianale. La caratteristica di ciò che non di rado sembra prendere la forma di una raffinata "opera d'arte", suscitando in noi un'impressione d'insieme così sbalorditiva, non è tanto la genialità universale quanto piuttosto l'impiego o la sequenza di piccoli elementi isolati, in sé generalmente molto semplici. Risponde alla loro mentalità ed alla loro concezione il fatto di possedere un'inclinazione quasi ingenua alla sopravvivenza, come se non esistessero problemi di tempo di gusti, né tendenze o fenomeni di moda.

Il mondo delle immagini e dei motivi, scaturito dalla fantasia dei maestri o degli artigiani giapponesi, è un mondo di serenità stoica e di pace interiore, non conosce artifici, sovrastrutture ideologiche, metamorfosi o eccessi dialettici, ma è profondamente ancorato nel mondo delle cose di tutti i giorni, nelle preoccupazioni per il pane quotidiano, o si ispira alla natura e alle sue stagioni. Temi ricorrenti sono i bambù e i pini, che da tempi immemorabili, con il loro sempre verde vigore, forniscono un ricco tesoro di motivi. Flora e fauna hanno stimolato all'infinito la creazione rappresentativa, così il modello del guscio di tartaruga deve aver sempre esercitato un fascino del tutto particolare sugli artisti giapponesi, come anche i ventagli e gli ombrelli, i cappelli di paglia ed altri semplici oggetti. I paesaggi e i fiumi giapponesi, soprattutto il mare, sono soggetti prediletti che ritroviamo in permanenza sugli arnesi di uso quotidiano. Pesci e frutti di mare hanno la stessa estrema importanza della montagna sacra: il Fujiyama.

Isolato da ogni altra cultura, e quasi sempre chiuso su se stesso in ragione del suo carattere insulare, il Giappone, in funzione di questa realtà, ha sviluppato una sua arte ornamentale semplice e di stile quasi paesano. Trova ancora oggi un suo impiego in innumerevoli piccoli modelli monocromi per i tessuti del kimono.

Anche se il flusso delle idee sembra pressochè illimitato, ed i motivi spesso semplici, si ha qualche volta l'impressione di una poesia con richiami addirittura fiabeschi e la maniera di rappresentare rimane alquanto ripetitiva. Il fascino che ne scaturisce non si basa certo soltanto sulla forza ispiratrice dello spirito giapponese, ma piuttosto su un mondo di idee chiuso che, con zelo quasi religioso, suggerisce ripetutamente all'osservatore, come un mulino delle preghiere, una forma di sicurezza, di pace interiore, di permanenza e di longevità.

Bist du auf der Suche nach dem Land der aufgehenden Sonne, in dem Geishas in kleinen Teehäusern inmitten liebevoll angelegter Ziergärten die Kunst des Zens zelebrieren oder in seidenen und farbenprächtig geschmückten Kimonos durch traditionsreiche Darbietungen huldigungsvoll Zerstreuung spenden, wo wildentschlossene Samurais sich voller Stolz und Würde beim leisesten Schimmer einer auch nur scheinbaren, persönlichen Niederlage weihevoll selbst entleiben? Bist du auf der Suche nach dem Land der ewigen Kirschblüte, die mit ihrem Duft alles zu verzaubern scheint, so wird dir Enttäuschung widerfahren: denn selbst in Japan sind dies längst keine Realitäten mehr. Allenfalls in Filmen oder in Büchern lassen sich solch versunkene Zeiten noch einmal zum Leben erwecken.

Doch willst du wenigstens einen Hauch jenes erregenden und betörenden Kirschblütenduftes spüren, eindringen in die Bilder- und Ideenwelt jenes fernöstlichen Inselreiches, das in den Überlieferungen und vor allem in unserer Phantasie wenigstens teilweise noch so fest verankert ist wie die Märchen aus der frühen Kindheit, so wirst du dich in eine Vielzahl von Kleinigkeiten versenken müssen, in jene wichtigen Einzelheiten, in denen die Japaner schon immer erhabene Meister waren. Vielleicht liegt hier der Schlüssel, der uns Zugang verschafft zu jenem Stück Legende, das wir Europäer hin und wieder so dringend benötigen, um unsere Vorstellungskraft mit neuen Illusionen, mit exotischen Reizbildern zu beleben und zu bereichern.

Wenngleich die hier gezeigten Muster und Motive auch nur Hintergrundmaterial für die japanische Tradition bilden, so sollen dabei doch einige wenige Fragmente zur Geltung kommen; jene so wichtigen, dekorativen Kleinode des Kunsthandwerks, die die Fama von der vollendeten Perfektion und von der Beachtung auch des nur kleinsten Details erst aufkommen ließen.

Das Ornament, das Dekorative, die Welt der Motive, das Arrangement, die Nuancen der Farben: all dies waren elementare Voraussetzungen, die beim Gestaltungsprozeß japanischer Kunstprodukte eine so wesentliche Rolle spielten. Ob in der Gartenkunst, bei der Teezeremonie, der Meditation im Zen, dem Kabukitheater, dem Herstellen von Kimonos oder auch im Bereich des Kunstgewerbes: der Hang zur handwerklichen Vollendung, zur autonomen Beherrschung von Material and Materie, ergibt die Summe dessen, was wir verblüffend als Resultat, als perfekte Harmonie und innere Ausgeglichenheit bestaunen. Oft fragen wir uns verwundert, ob das Ergebnis denn den Aufwand und die Mühe gelohnt habe. Doch den Japaner plagt diese leidige Frage nicht. Für ihn ist der Weg das Ergebnis und nicht das Endprodukt.

Was beim näheren Hinsehen dann auch so immens beeindruckt, ist oft nur eine Vielzahl kleiner Einzelheiten, die perfekt ablaufen und gekonnt ausgeführt wurden. Und der Beherrschung der Mittel liegt fast immer eine enorme handwerkliche Leistung zugrunde. Was sich nicht selten zu einem raffinierten "Kunstwerk" zu formen scheint und bei uns einen so verblüffenden Gesamteindruck hinterläßt, ist weniger geprägt von einer universalen Genialität, als vielmehr von der Verwendung oder Reihung kleiner Einzelschritte, die in sich meistens sehr einfacher Natur sind. Es entspricht ihrer Mentalität und ihrer Konzeption, daß sie mit einem fast unverfänglichen Hang zum Überleben ausgestattet sind, als gäbe es keine Zeit- und Geschmacksprobleme, keine Trends oder Modeerscheinungen.

Die Bilder- und Motivwelt, die der Phantasie der japanischen Meister oder Kunsthandwerker entspringt, ist eine Welt stoischer Gelassenheit und innerer Ruhe. Sie kennt keine Kunstgriffe, keinen ideologischen Überbau, keine Metamorphosen und keine dialektischen Sprünge. Sie ist tief verwurzelt in der Dingwelt des Alltags, in der Sorge um das tägliche Brot oder inspiriert von der Natur und ihren Jahreszeiten. Ständig wiederkehrende Themen sind der Bambus oder die Pinie, die mit ihren immergrünen Lebenskräften seit Gedenken einen reichen Motivschatz liefern. Unbegrenzt haben Flora und Fauna zu Darstellungen angeregt. Das Muster des Schildkrötenpanzers muß dabei stets eine ganz besondere Faszination auf die japanischen Künstler ausgeübt haben, ebenso wie Fächer oder Schirme, Strohhüte oder ähnlich Simples. Landschaften, Flüsse und vor allem das Meer sind bevorzugte Sujets, die sich fortdauernd auf Gebrauchsgegenständen des täglichen Lebens wiederfinden. Fische und Meeresfrüchte sind dabei ebenso von zentraler Bedeutung wie der heilige Berg, der Fudschijama.

Abgeschlossen von allen Kulturen und durch den Inselcharakter im wesentlichen auf sich selbst gestellt, hat sich in Japan eine entsprechend einfache, fast bäuerlich wirkende Ornamentik entwickelt. In unzählig kleinen Monochrom-Mustern findet sie noch heute für Kimonostoffe Verwendung.

Obwohl der Ideenstrom schier unbegrenzt zu sein scheint und die oft sehr schlichten Motive manchmal poetisch anmuten, nicht selten sogar ans Märchenhafte erinnern, bleibt die Darstellungsweise eher repetitiv. Die Faszination, die sich einstellt, basiert sicher nicht allein auf der inspirativen Kraft japanischen Geistes, als vielmehr auf der geschlossenen Ideenwelt, die in fast religiösem Eifer ständig aufs neue, Gebetsmühlen gleich, dem Betrachter eine Form der Sicherheit, der inneren Ruhe, der Beständigkeit und der Langlebigkeit suggeriert.

¿Buscas el país de sol naciente, donde las geishas, en pequeñas casas de té, rodeadas de jardines floridos cultivados con amor, celebran el arte Zen; o bien envueltas en sus kimonos de seda de llamativos colores, conceden con reverente deferencia, pasatiempos con espectáculos de ricas tradiciones, en las que soberbios samurai se suicidan solemnemente con salvaje determinación ante la más mínima sospecha de una derrota personal? ¿Buscas el país de las eternas flores de cerezo, cuya fragancia parece embrujar todo? Si algo de ésto buscas, te desilucionarás: Si bien todo ello continúa vivo en la literatura y en el cine, en el mismo Japón ya no existe.

Pero si de todas maneras deseas captar por lo menos un efluvio de aquel excitante y cautivante perfume de cerezo en flor, y entrar en el mundo de imágenes e ideas de aquel imperio insular del Extremo Oriente, aún hoy fuertemente anclado en las tradiciones, y sobre todo en nuestra fantasía, como las fábulas de nuestra primera infancia, entonces deberás sumergirte en una miriades de cosas: en esos detalles esenciales de los que los japoneses fueron siempre enminentes maestros. Posiblemente sea ésta la clave que permita acceder a ese escorzo de leyenda de la cual nosotros europeos tenemos urgente necesidad para estimular y enriquecer nuestra imaginación con nuevas ilusiones y exóticas representaciones.

Aunque los modelos y motivos representados en este volumen son solamente un fondo de aquellas tradiciones japonesas, es necesario poner en relieve algunos modelos; destacar joyas decorativas de la artesanía artística que dieron origen a la fama de acabada perfección, de escrupulosa atención de los más mínimos detalles.

Ornamento, decoración, mundo de motivos, disposición, matices de colores:

tales las premisas esenciales que protagonizaron el proceso creativo de la producción artística japonesa. Ya sea en el arte de la jardinería, en la ceremonia del té, en la meditación Zen, en el teatro kabuki, en la confección del kimono y en el arte aplicado, la tendencia a alcanzar la perfección en el trabajo artesanal, sumada a la maestría en la elaboración y conocimiento del material y la materia, producen un todo, una concordancia perfecta, un equilibrio interior que admiramos con estupor. Y, con frecuencia, nos preguntamos maravillados si el resultado justifica el notable esfuerzo realizado. Nuestra duda no les preocupa a los japoneses. Para ellos el resultado no es el producto terminado sino el camino recorrido.

Lo que realmente impresiona, mirando atentamente de cerca, es la cantidad de minúsculos detalles que se corresponden perfectamente. El dominio de los medios es casi siempre el fruto de una extraordinaria dedicación artesanal. La característica de lo que generalmente parece tomar la forma de una refinada "obra de arte", provocando en nosotros una sorprendente impresión global, no es tanto una genialidad universal sino más bien el empleo o la secuencia de pequeños elementos aislados, de por sí muy simples. Responde a su mentalidad y concepción el hecho de poseer una inclinación casi ingenua hacia la supervivencia, como si no existieran problemas de tiempo y de gusto, ni tendencias o fenómenos de moda.

El mundo de las imágenes y motivos fluyentes de la fantasía de los maestros y artesanos japoneses, es un mundo de estoica serenidad y paz interior. No concede artificios, sobreposición de estructuras ideológcas, metamorfosis ni eccesos dialécticos. Está profundamente radicado en el mundo de las cosas cotidianas, en la procupación del pan diario, o se inspira en la naturaleza y sus estaciones. Temas frecuentes son el bambú y los pinos que, desde tiempos inmemoriales, dan lugar a un rico tesoro de motivos. La flora y la fauna estimulan infinitamente la creación representativa. De esta manera, la caparazón de la tortuga debe haber ejercitado siempre un especial encanto en los artistas japoneses, como así también los abanicos y los paraguas, los sombreros de paja y otros objetos simples. Los paisajes y los ríos japoneses, y sobre todo el mar, son sujetos predilectos que encontramos permanentemente en utensilios de uso diario. Peces y mariscos adquieren tanta importancia como la montaña sagrada, el Fujiyama.

Aislado de cualquier otra cultura, está casi siempre cerrado en sí mismo en razón de su caracter insular. En función de esta realidad, el Japón ha desarrollado un arte ornamentalmente simple y de estilo casi aldeano. Aún hoy encuentra lugar en inumerables pequeños modelos para tejidos del kimono cotidiano.

Si bien el flujo de ideas parece ser ilimitado, y los motivos simples dan, a veces, la impresión de una poesía con perfiles de fábula, la manera de representar es repetitiva. El encanto que de ella emana no está basado solamente en la fuerza inspiradora del espíritu japonés, sino más bien en un mundo hermético de ideas que, con celo casi religioso, sugiere repetidamente al observador, como un molino de plegarias, una forma de seguridad, de paz interior, de permanencia y de longevidad.

Es-tu à la recherche du pays du soleil levant, où des geishas, dans de petites maisons de thé au milieu de jardins d'agrément aménagés avec amour, célèbrent l'art du zen, ou encore, dans leurs kimonos en soie aux couleurs somptueuses, distraient leurs hôtes, en hommage respectueux, avec des spectacles riches en traditions, où de fiers et dignes samouraïs se suicident solennellement au moindre soupçon de défaite personnelle, ne fut-elle qu'apparente? Si tu recherches le pays des fleurs de cerisier éternelles, dont la senteur semble ensorceler tout ce qui les entoure, attends-toi à être déçu: car même au Japon, ces choses ont cessé d'être une réalité. Tout au plus, les temps révolus revivent-ils encore dans les films et dans la littérature.

Mais si tu désires avoir au moins un soupçon de cette odeur de fleurs de cerisier, si excitante et envoûtante, et pénétrer dans le monde d'images et d'idées de cet empire insulaire d'Extrême-Orient, encore si solidement ancré, au moins en partie, dans les traditions et surtout dans notre fantaisie, comme les fables de notre tendre enfance, tu devras alors te plonger dans une multitude de petits riens, dans ces détails si importants où les Japonais ont toujours été des maîtres éminents. Ici se trouve peut-être la clé qui donne accès à ce fragment de légende dont nous, Européens, avons tant besoin pour stimuler et enrichir notre imagination de nouvelles illusions et de figures exotiques captivantes.

Et même si les modèles et motifs présentés dans cet ouvrage ne constituent qu'une toile de fond de cette tradition japonaise, quelques exemples méritent d'être mis en valeur; entre autres, ces remarquables joyaux décoratifs de l'artisanat artistique qui ont tout d'abord créé la réputation de perfection accomplie, de minutie dans l'exécution du moindre détail.

Ornement, art décoratif, monde des motifs, aménagement, nuances dans les couleurs: ce sont là les données essentielles qui ont joué un rôle si important dans le processus créatif des productions de l'art japonais. Qu'il s'agisse de jardin d'agrément, de cérémonie du thé, de méditation zen, de théâtre kabuki, de confection de kimonos, ou même d'art appliqué, le penchant à la perfection artisanale, à la maîtrise autonome du matériel et de la matière, a produit un ensemble dont nous admirons avec stupéfaction l'harmonie parfaite et l'équilibre intérieur. Et nous nous demandons souvent si le résultat justifie une telle prodigalité et de tels efforts. Mais cette question importune ne tourmente nullement les Japonais. Pour eux, c'est le chemin parcouru, et non pas le produit fini, qui est le résultat.

Vu de plus près, ce qui impressionne énormément, c'est souvent la multitude de petits détails qui s'ordonnent admirablement et qui ont été exécutés avec art. Et la maîtrise des moyens a presque toujours pour origine une extraordinaire performance artisanale. Ce qu'il n'est pas rare de voir prendre la forme d'une "oeuvre d'art" raffinée, et qui nous laisse une impression d'ensemble aussi étonnante, est marqué non pas tant par une génialité universelle que par l'emploi ou la succession d'éléments isolés, eux-mêmes généralement très simples. Le fait d'être doués d'une inclination presque ingénue à la survie, comme s'il n'existait aucun problème de temps ni de goût, aucune tendance ou phénomène de mode, répond à leur mentalité et à leur conception.

Le monde des images et des motifs issu de la fantaisie des maîtres et artisans japonais, est un monde de sérénité stoïque et de paix intérieure. Il ne connaît ni artifices, ni superstructures idéologiques, ni métamorphoses ni écarts dialectiques. Il est profondément enraciné dans le monde des choses de tous les jours, dans le souci du pain quotidien, ou alors il s'inspire de la nature et de ses saisons. Les thèmes qui reviennent constamment sont ceux des bambous ou des pins, dont l'éternelle vigueur fournit, depuis des temps immémoriaux, un trésor riche en motifs. La faune et la flore ont suggéré un nombre illimité de représentations. Ainsi, le modèle de la carapace de tortue doit avoir exercé de tous temps un charme très particulier sur les artistes japonais, de même que les éventails et les parapluies, les chapeaux de paille et autres objets courants. Les paysages et les fleuves, et surtout la mer, sont parmi les sujets préférés qu'on retrouve sans cesse sur les ustensiles d'usage quotidien. Poissons et fruits de mer ont une importance aussi grande que la montagne sacrée, le Fujiyama.

Isolé de toutes les cultures, et à peu près toujours livré à lui-même en raison de son caractère insulaire, le Japon, en fonction de cette réalité, a vu se développer un art de l'ornement très simple et d'un style presque paysan. Aujourd'hui encore, il trouve une application dans l'infinité de petits modèles monochromes pour les tissus des kimonos.

Même si le courant des idées est apparemment illimité, et si la simplicité des motifs donne parfois l'impression de la poésie, et fait même souvent penser aux contes de fée, le mode de représentation demeure plutôt répétitif. Le charme qui en découle ne se base pas uniquement sur la force d'inspiration de l'esprit japonais, mais particulièrement sur un monde d'idées fermé qui, avec un zèle presque religieux, suggère sans cesse à l'observateur, comme un moulin à prières, une forme de sécurité, de paix intérieure, de continuité et de longévité.

JAPAN IDEABOOK PART I
JAPAN MOTIFS

More than 200 intricate, sophisticated designs, deriving from the most intimate interrelation with Japanese art, represent mainly floral and graphic motifs. They are produced by the traditional crafts, in the majority of cases for decorative purposes.

Flora and fauna motifs, decorative ornamentation and geometric patterns express the Japanese simplified yet creative view of their every day life. What at first sight may seem to be merely a simplification of reality, is actually a highly sophisticated and careful study of the natural world, which then is transformed into an elaborate, abstract observation.

These designs are then applied to, among other things, fabrics and textiles, kimonos, gift wrapping paper, rice paper, book and print decoration, as well as in the adornment of the most varied kinds of commercial products.

The simple symbolism, the graphic clarity and the signal character of the motifs, their arrangement in rows reiteration, duplication or mirroring, their repeat or their symmetry, bear unmistakably the hallmarks of stamp or wood block printing, which suggests that they came into use very early.

We see in detail the Japanese world in this book through their graphic interpretation of a bird in flight, the bamboo gardens, the rolling of the waves and other similar visual encounters. Such decorative episodes reflect the high sensitivity to form of the Japanese ornamental style.

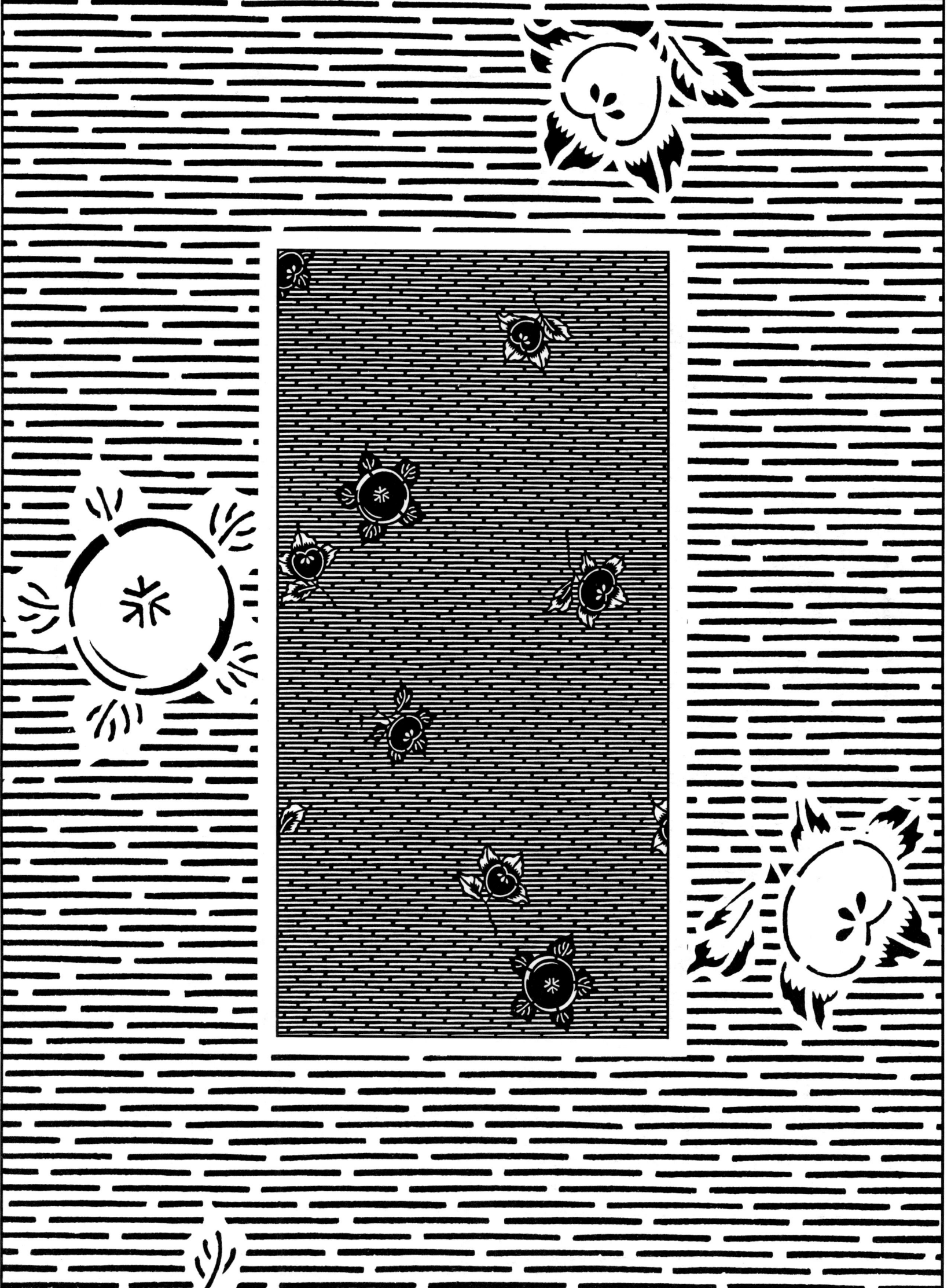

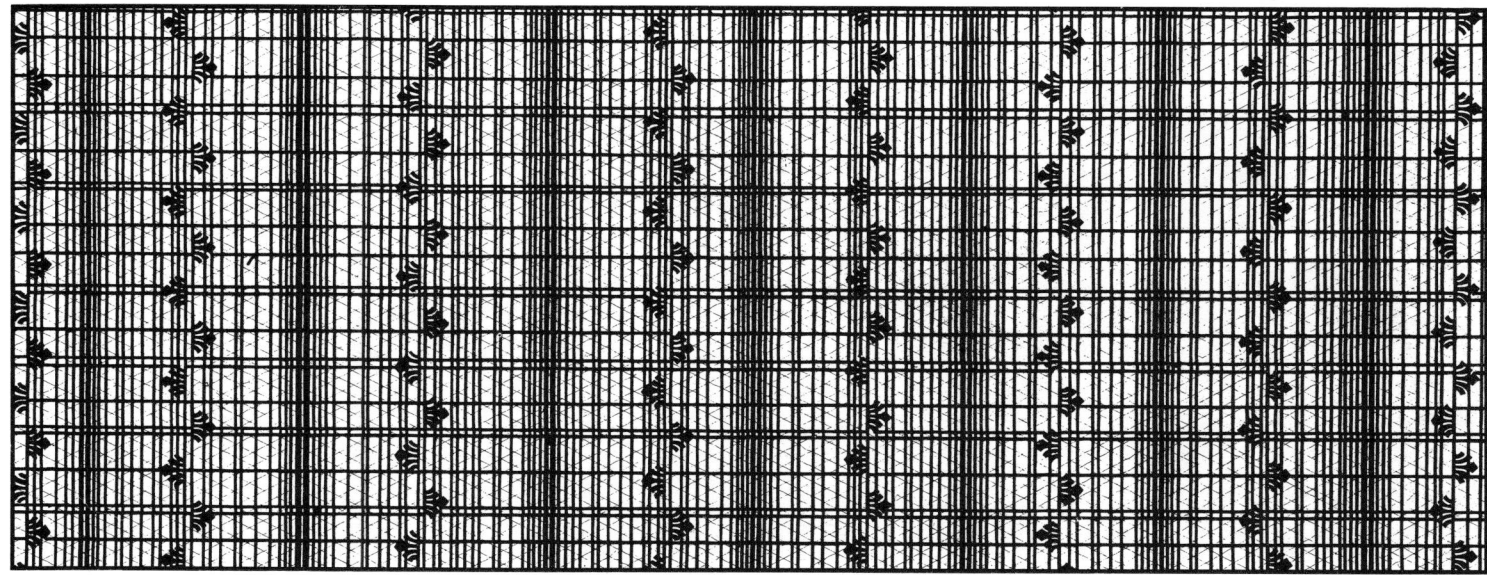

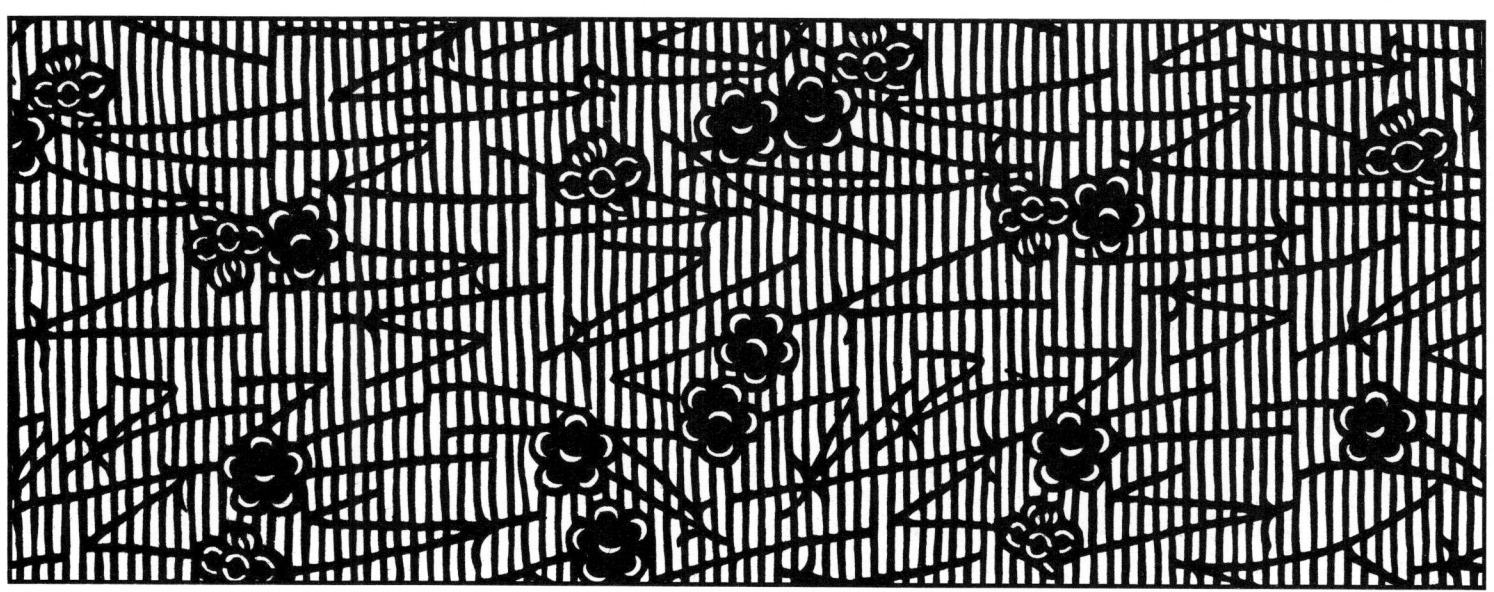

8

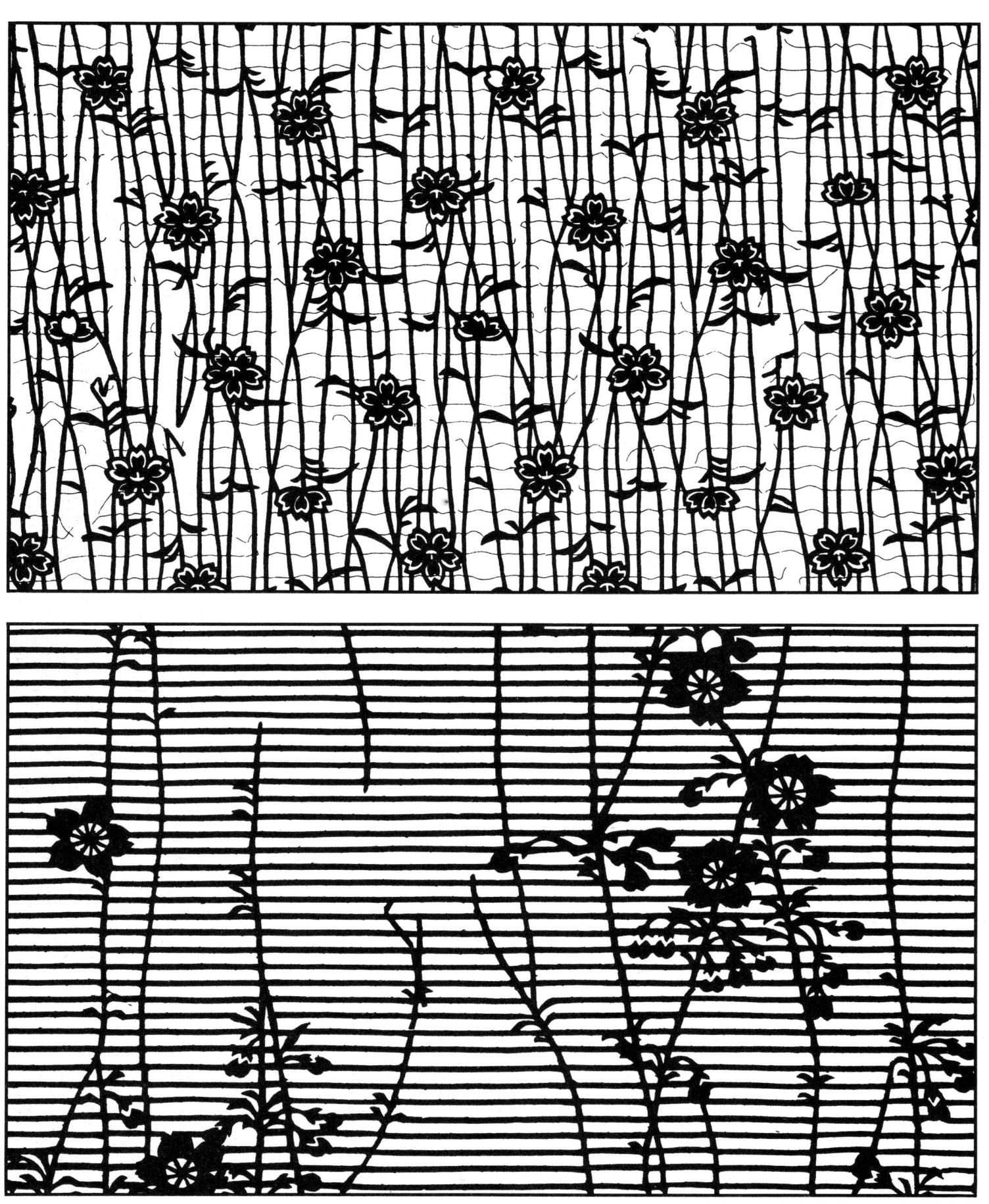

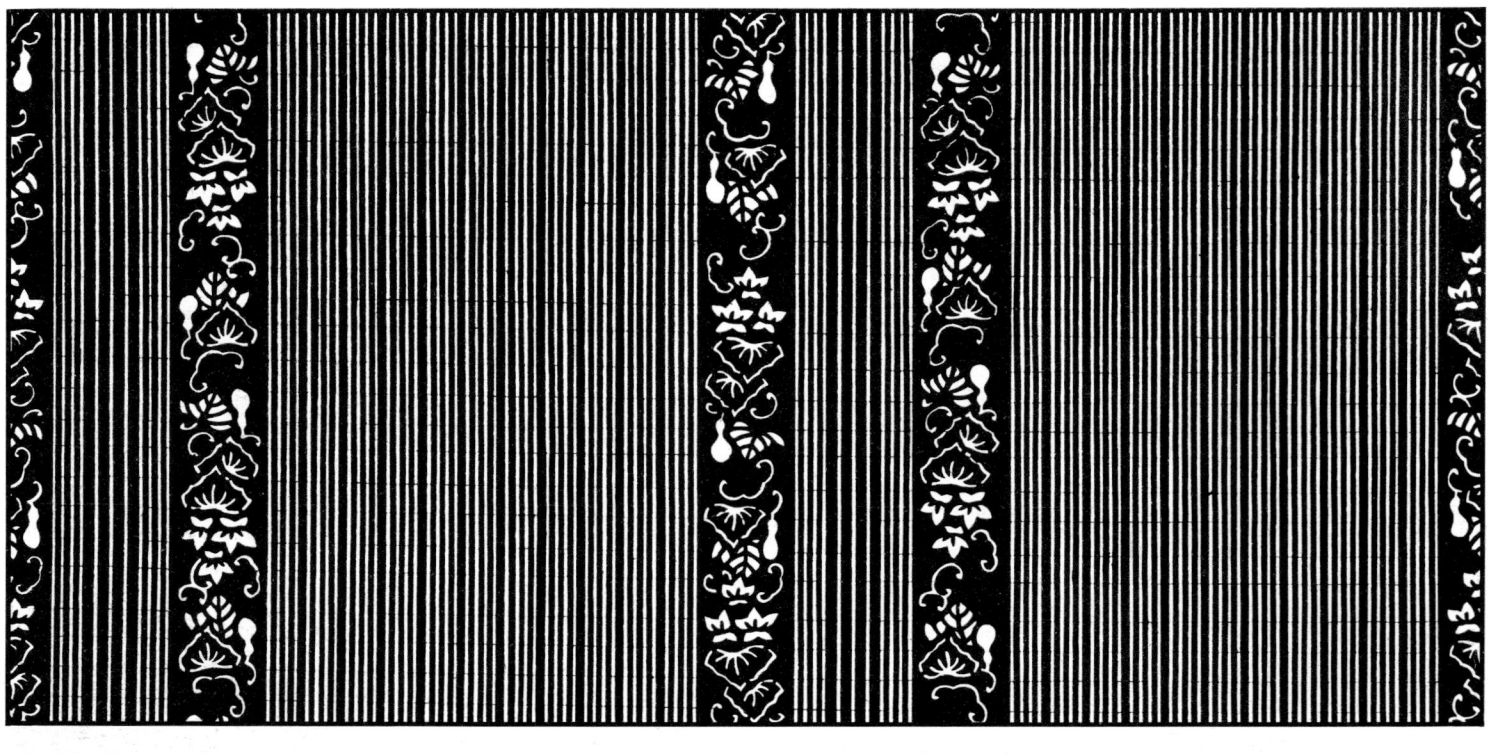

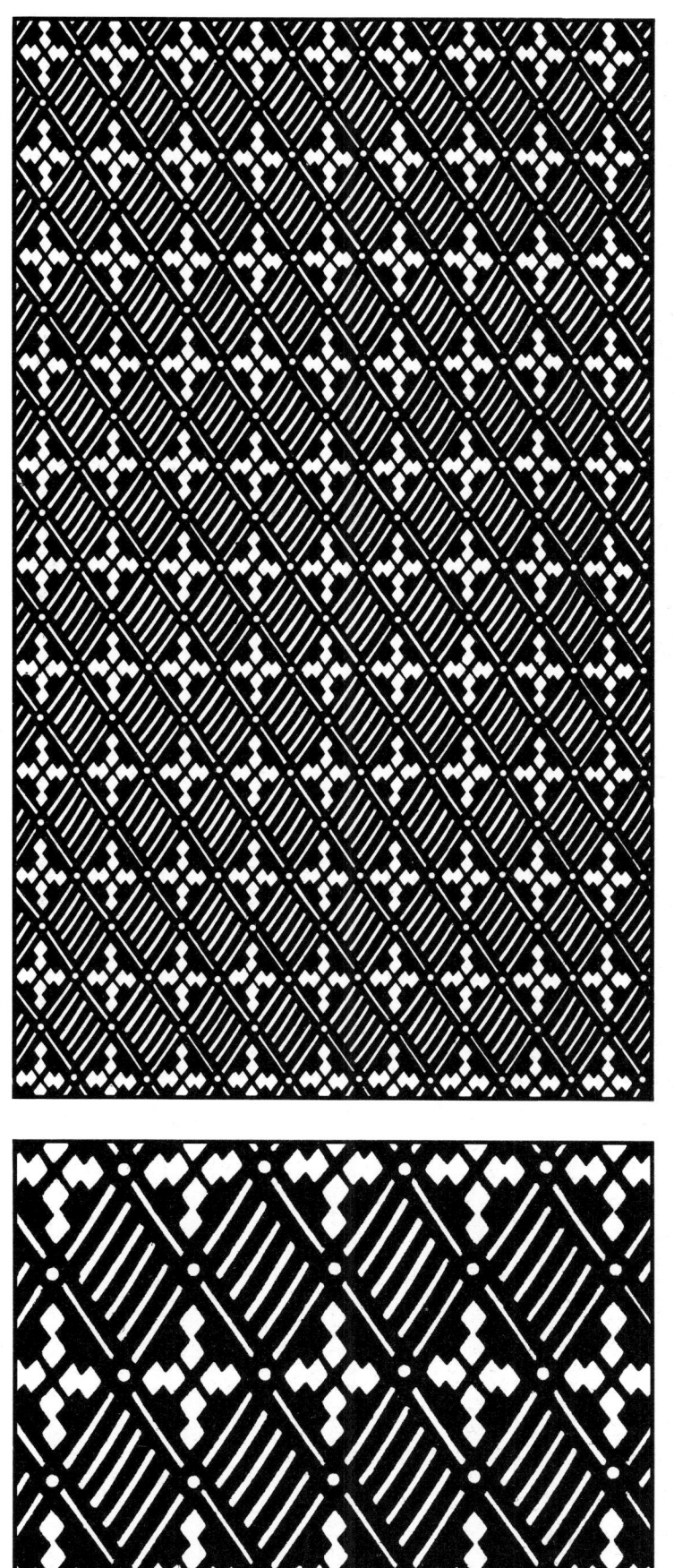

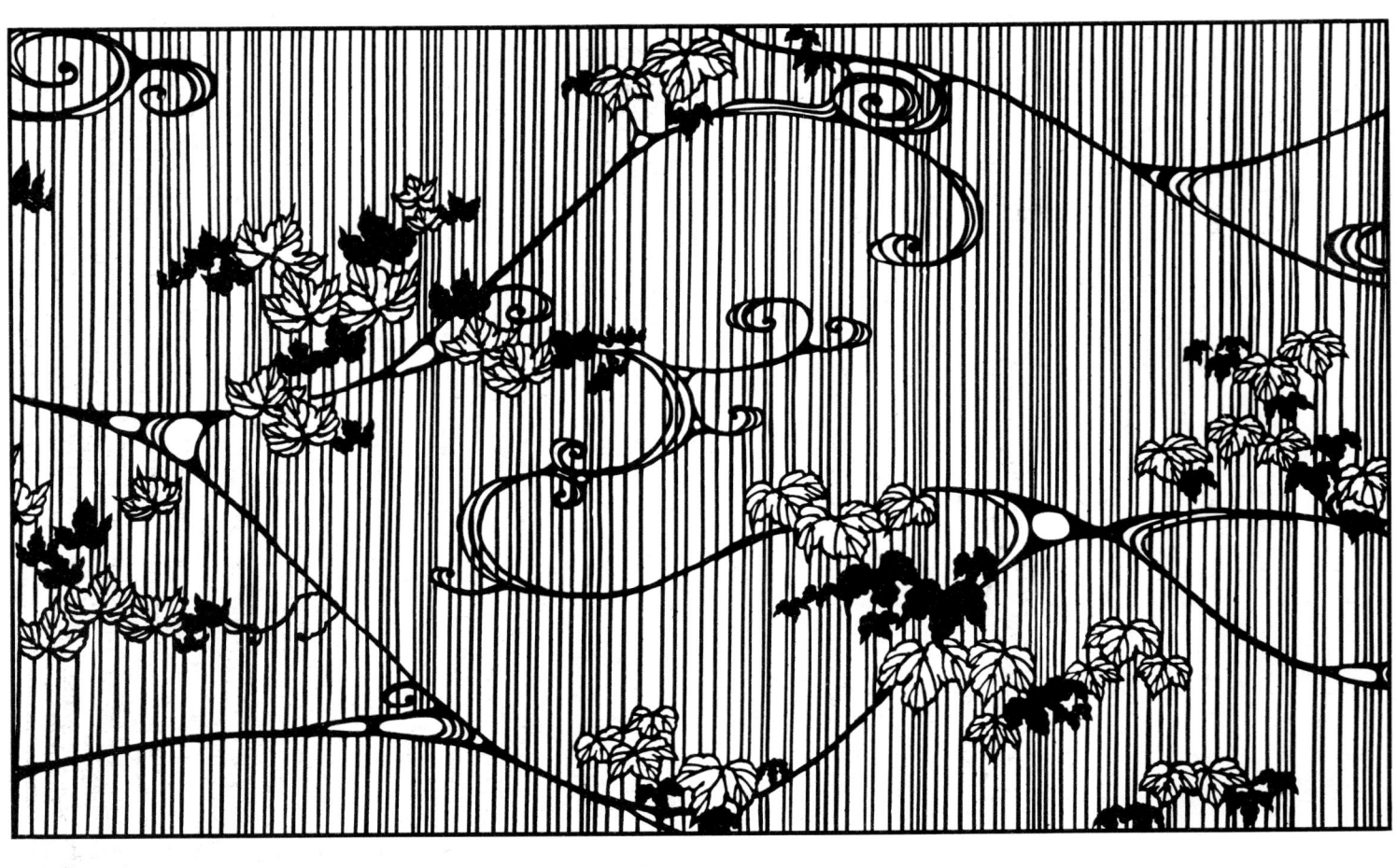

17

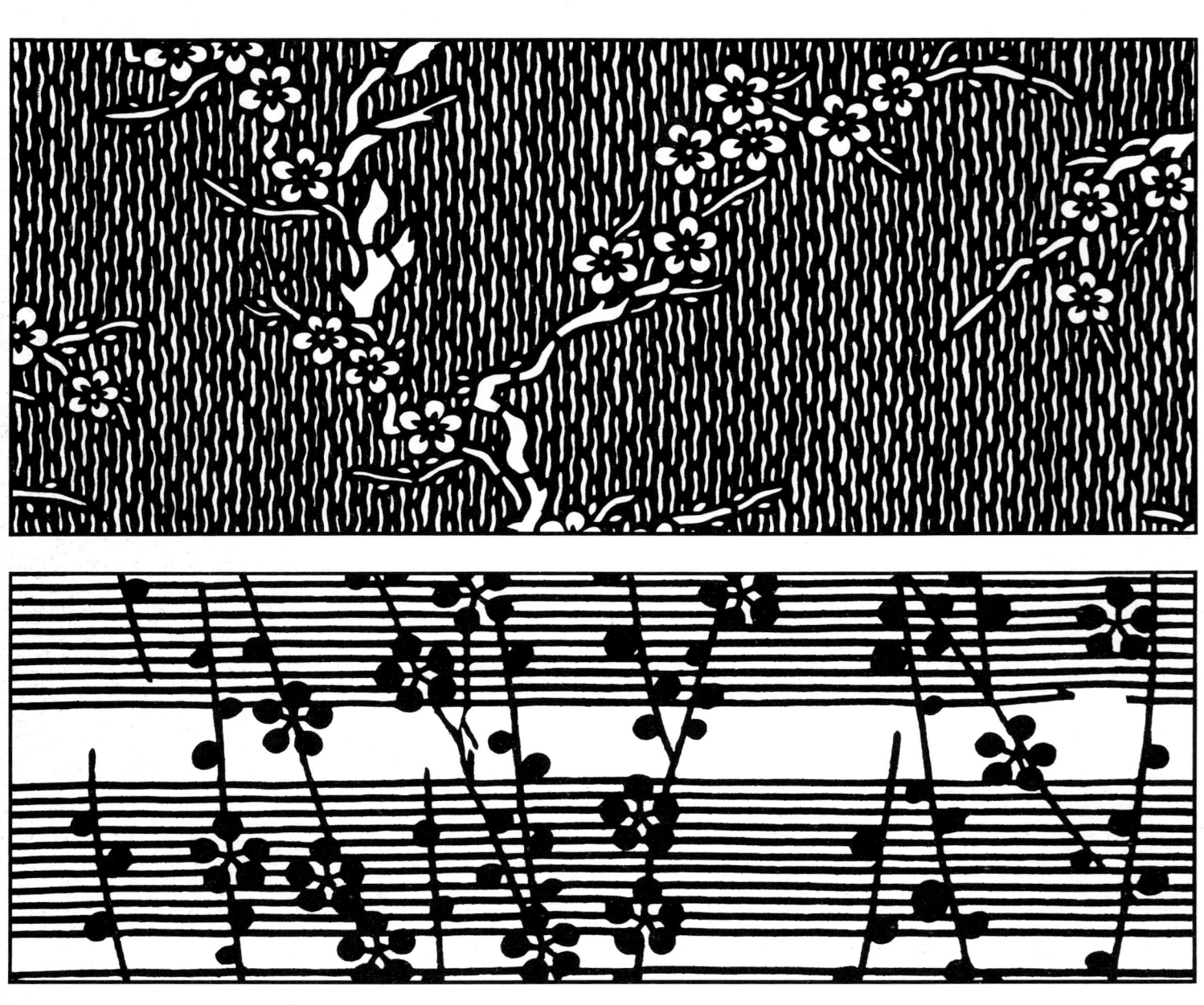

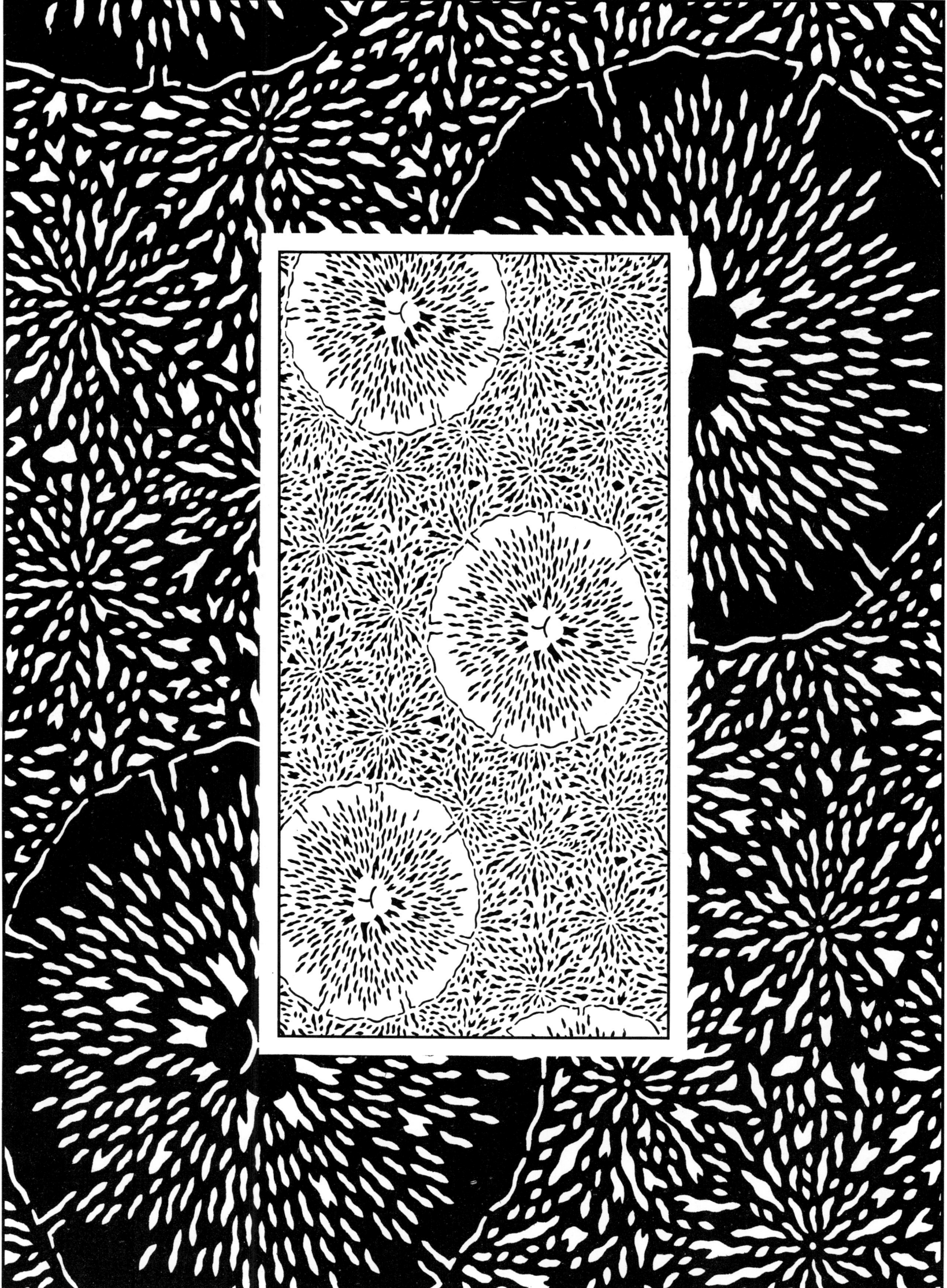

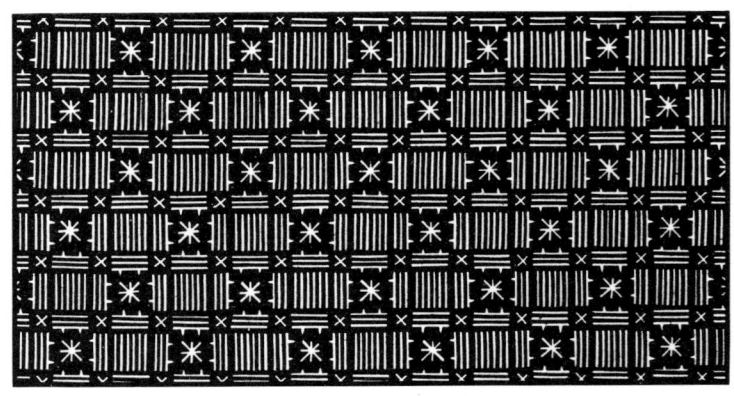

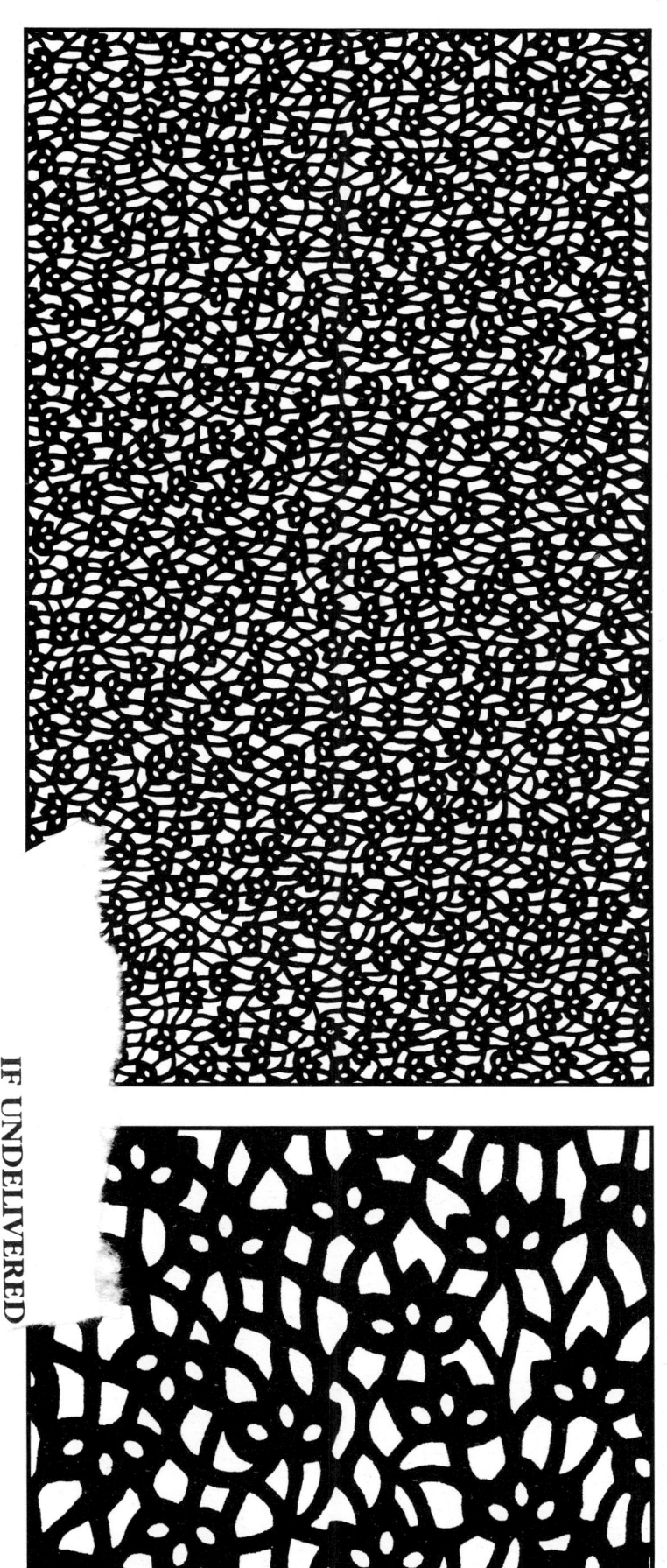

26

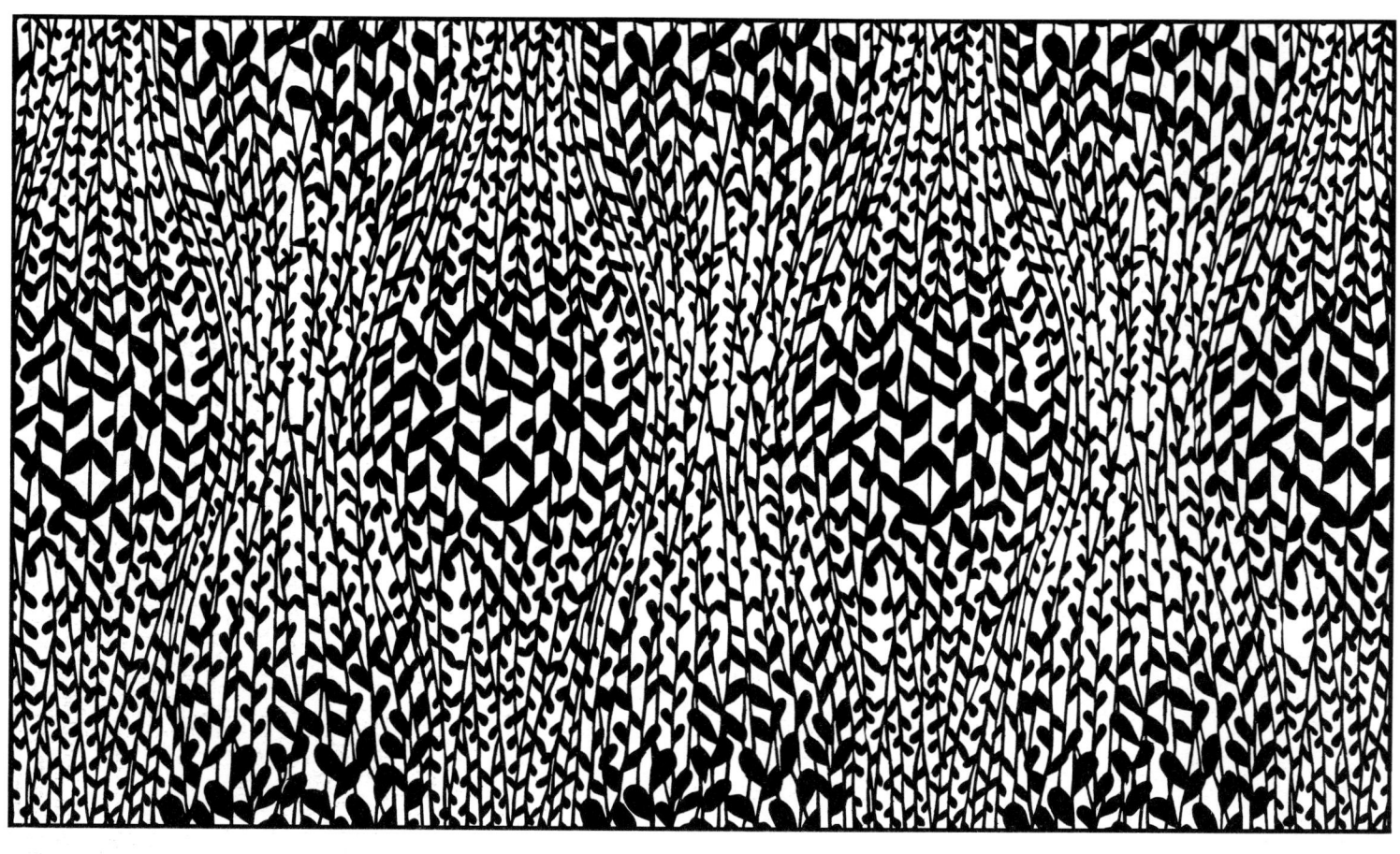

28

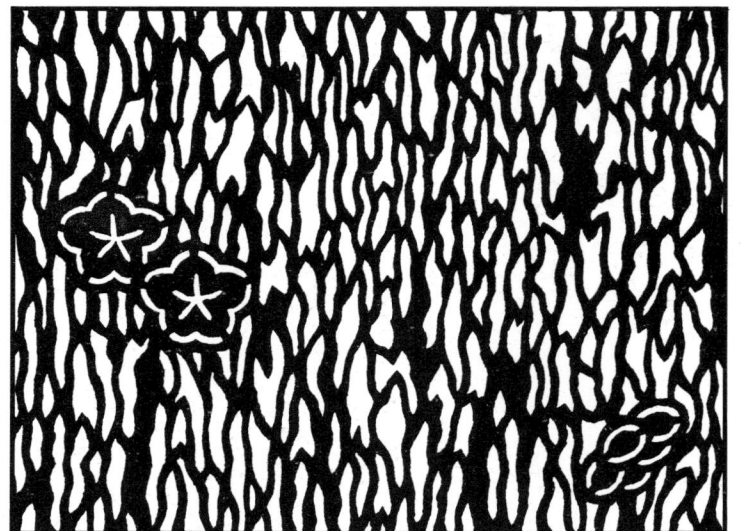

32

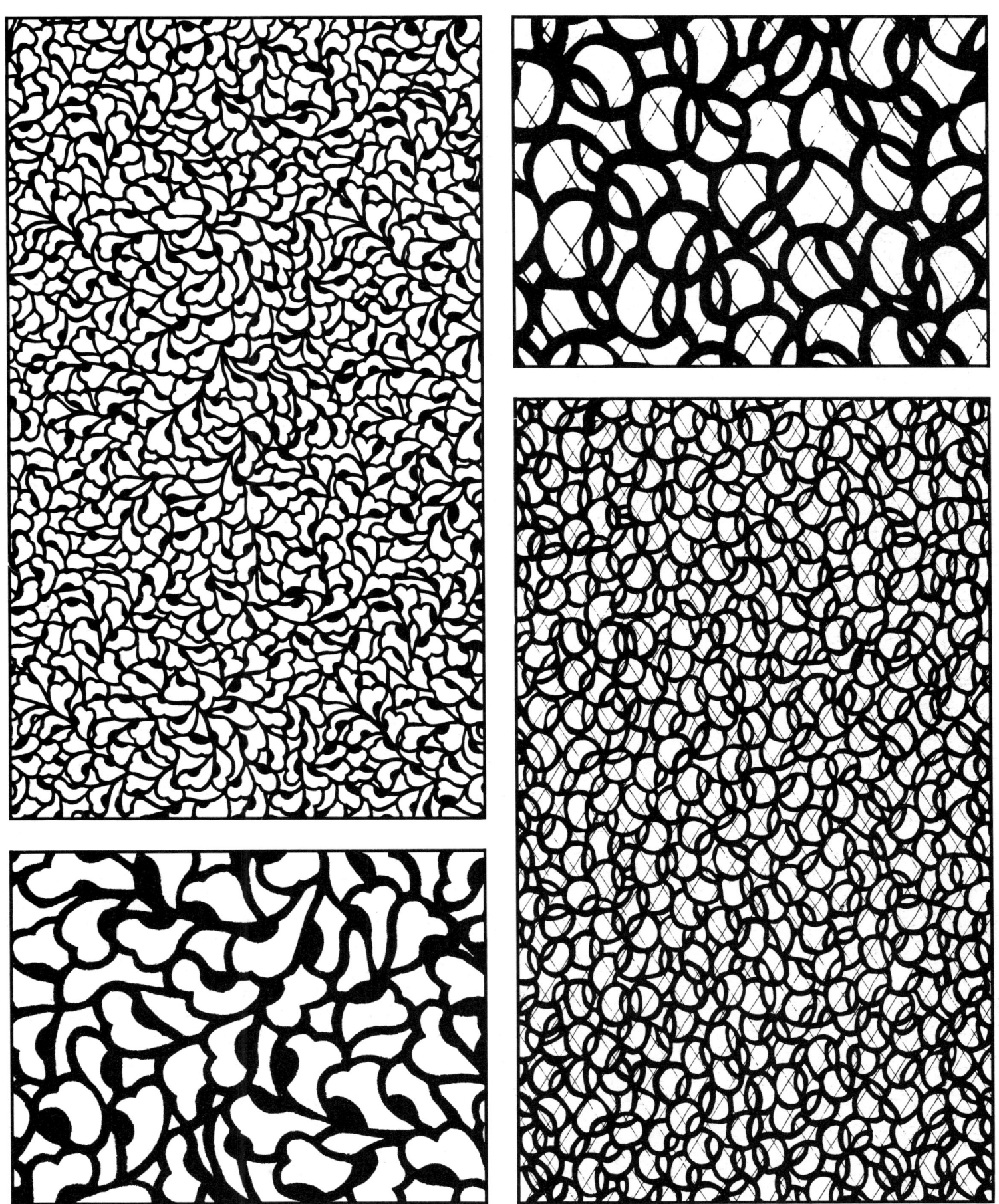

33

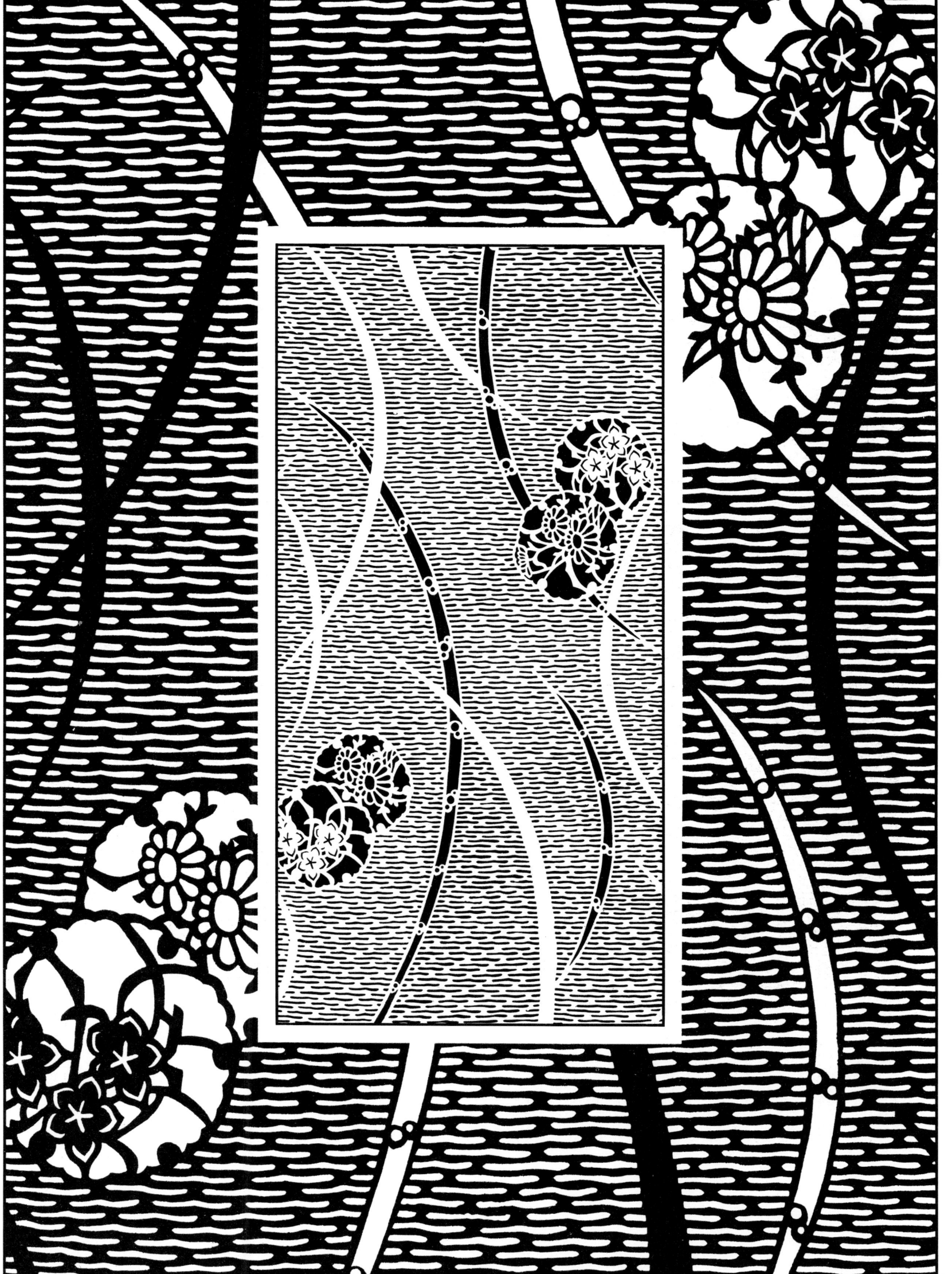

36

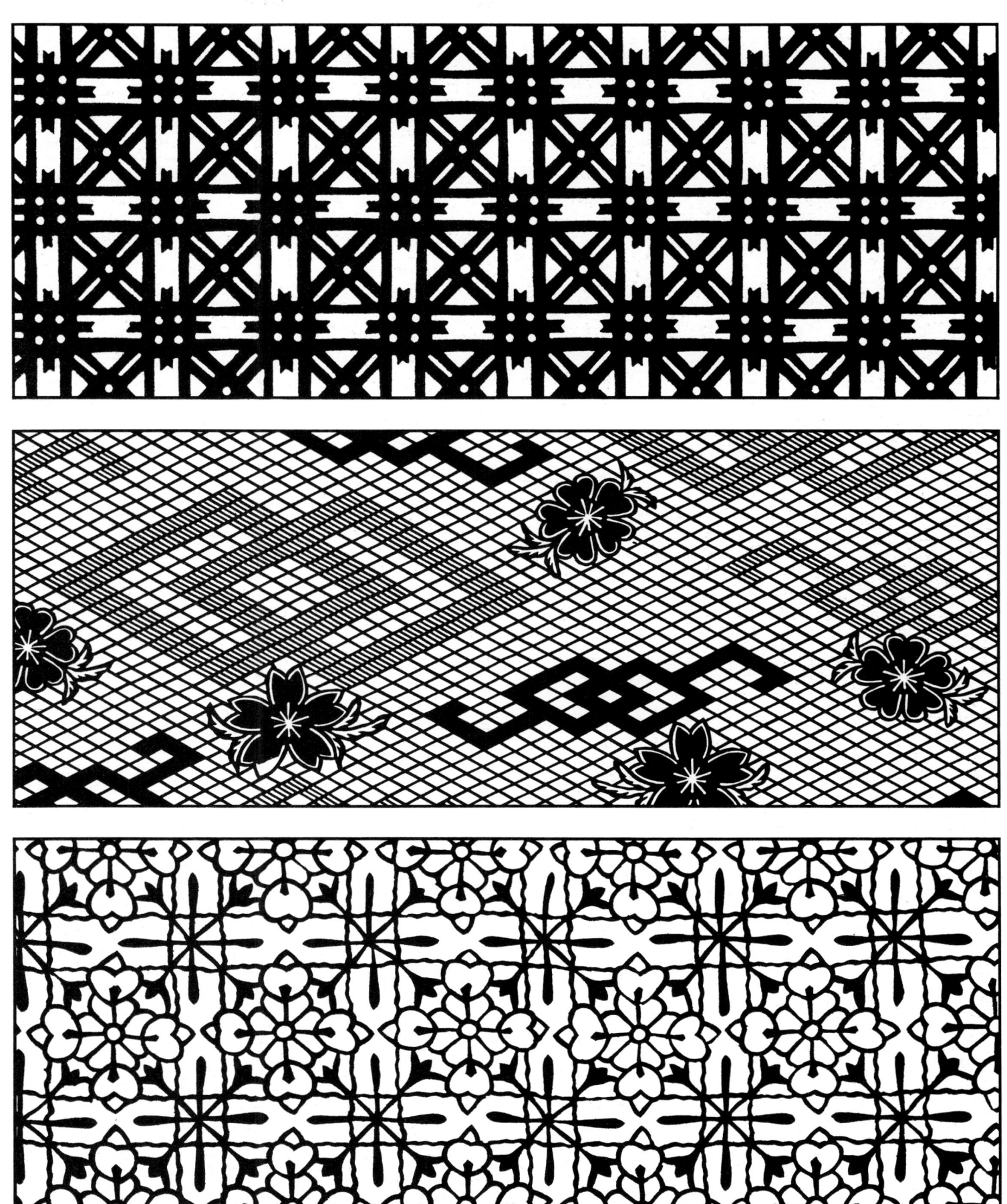

45

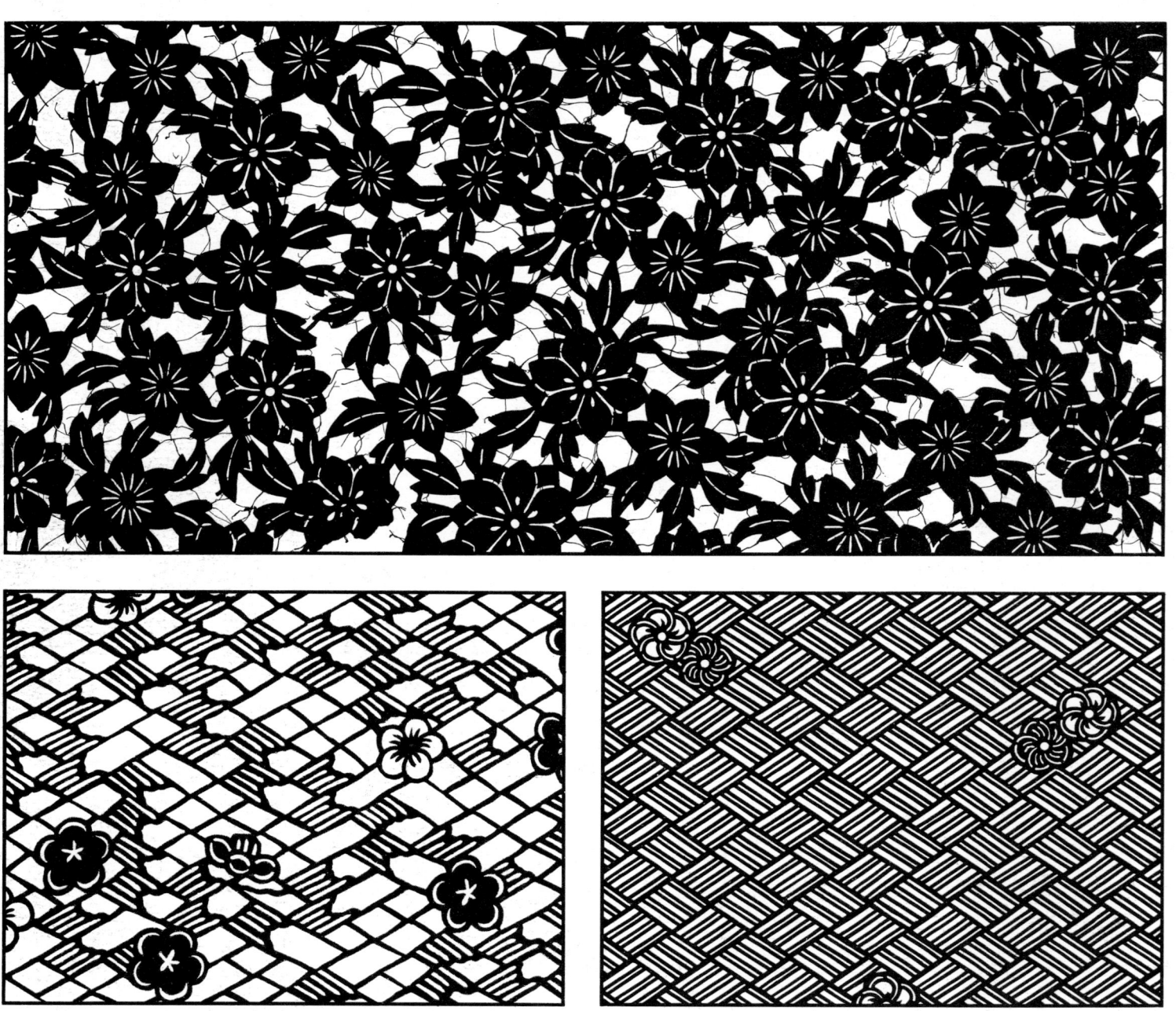

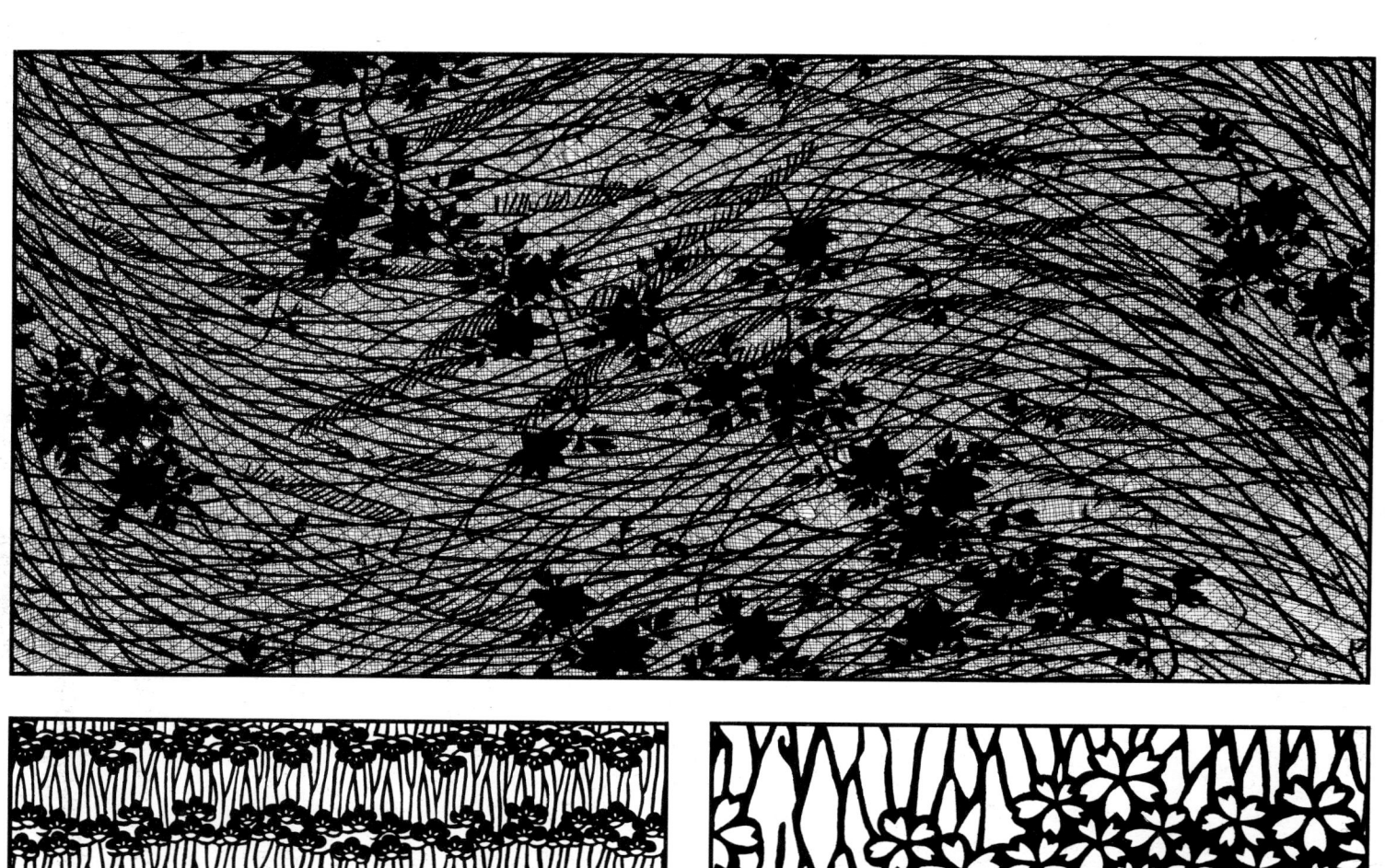

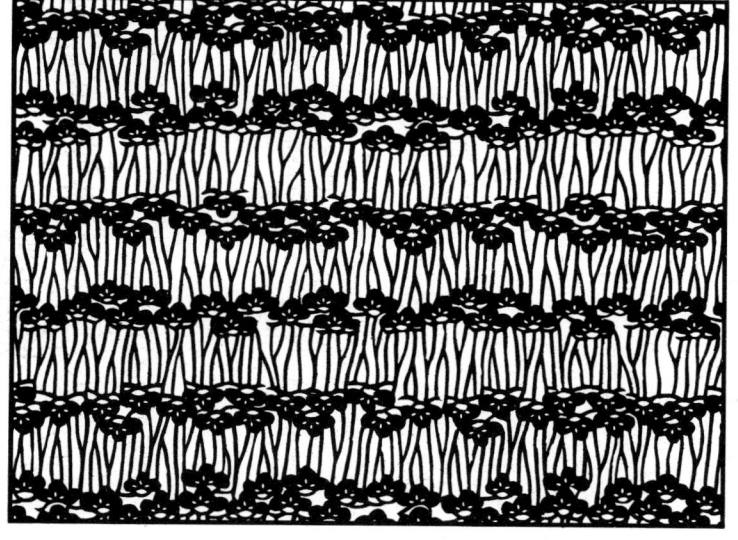

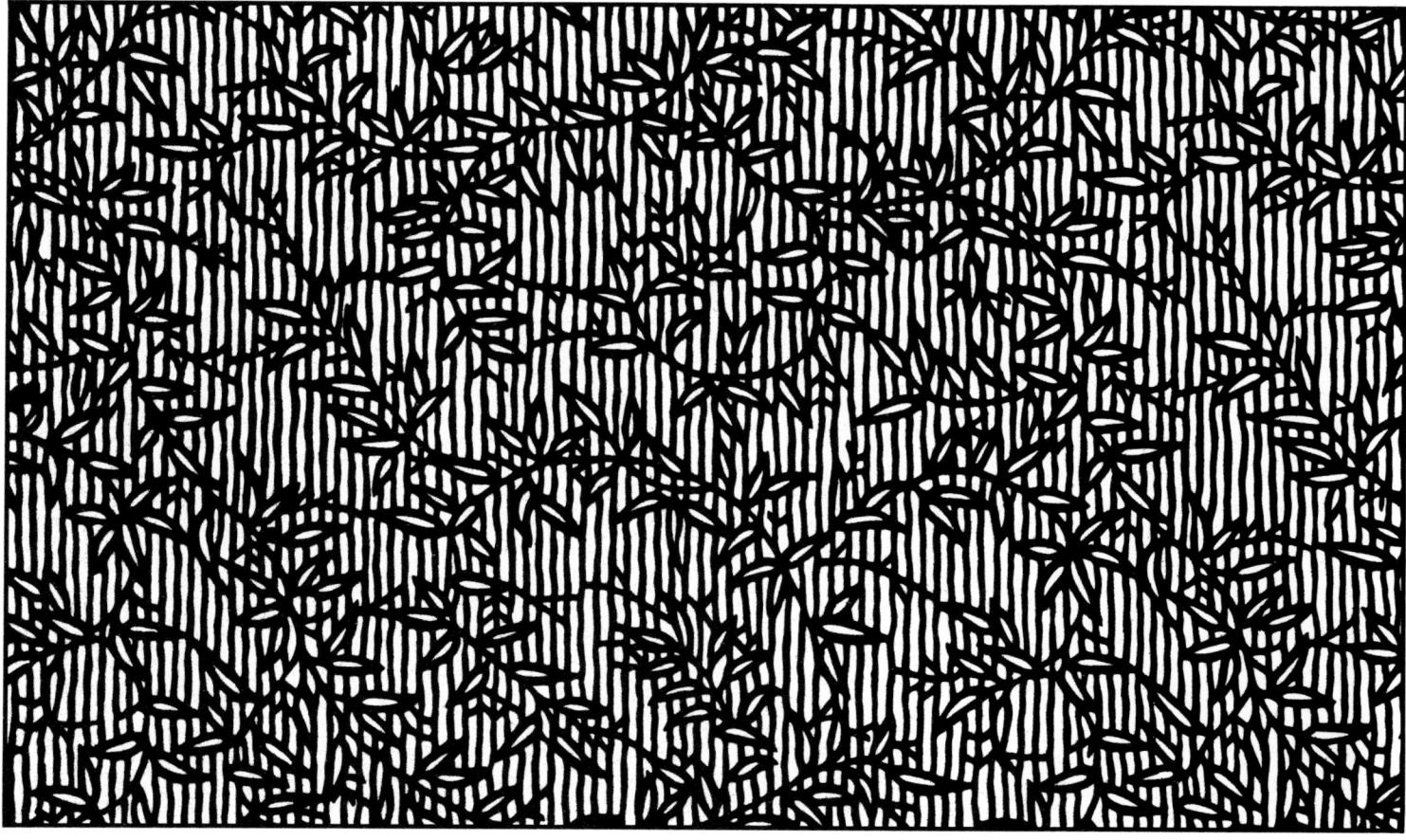

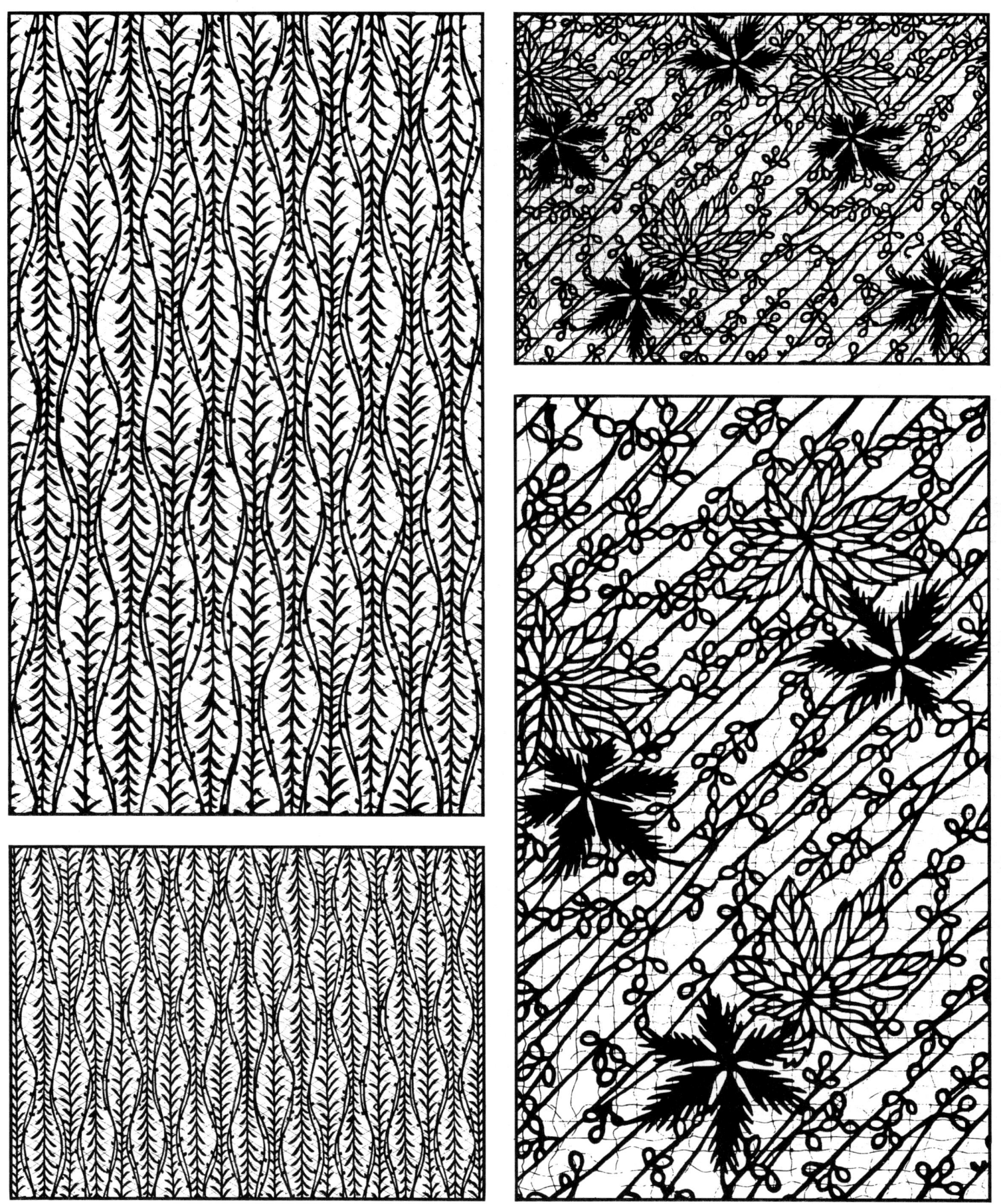

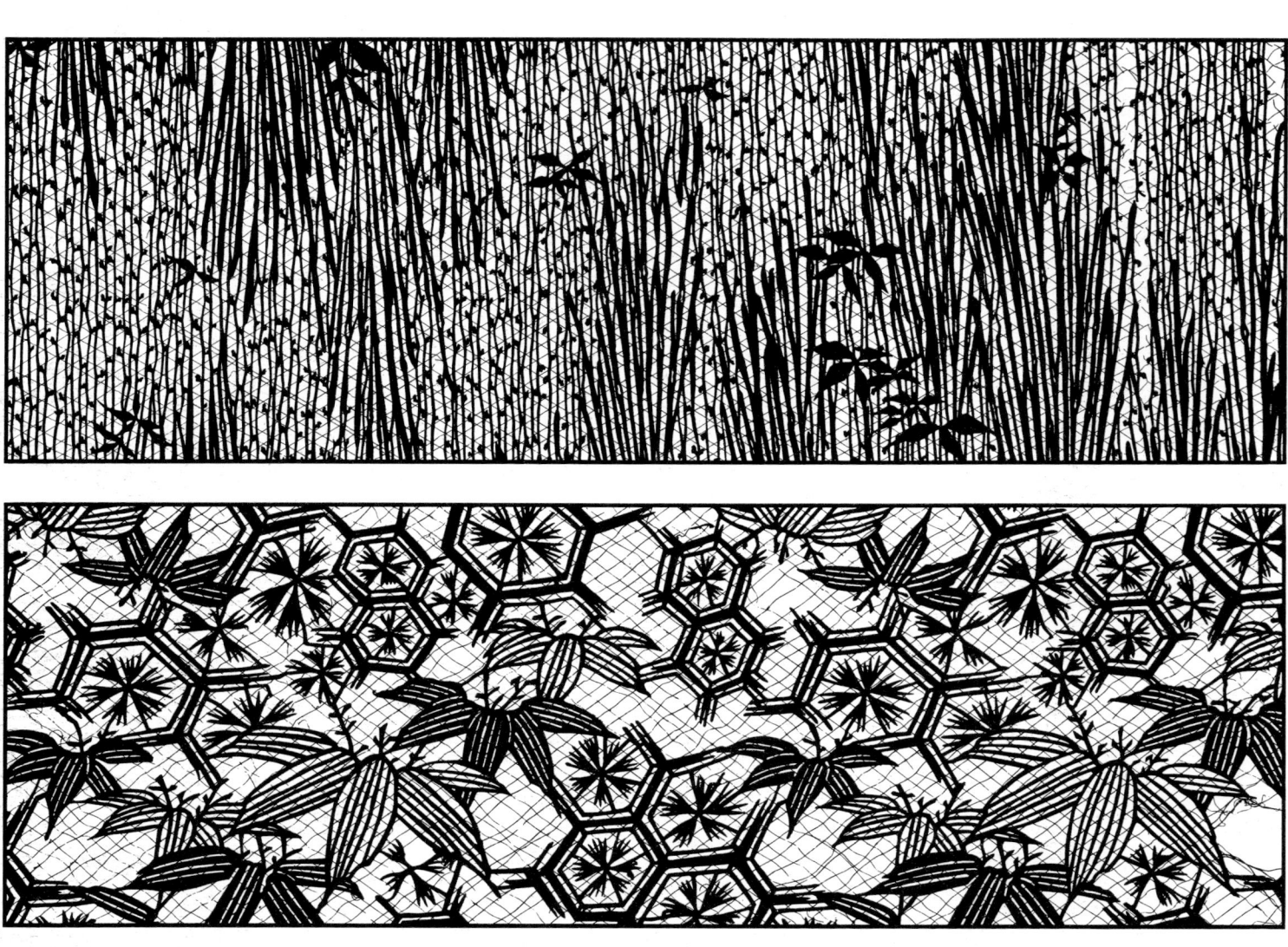

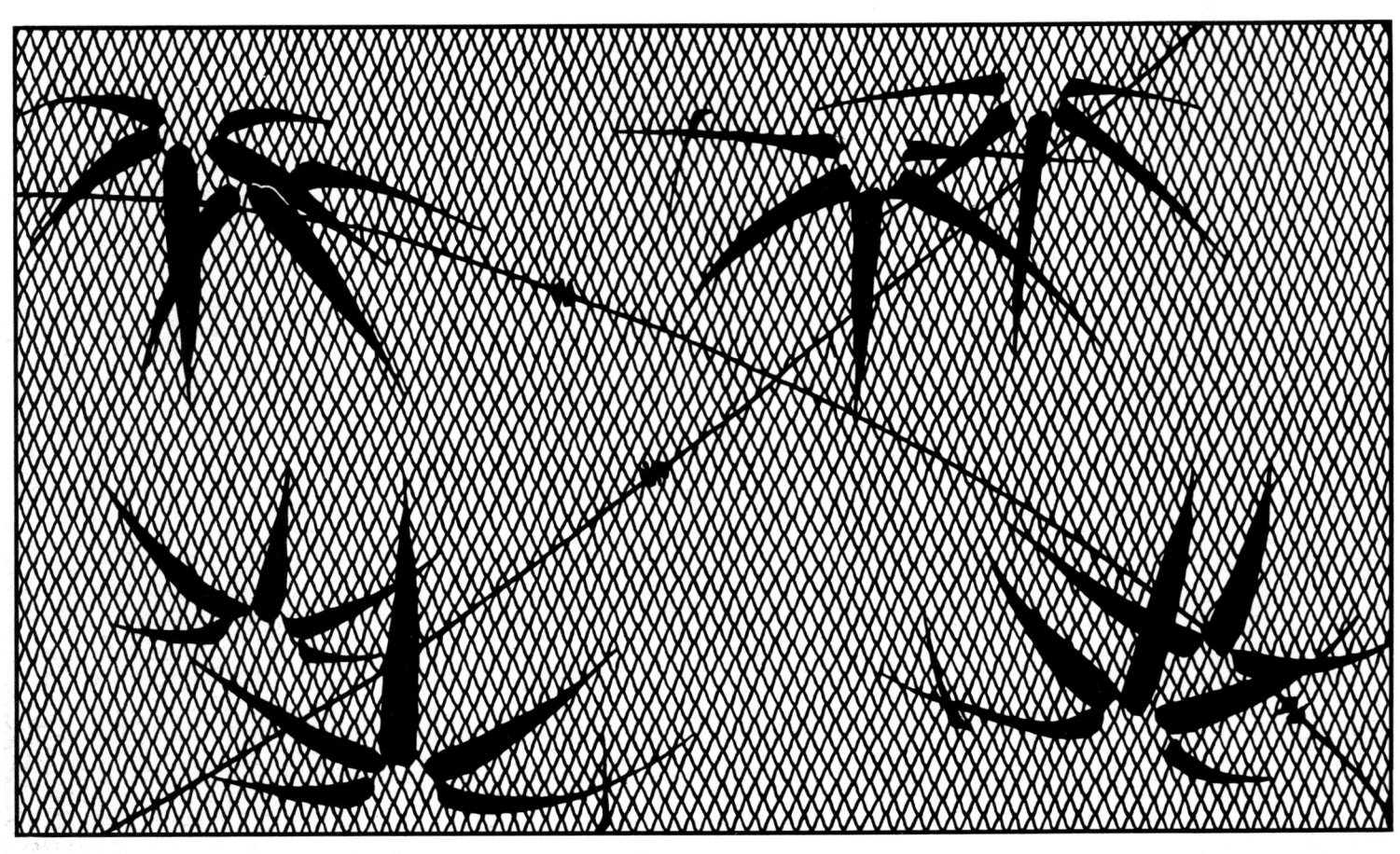

65

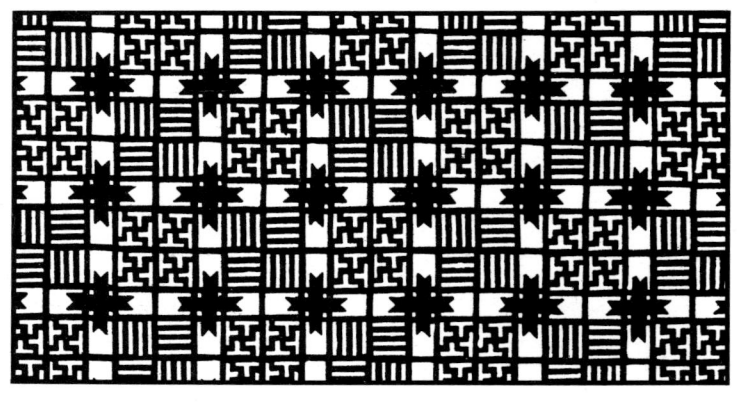

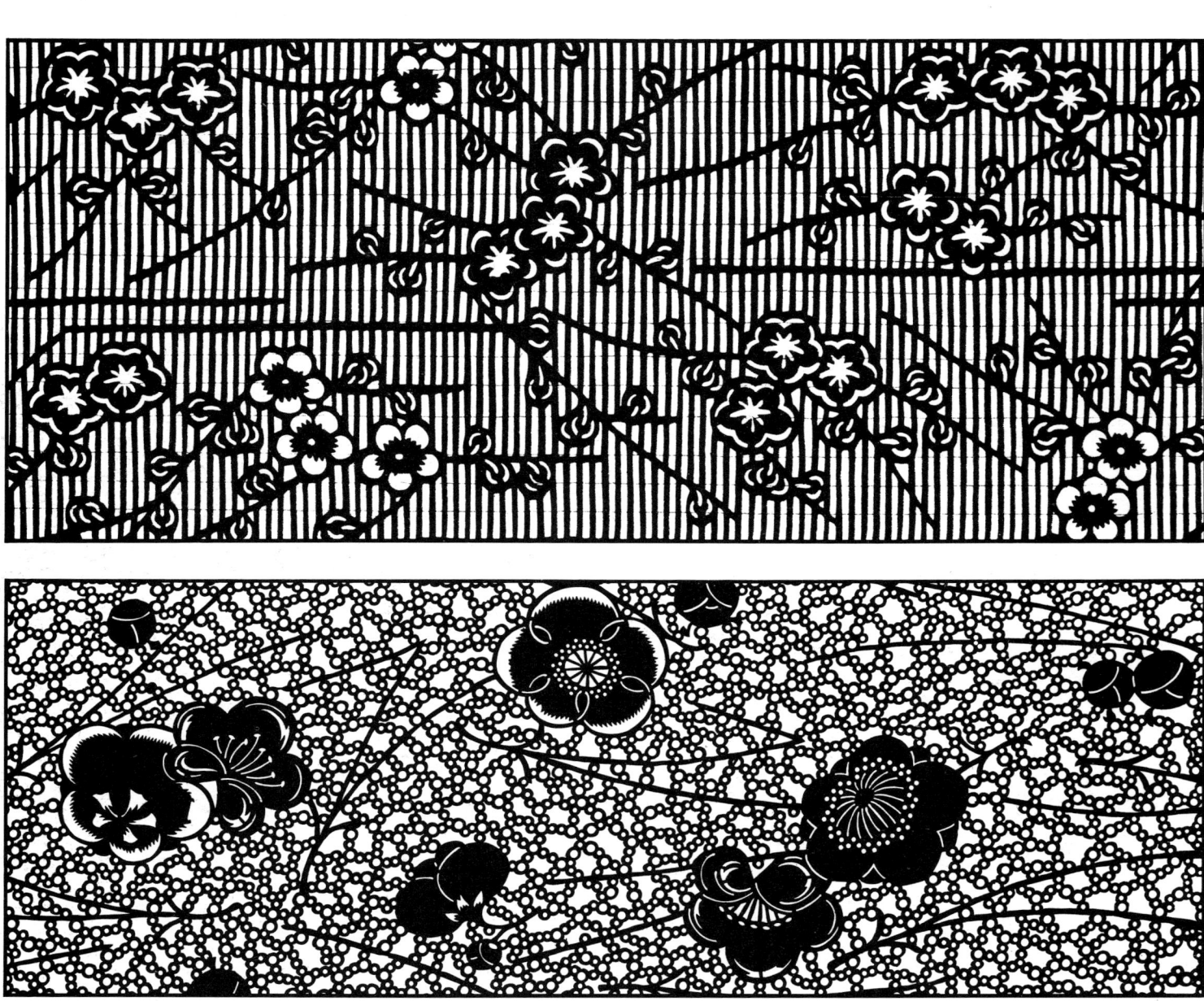

68

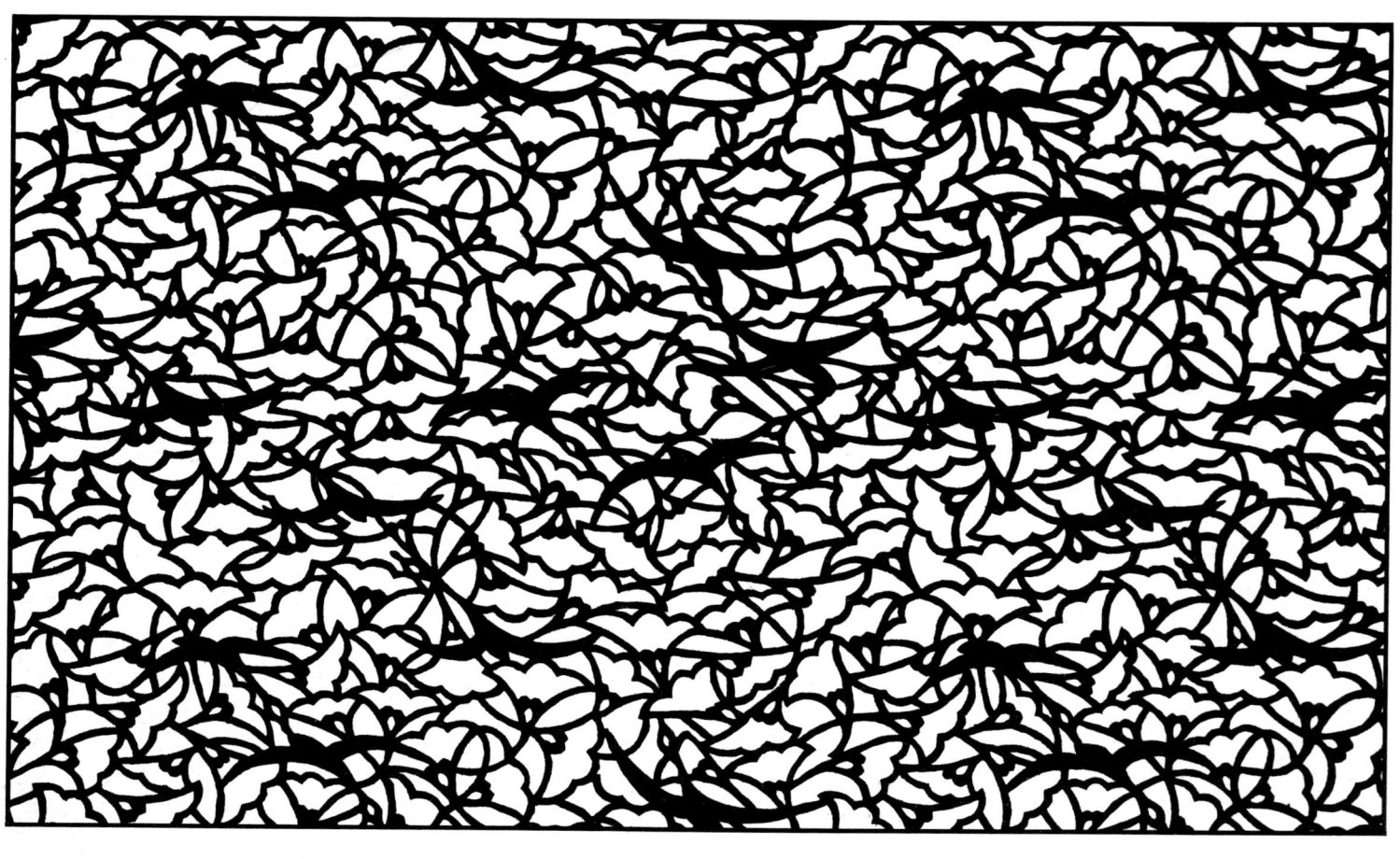

74

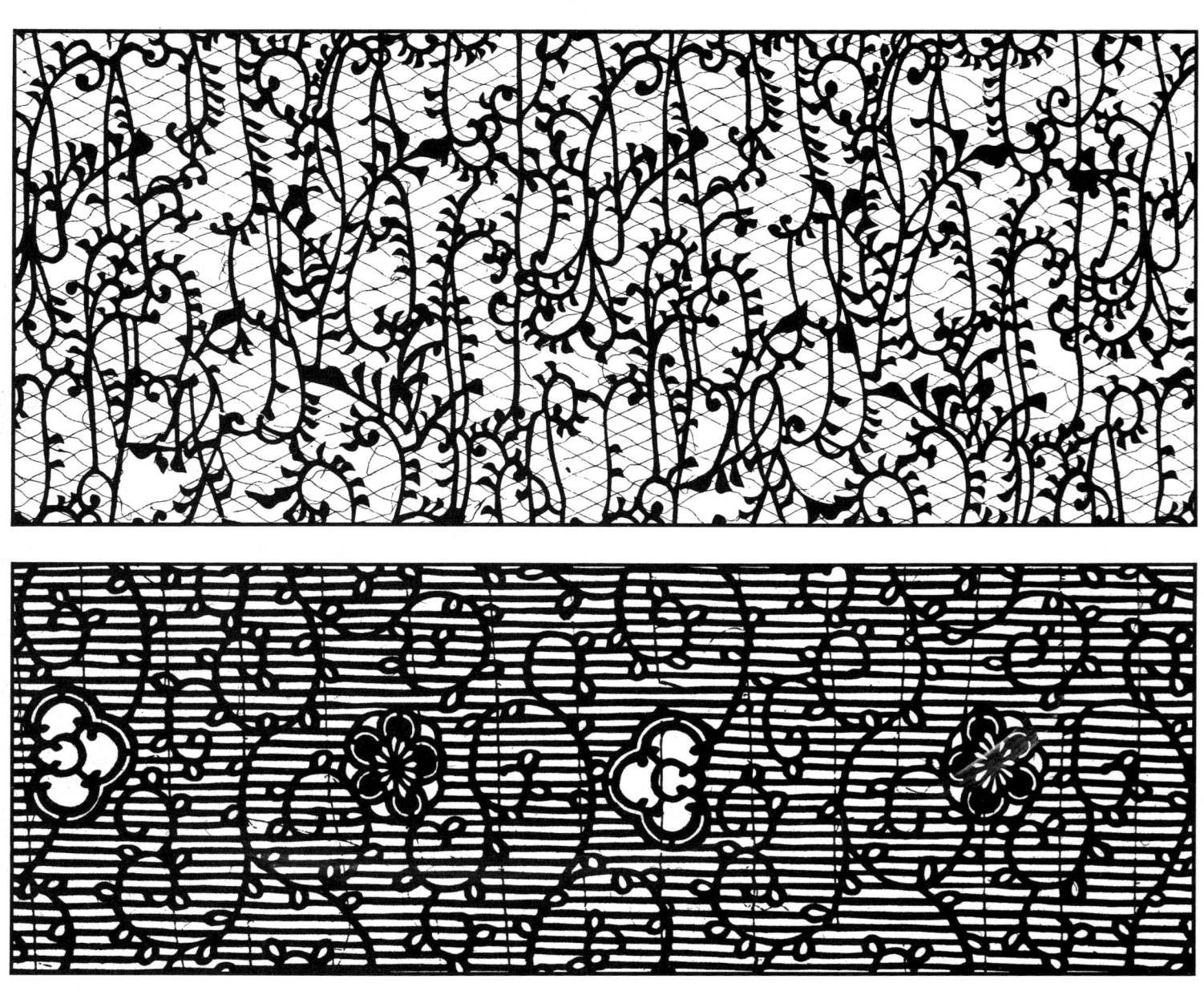

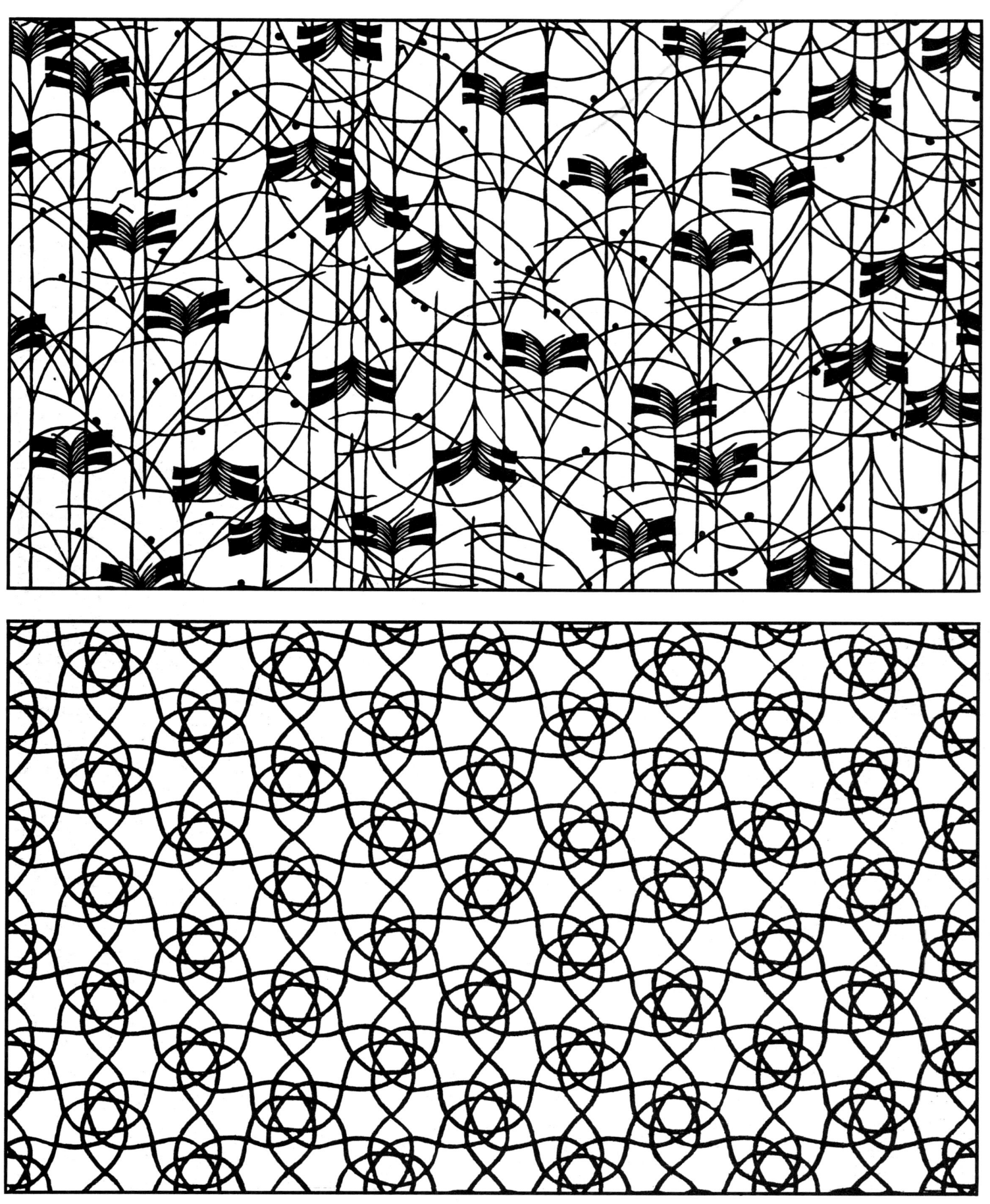

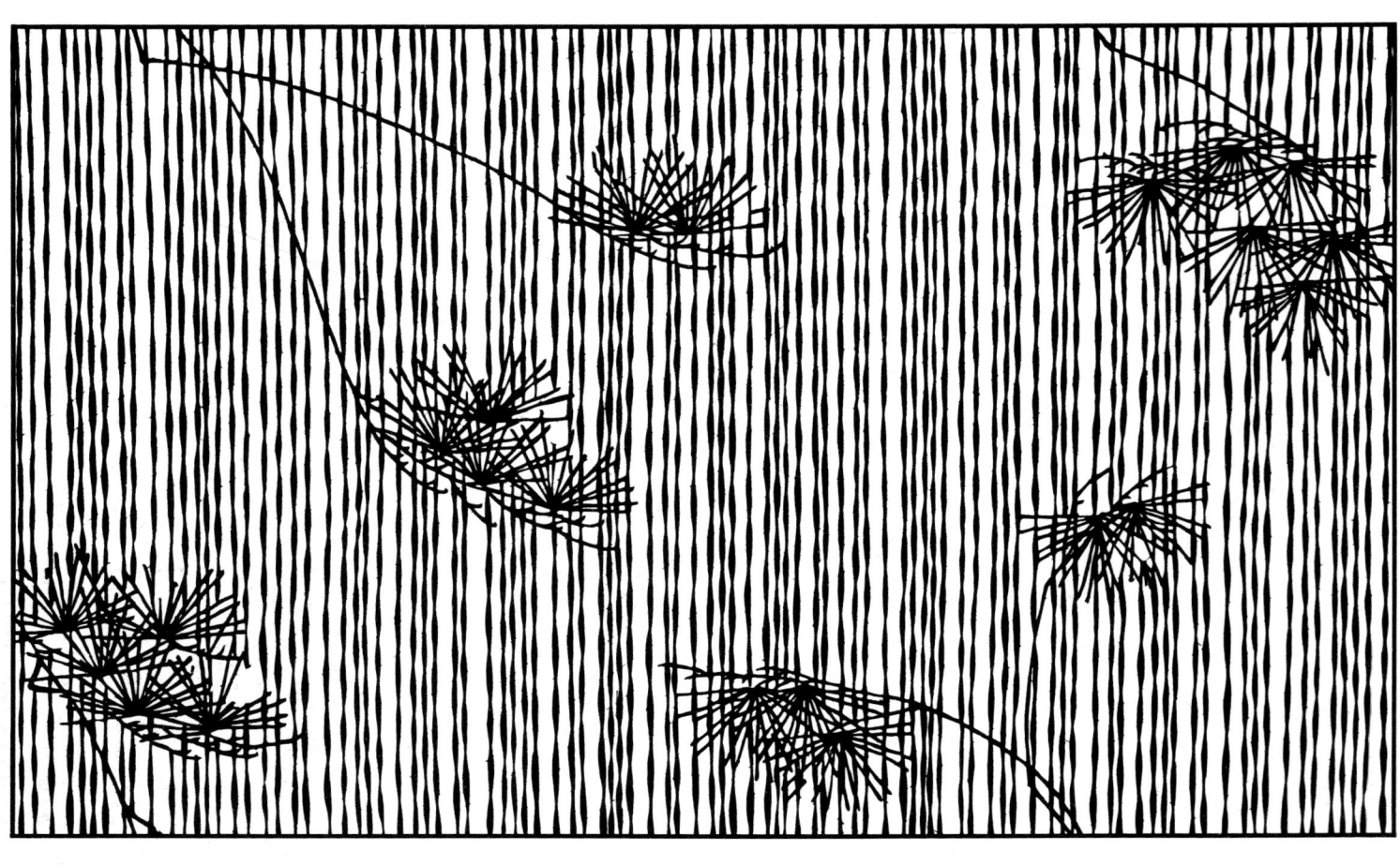

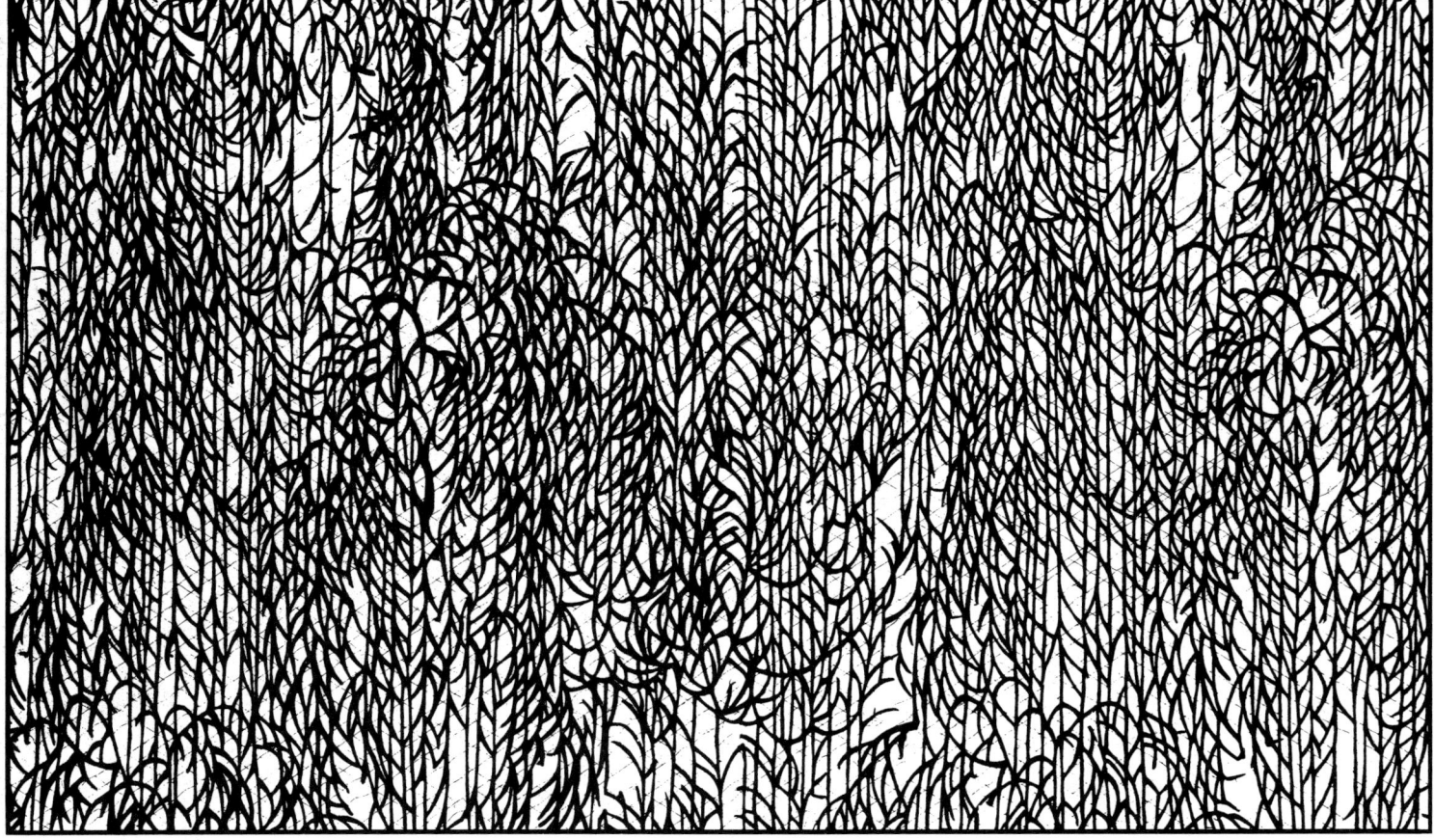

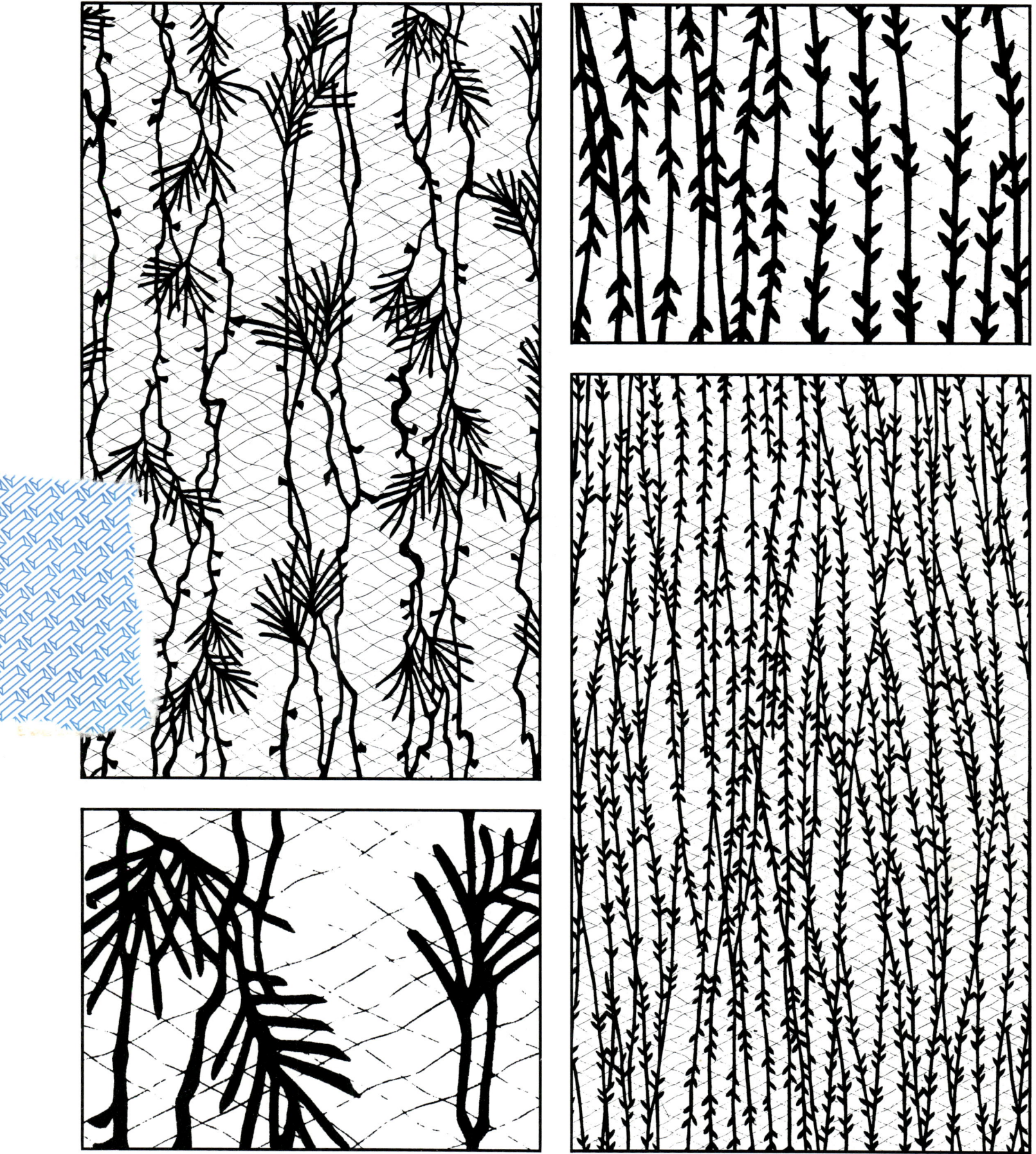

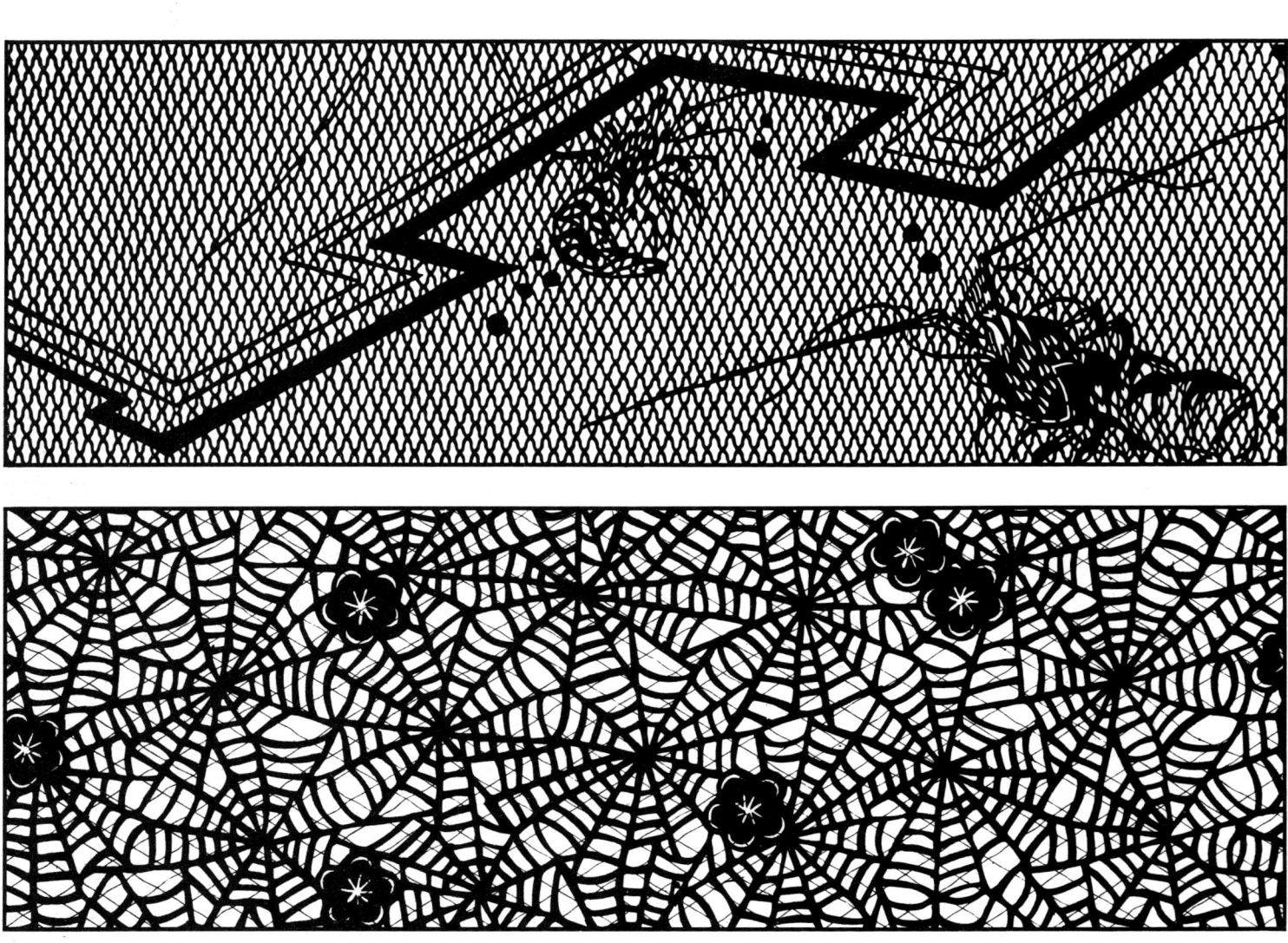

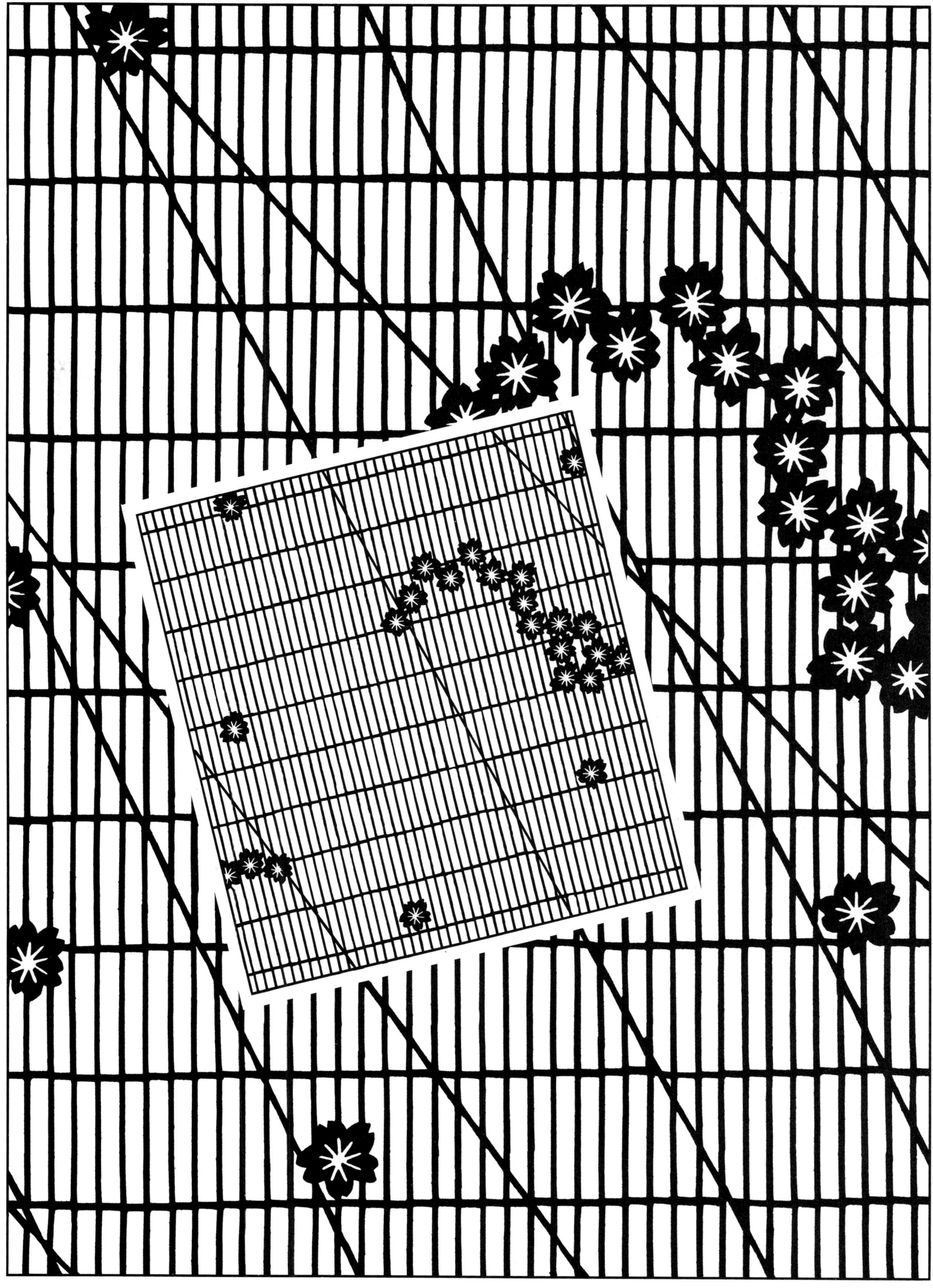

86

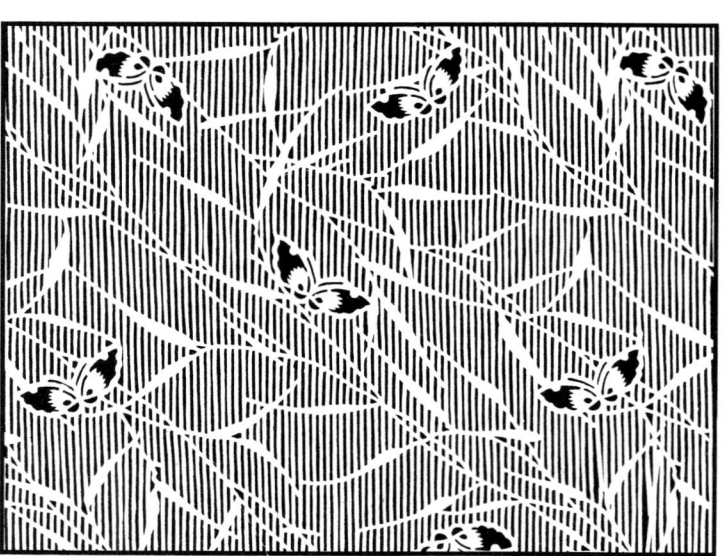

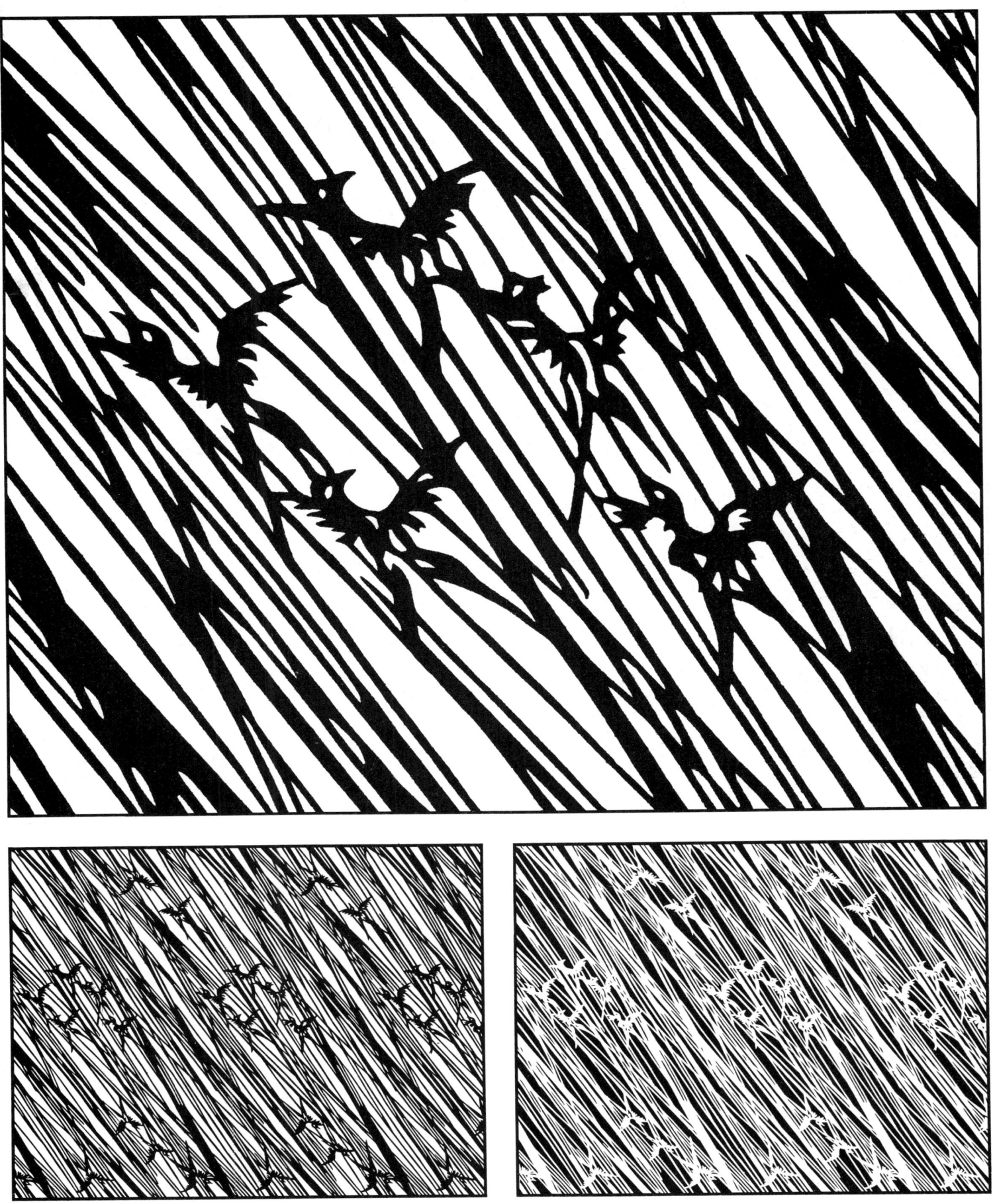

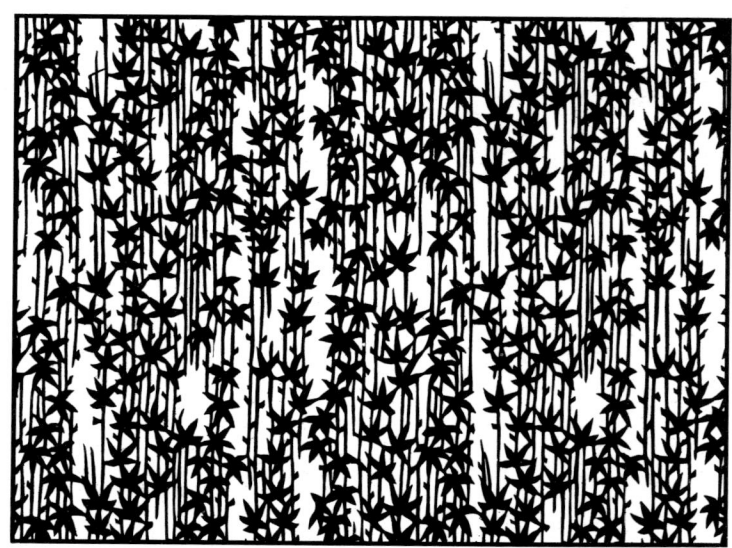

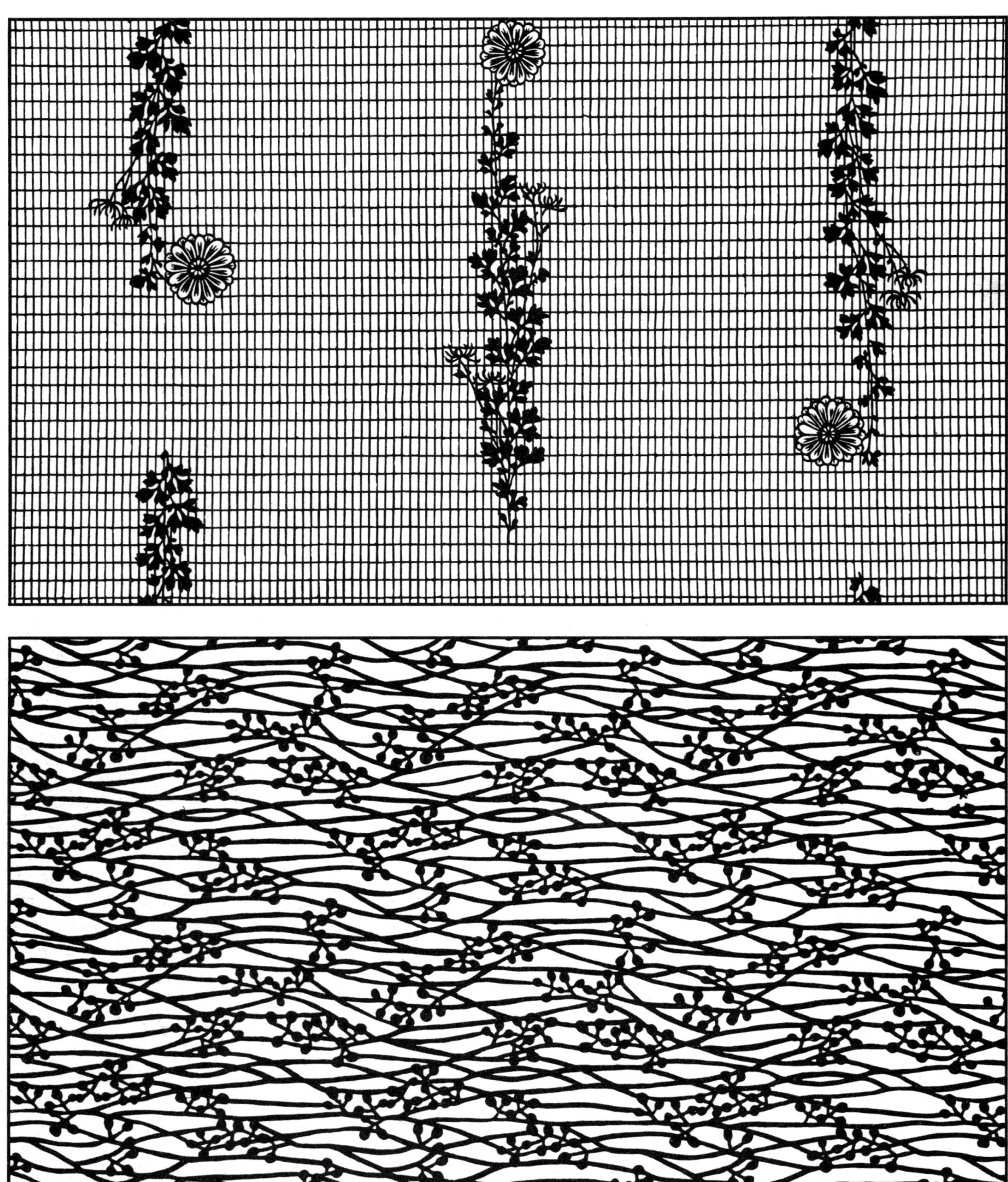

94

JAPAN IDEABOOK
PART II
JAPAN PATTERNS

This book shows more than 500 designs with the graphic motifs, produced in the majority of cases for decorative purposes, mainly by the traditional crafts, out of the most intimate interrelation with Japanese Art.

Designs and ornamentation found application in, among other things, fabrics and textiles, kimonos, gift wrapping paper, book decoration, as well as in adornment of the most varied kinds of commercial products.

A decor which is enriched with very simple basic graphic elements, and reflects, in its ordering, the high sensitivity to form of the Japanese ornamental style.

The simple symbolism, the graphic clarity, and the signal character of the motifs, their arrangement in rows, reiteration, duplication or mirroring, their repeat or their symmetry, bear unmistakably the hallmarks of stamp or block printing, which suggests that they early came into use.

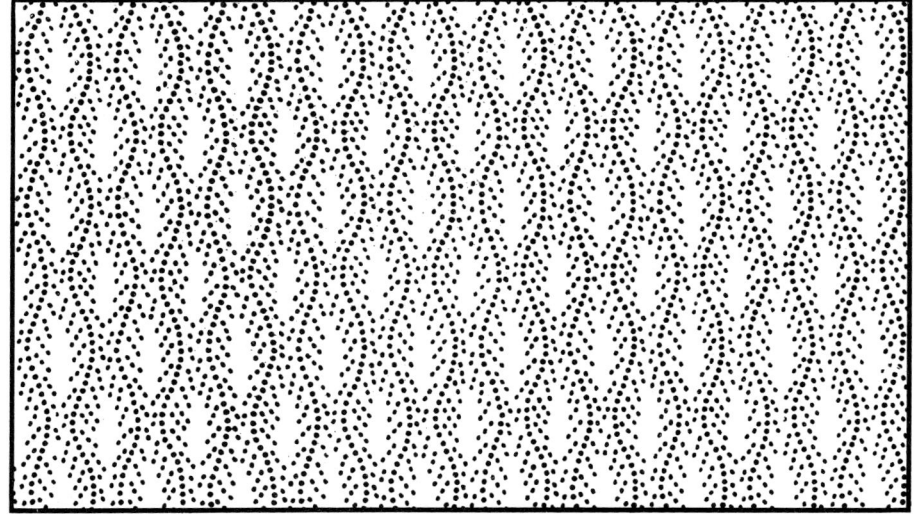

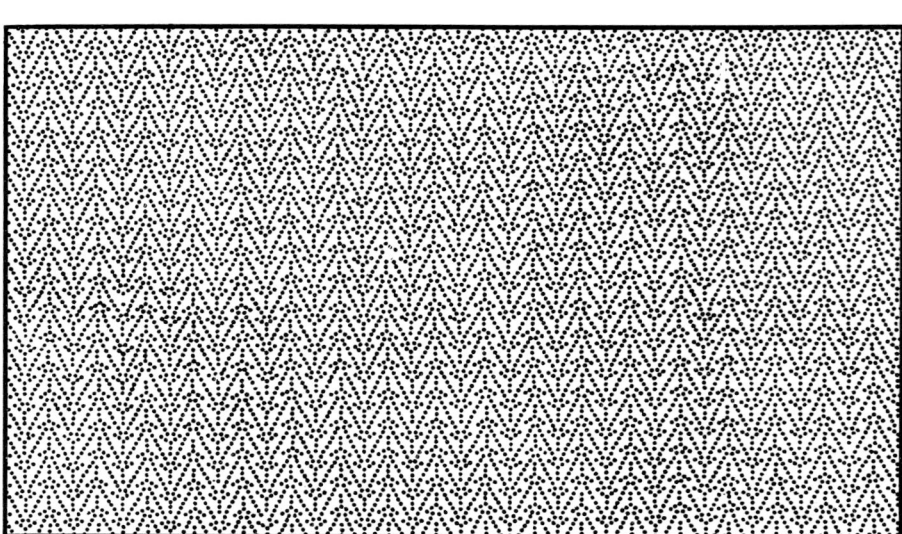
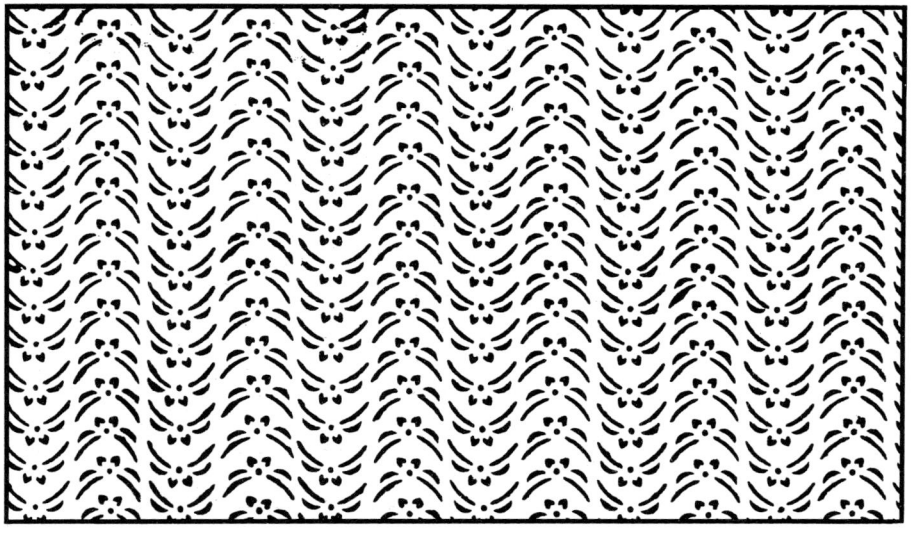

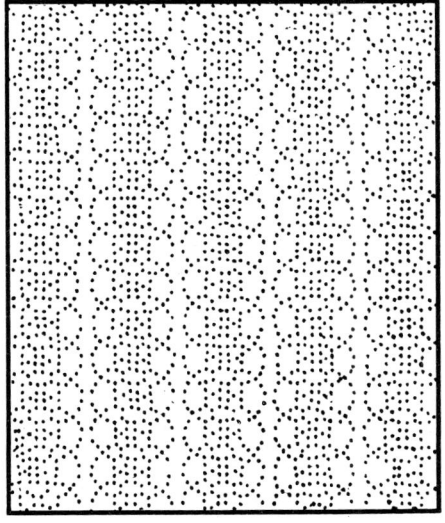

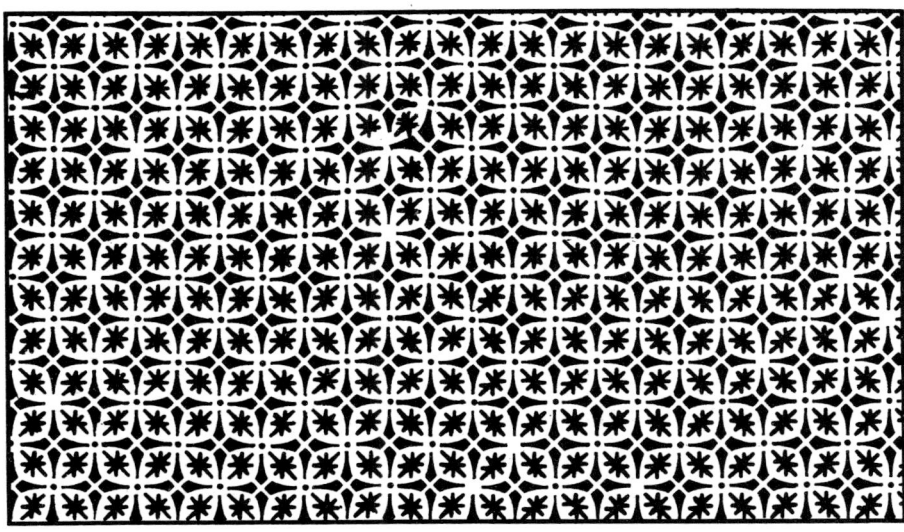
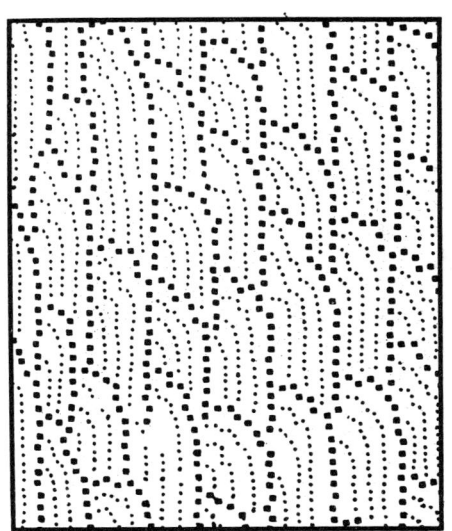
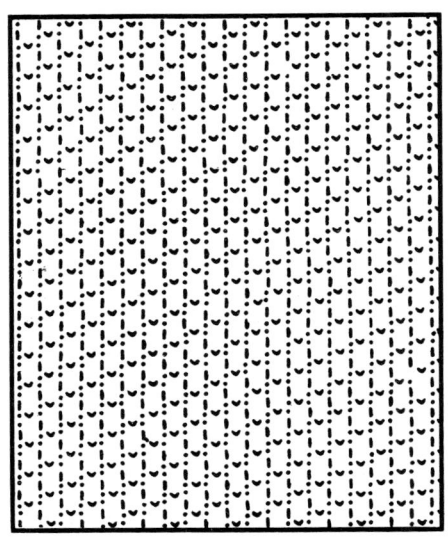

5

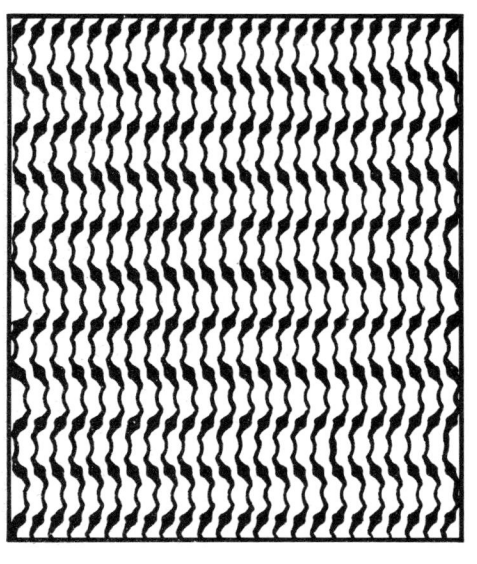

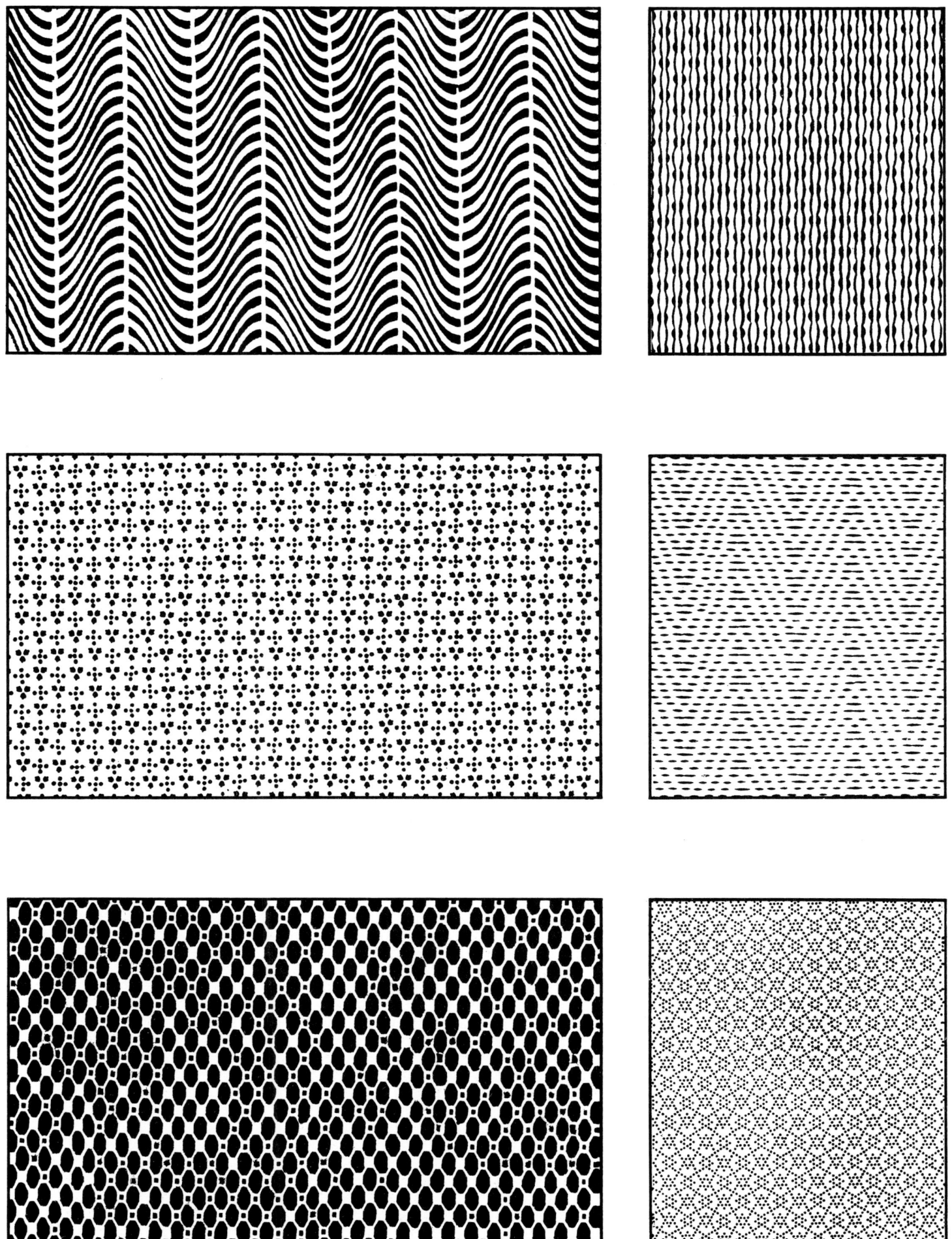

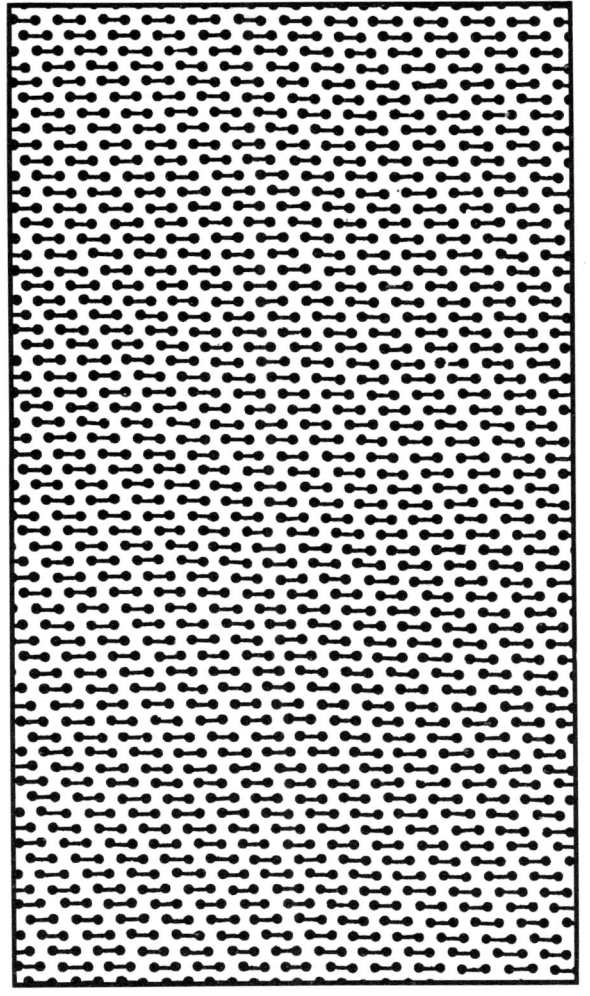

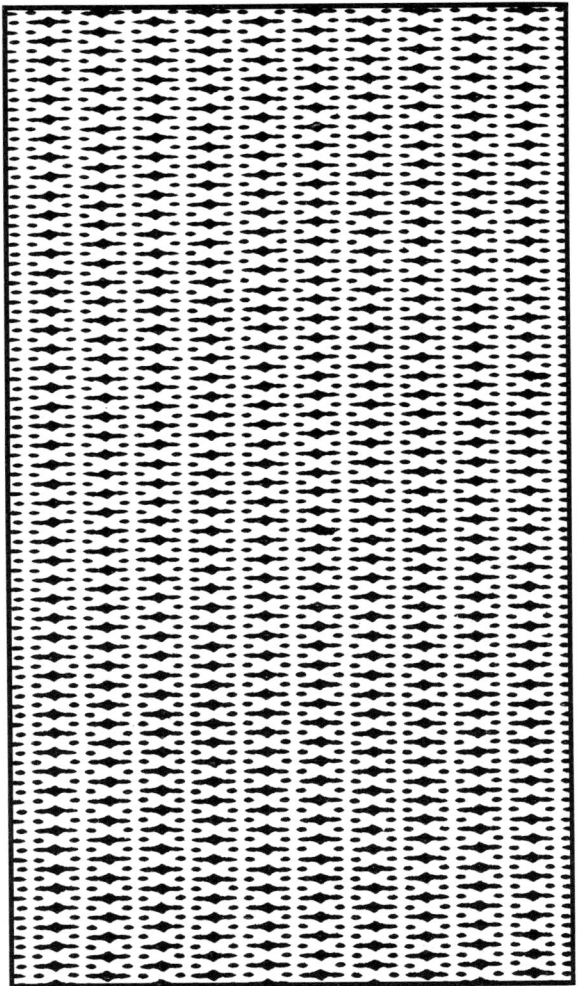

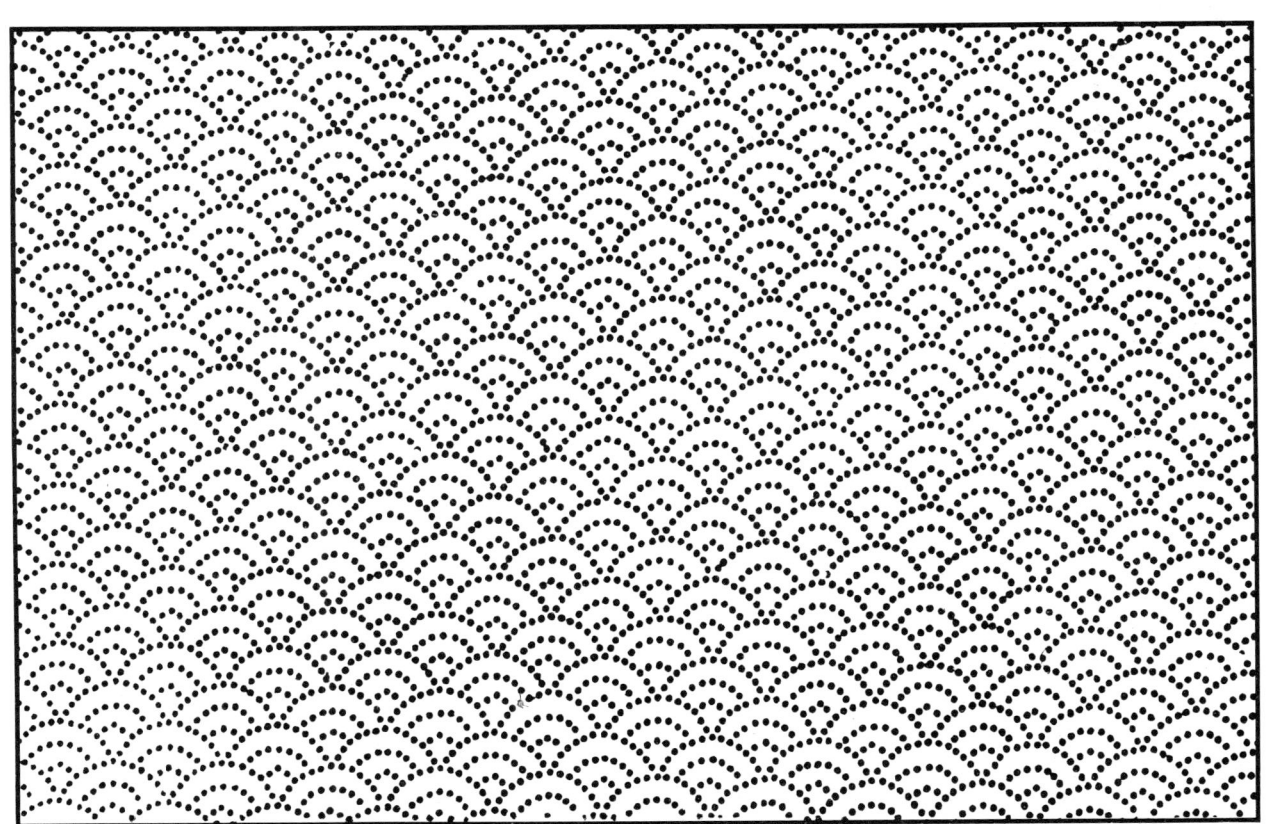

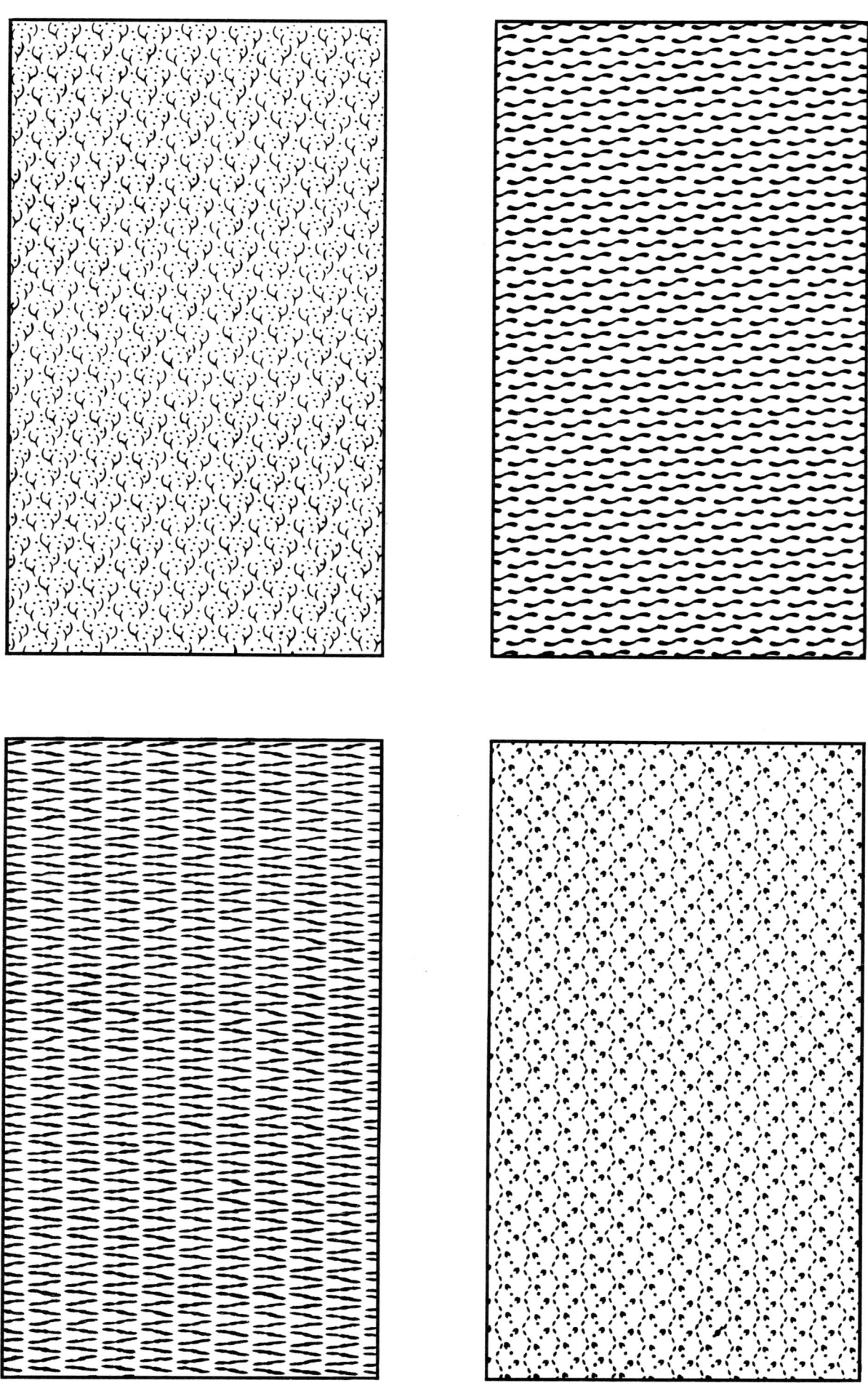

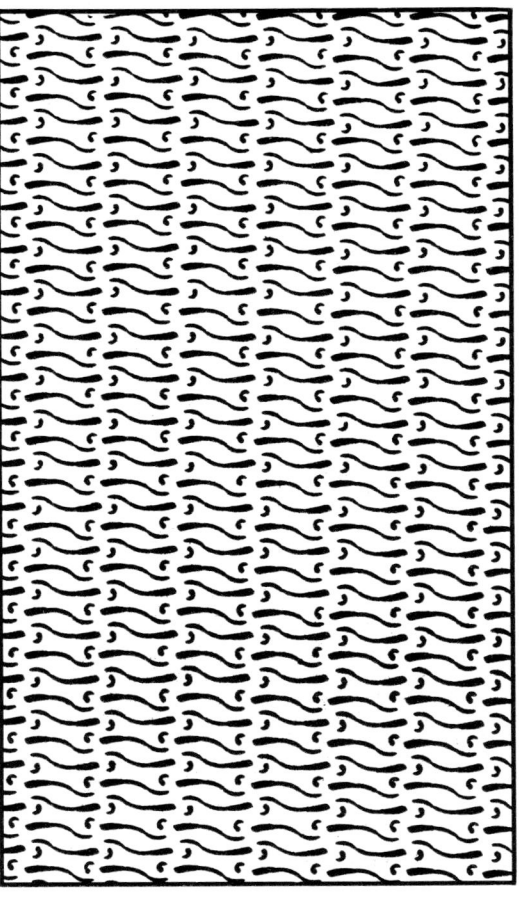

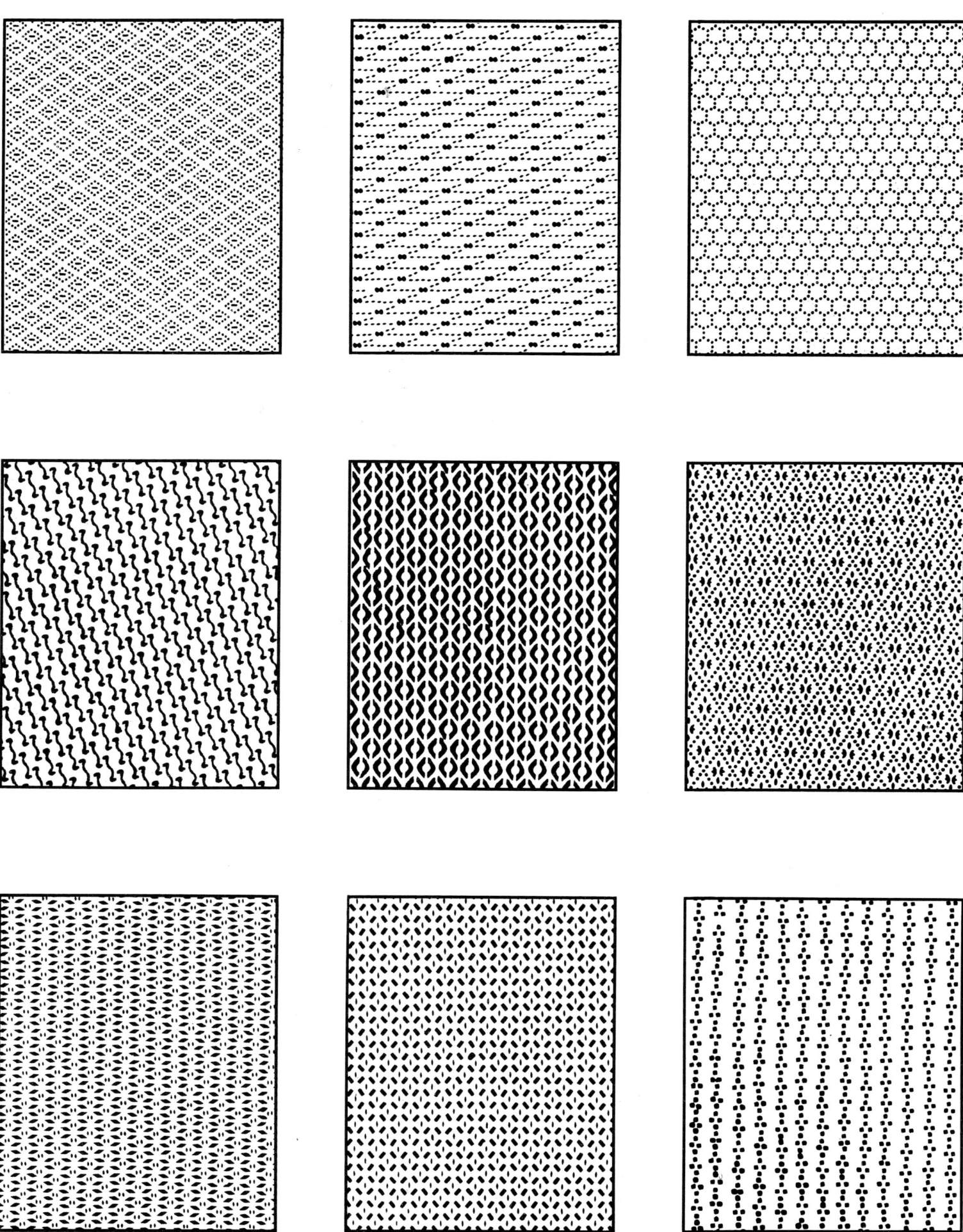

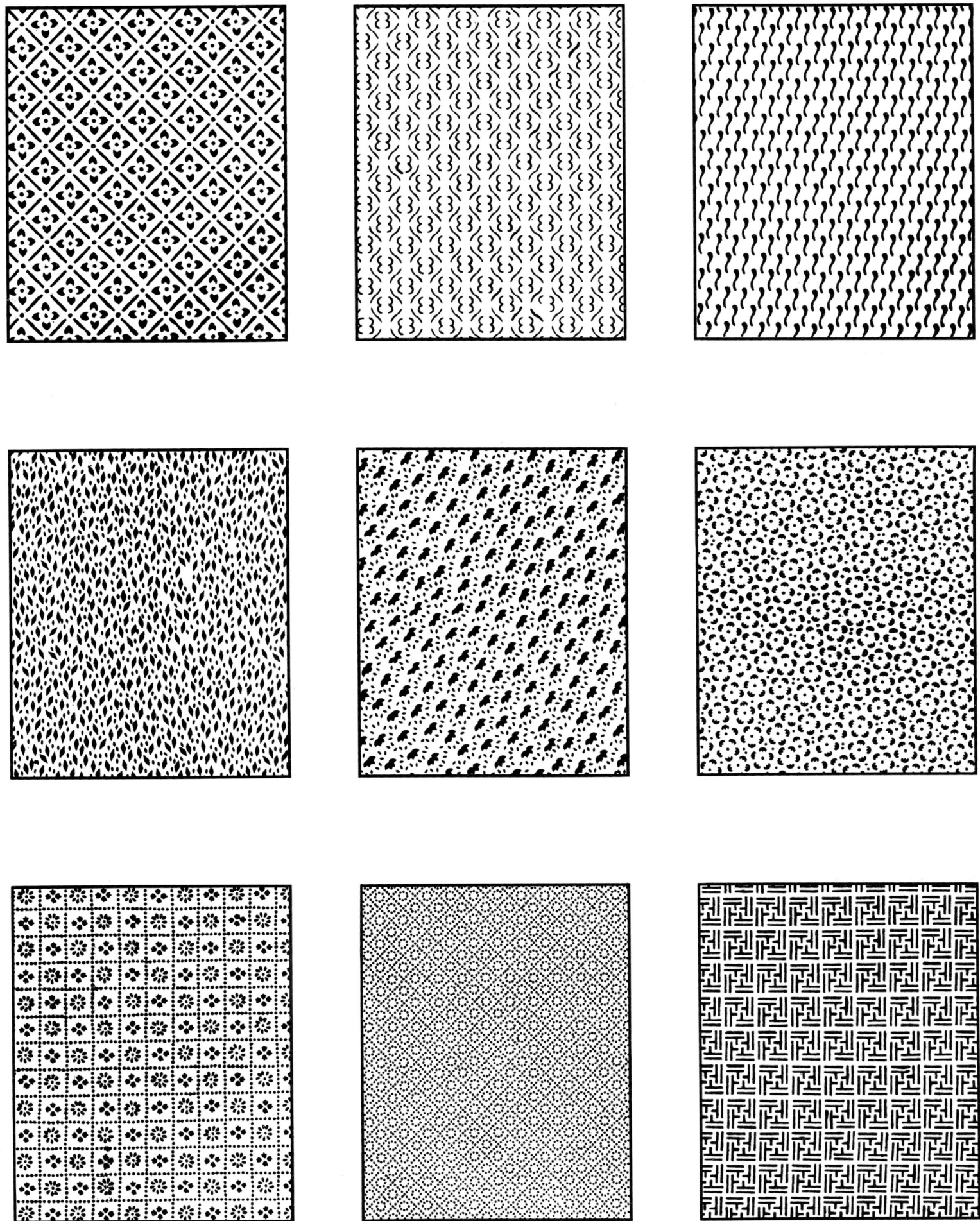

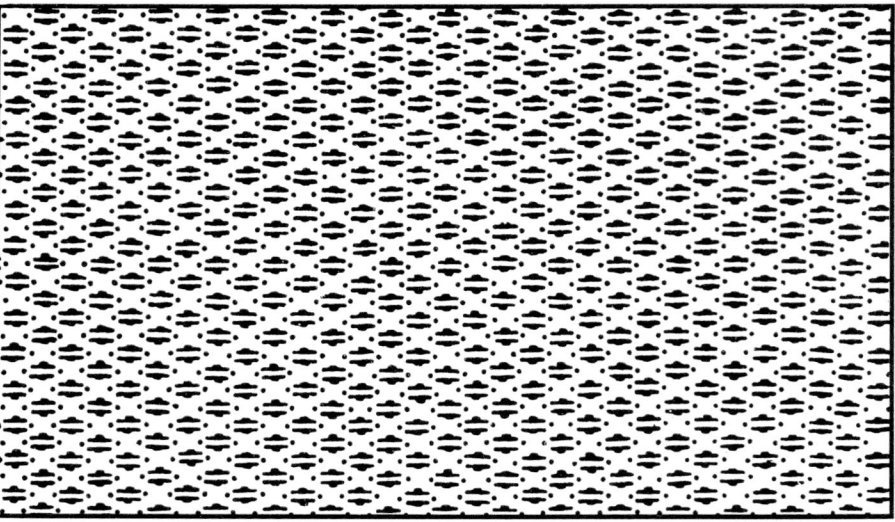

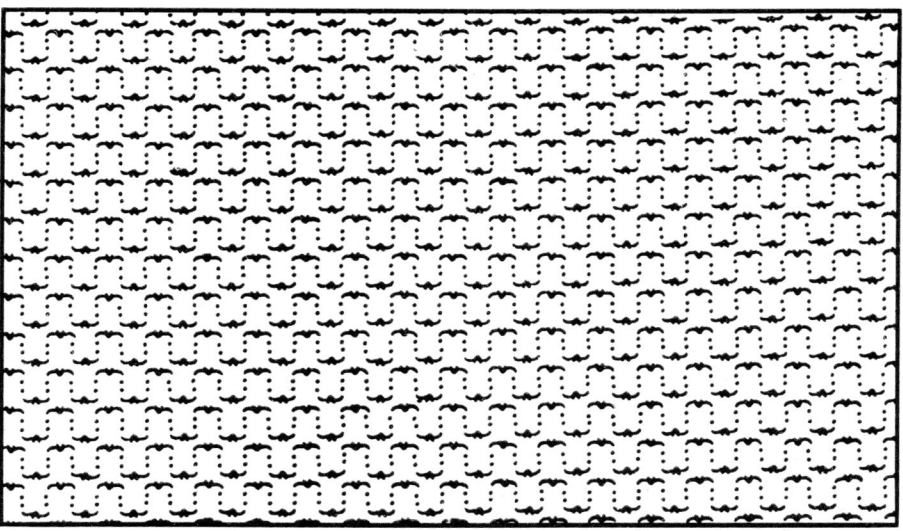

14

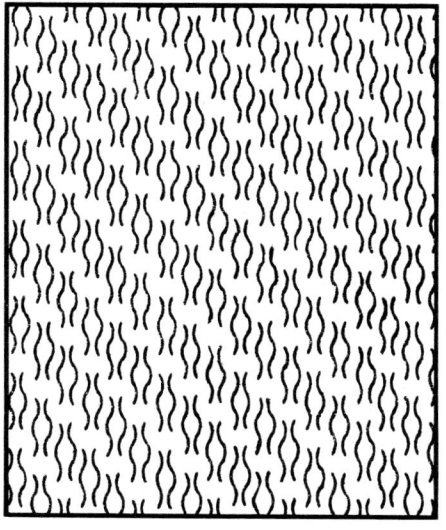

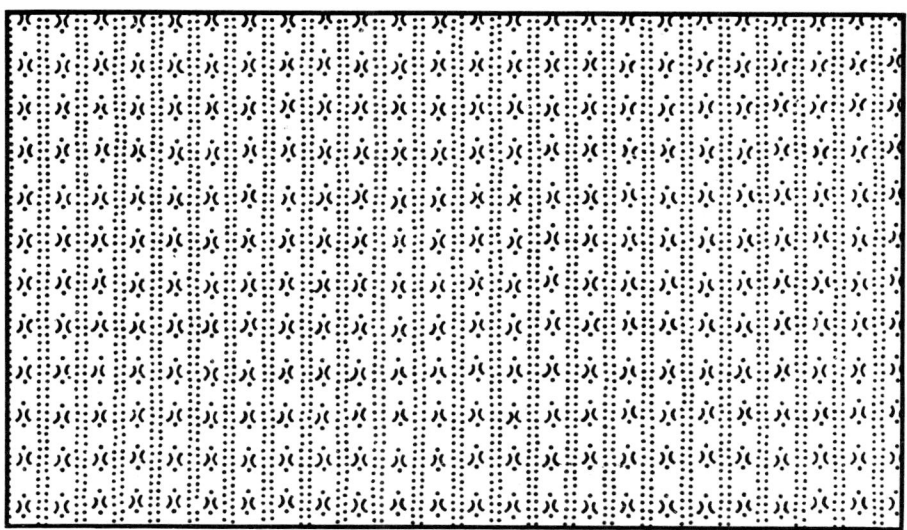

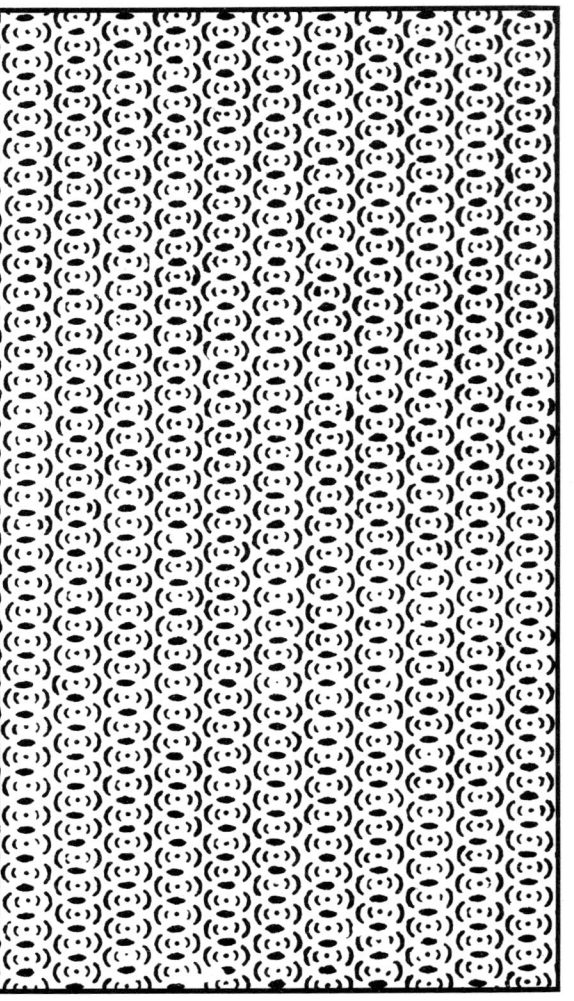

16

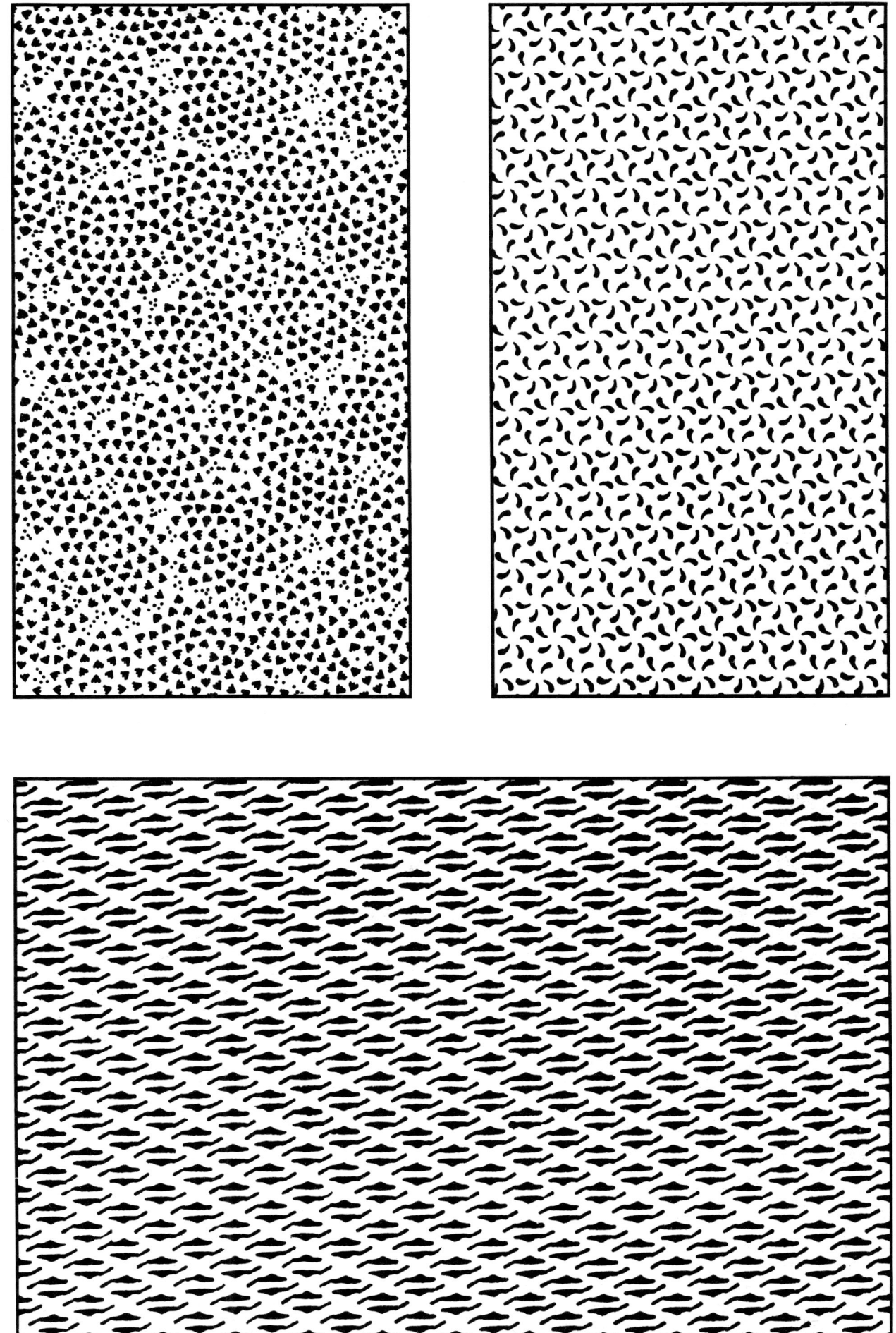

18

19

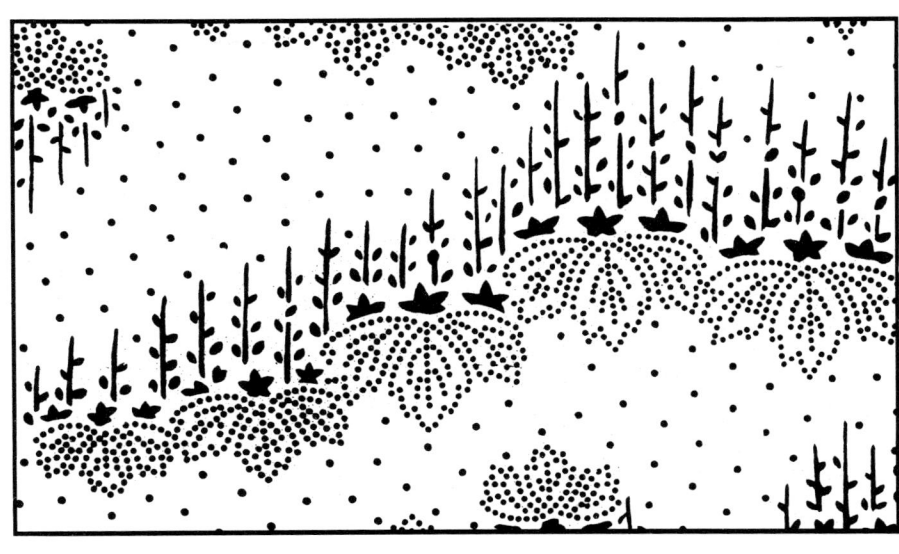

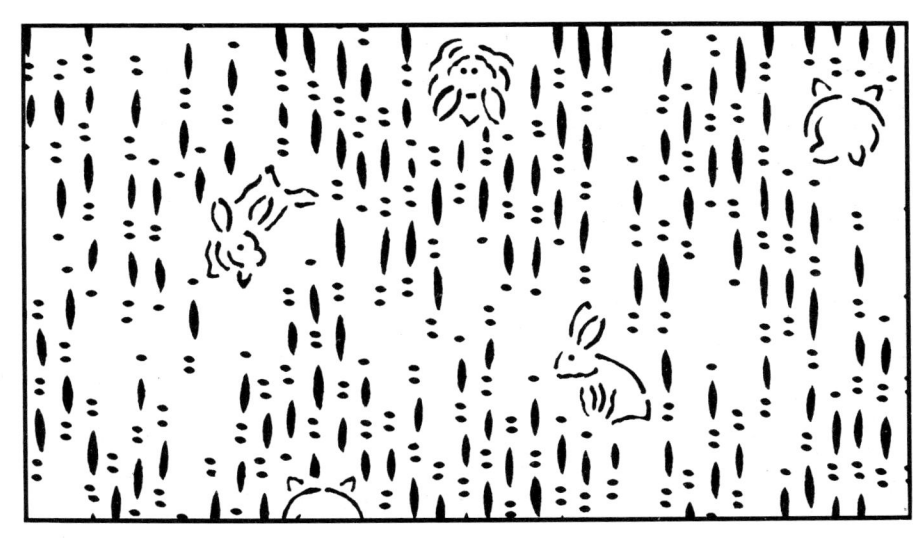

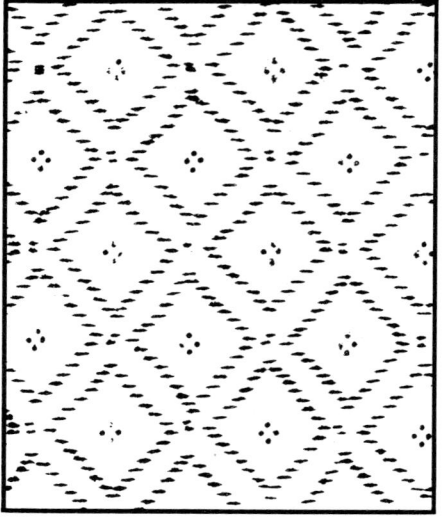
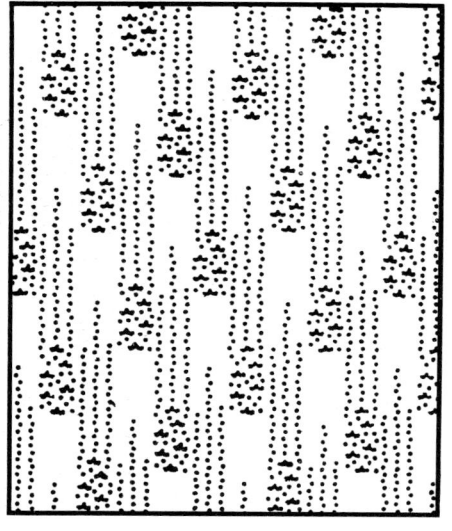

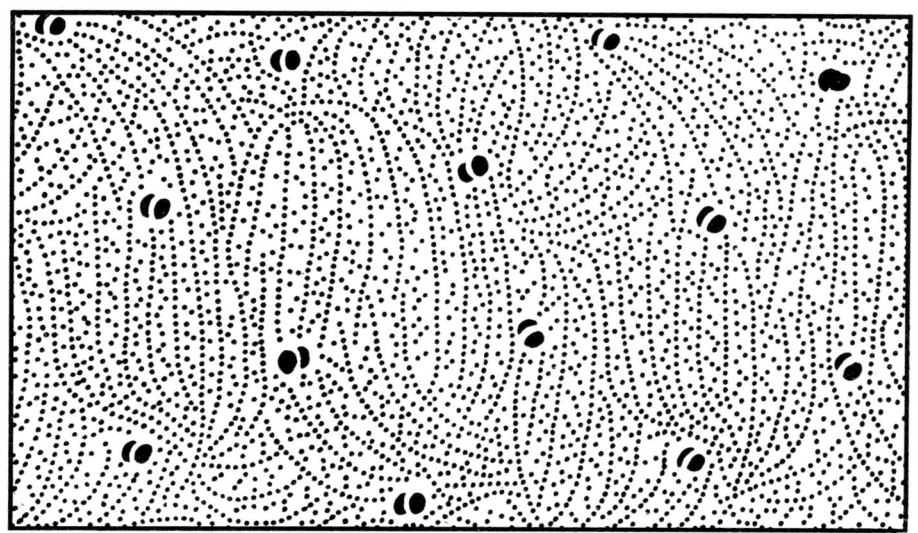
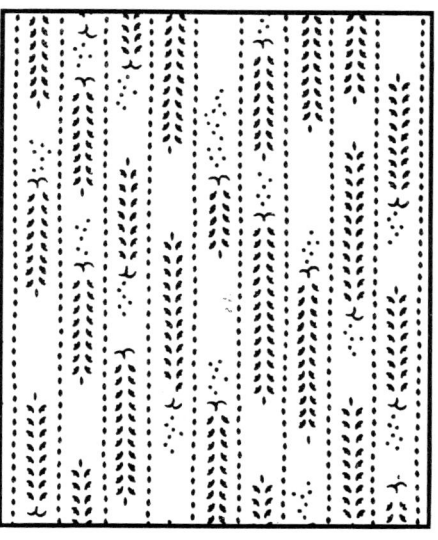

24

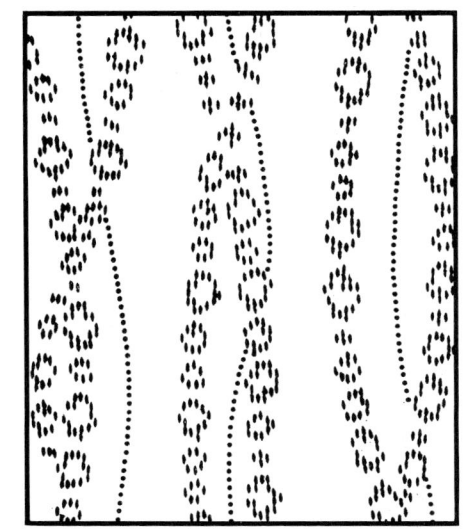

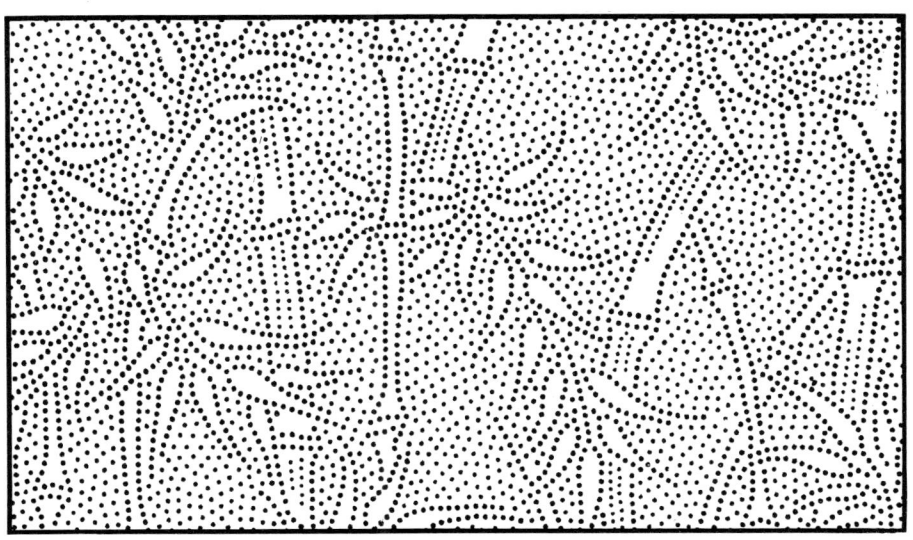
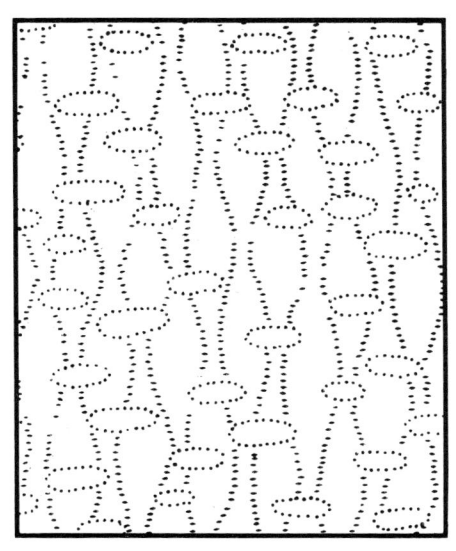

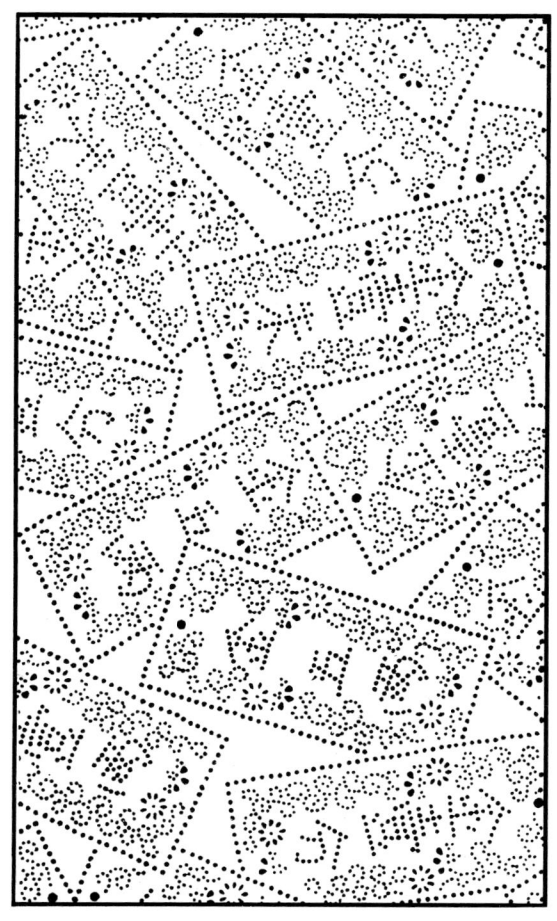
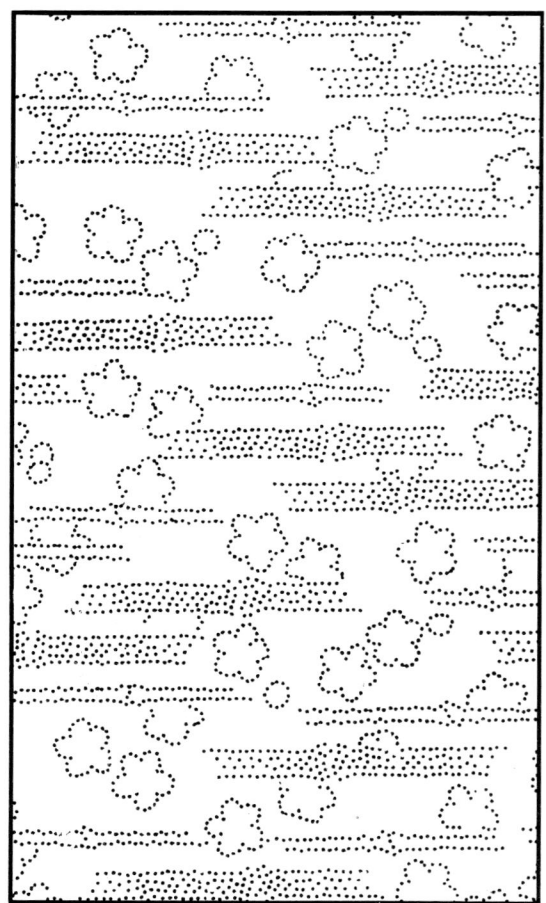

26

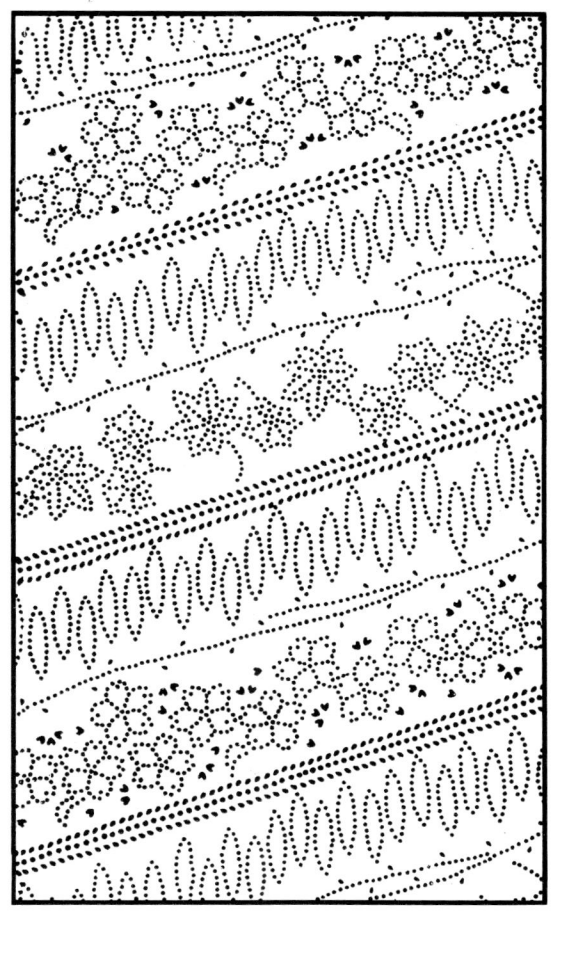

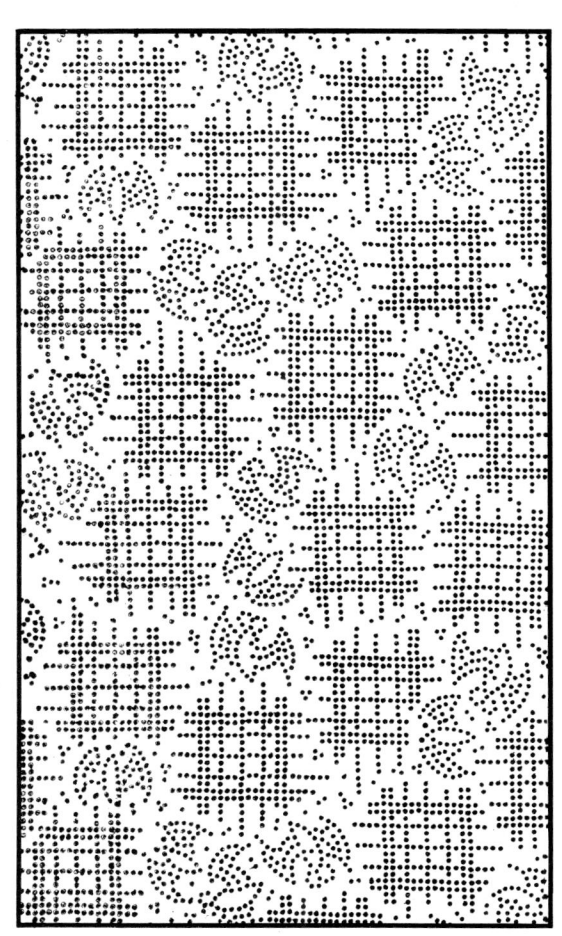

29

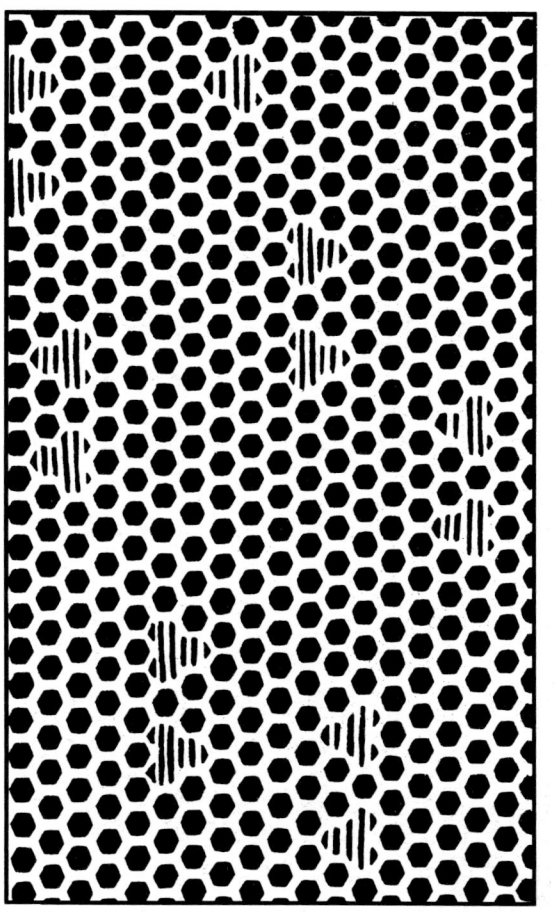

31

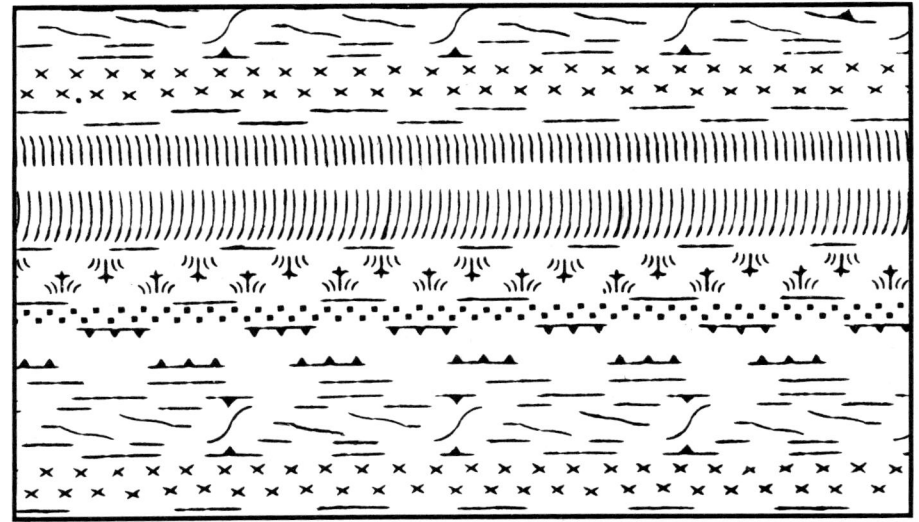

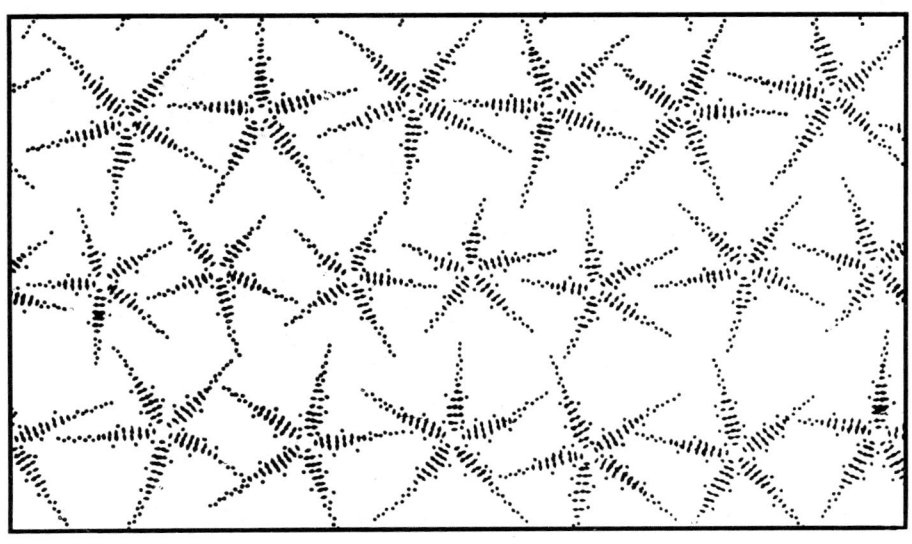
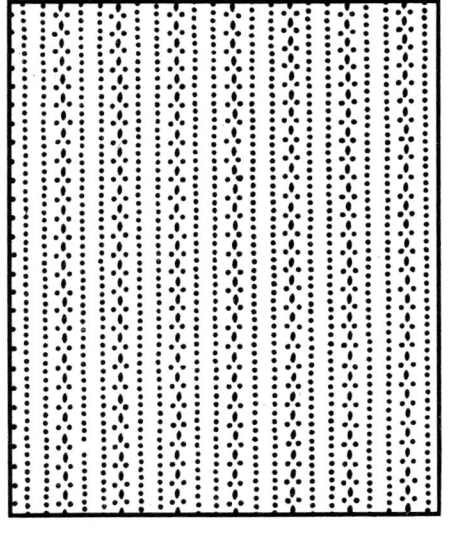

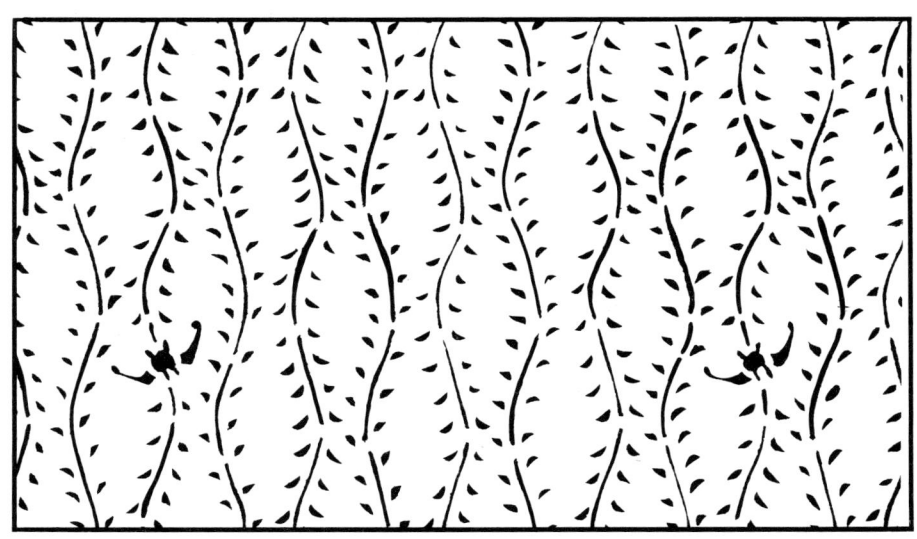

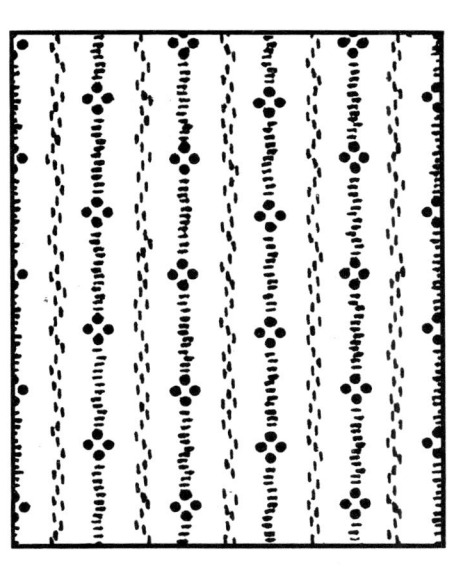

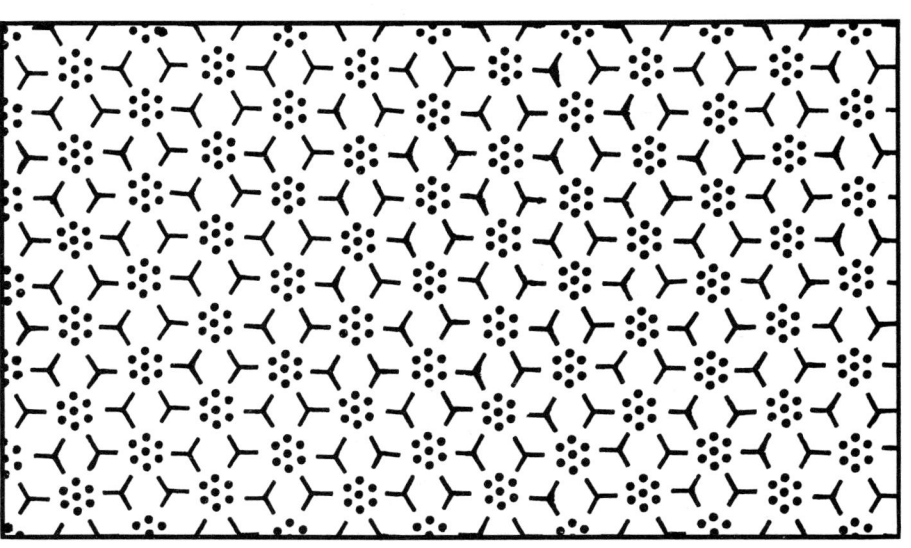

33

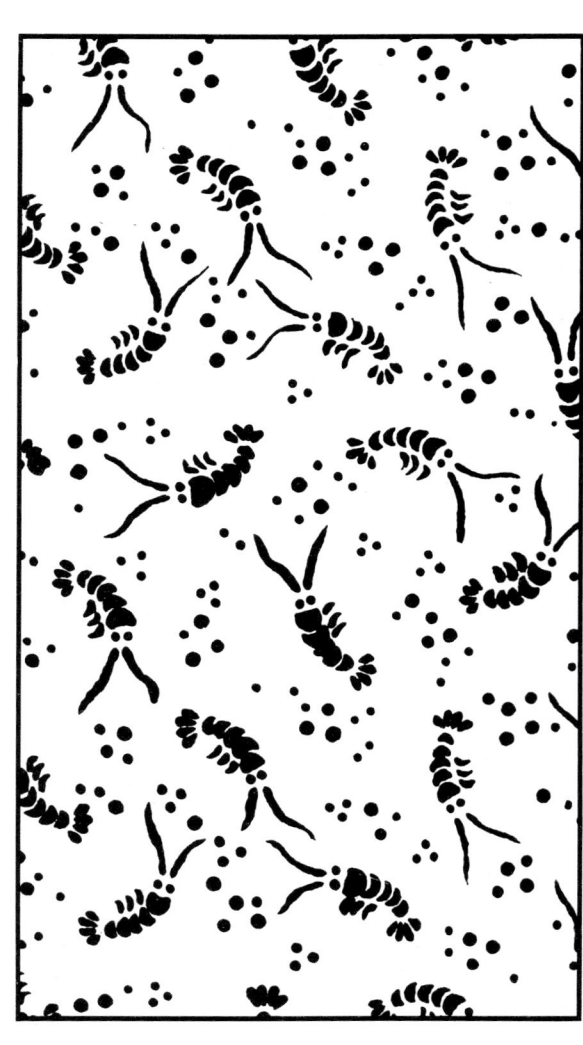

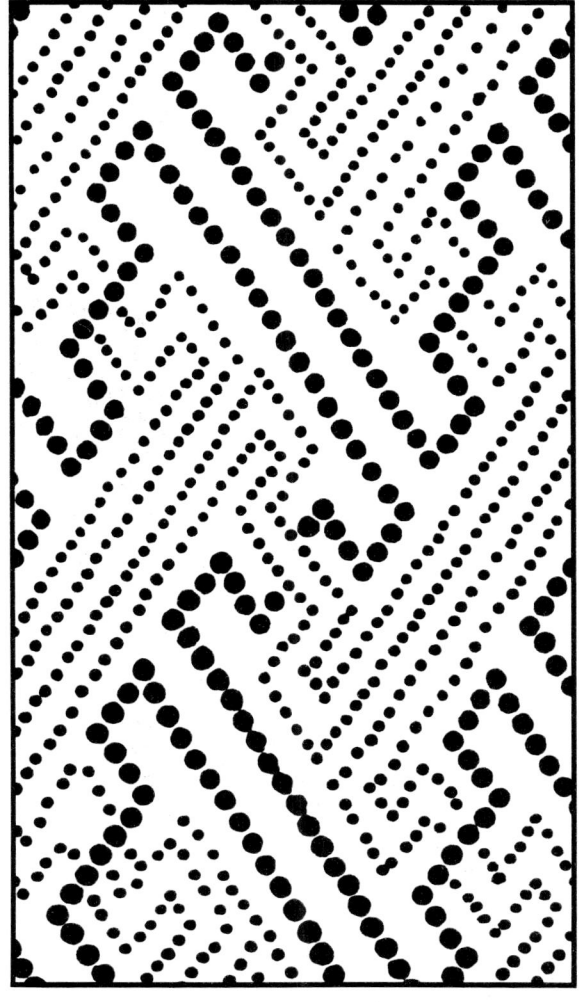

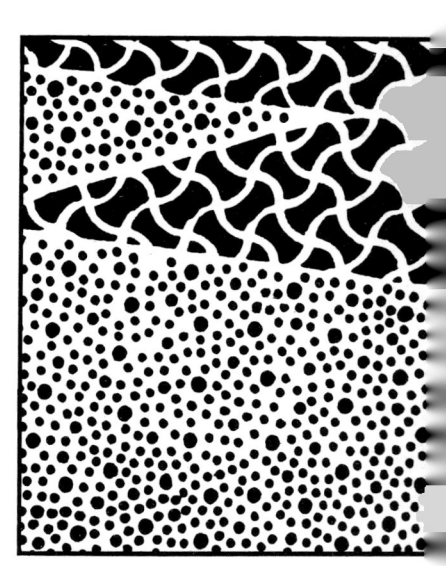

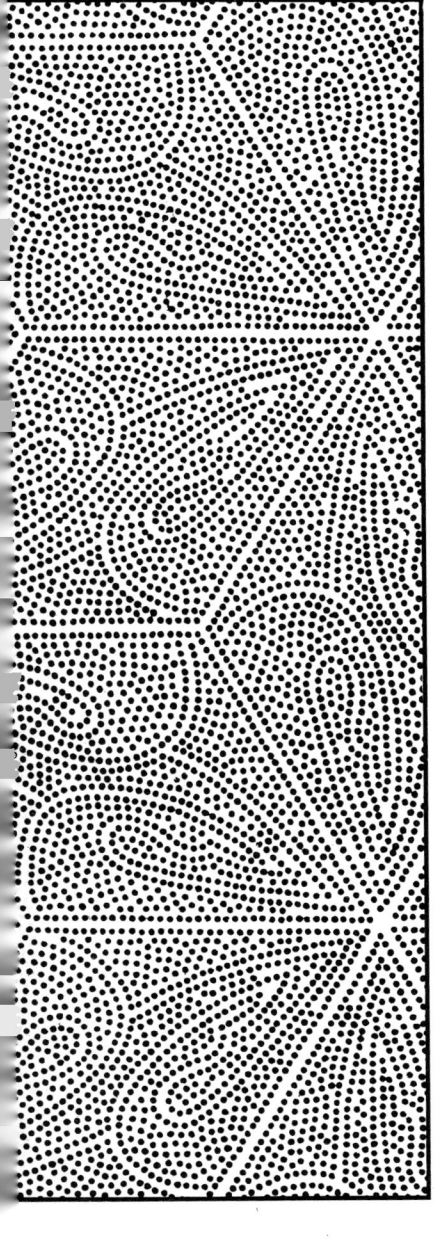

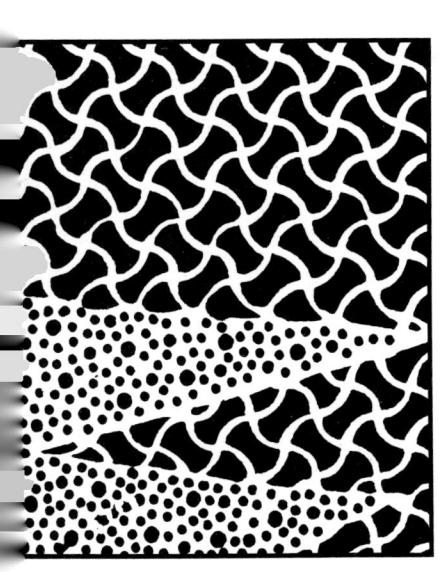

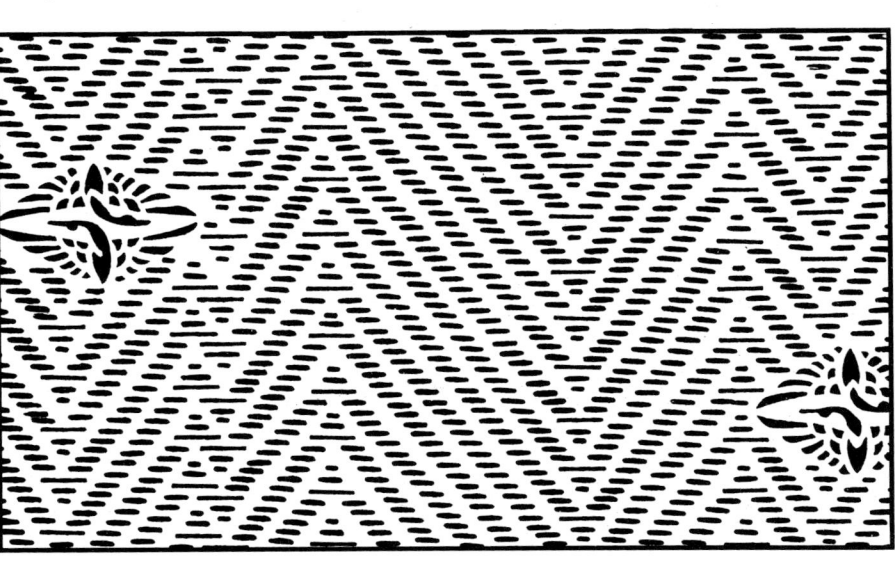

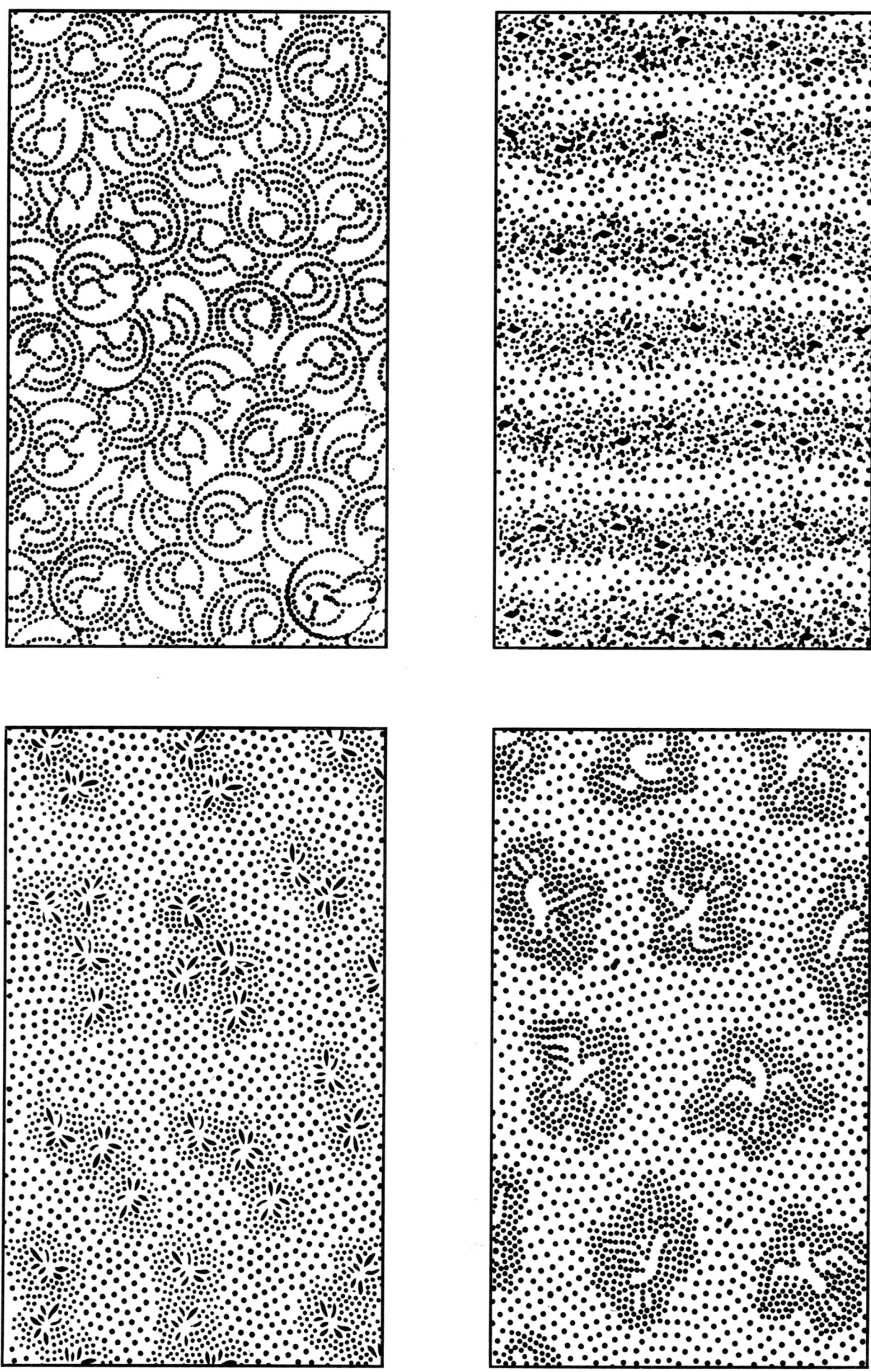

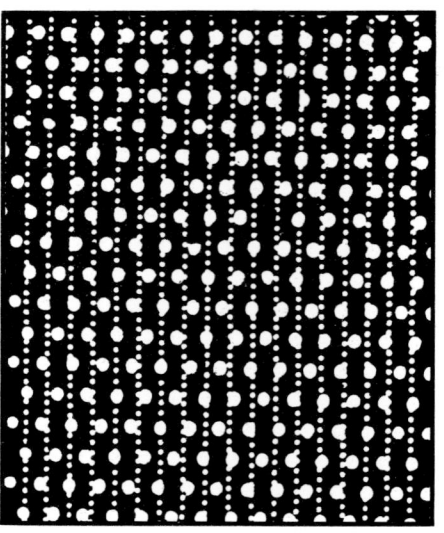

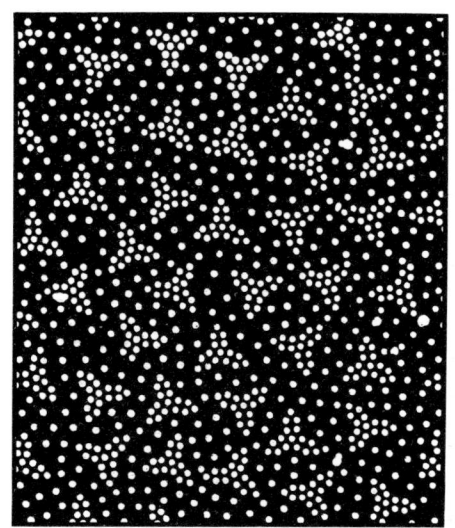

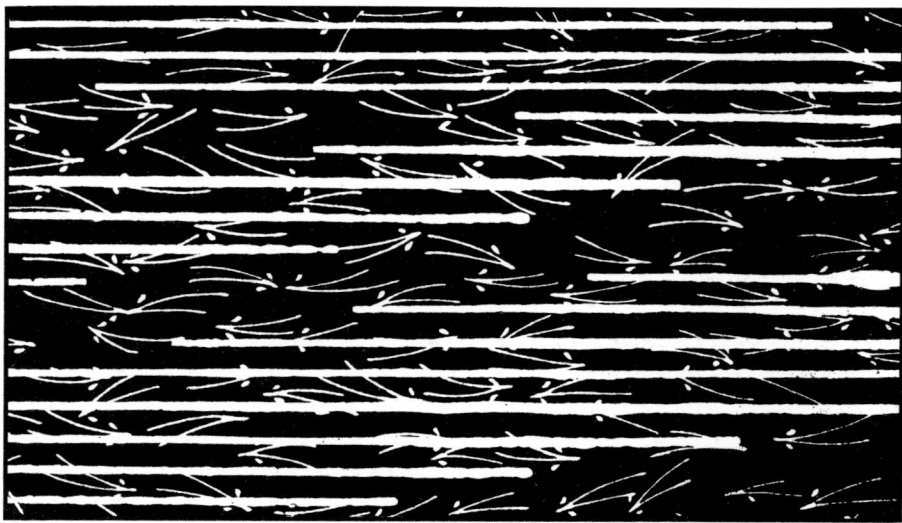

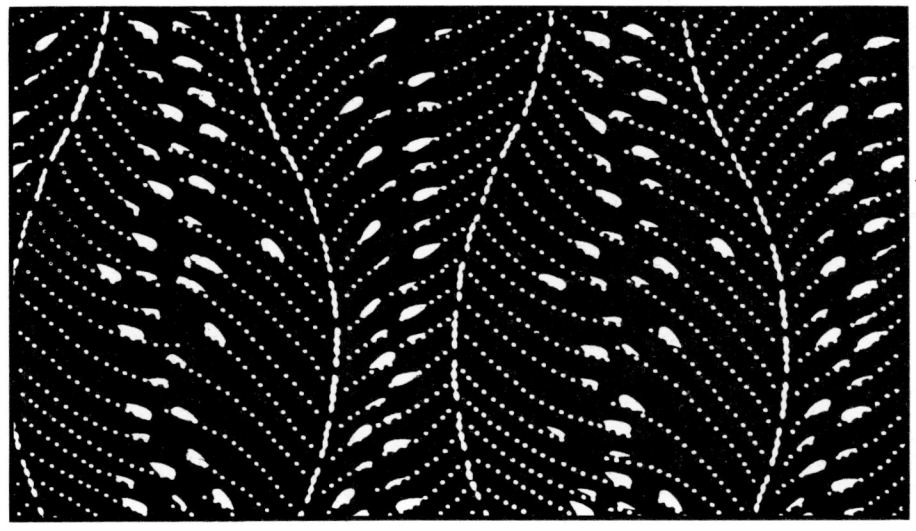

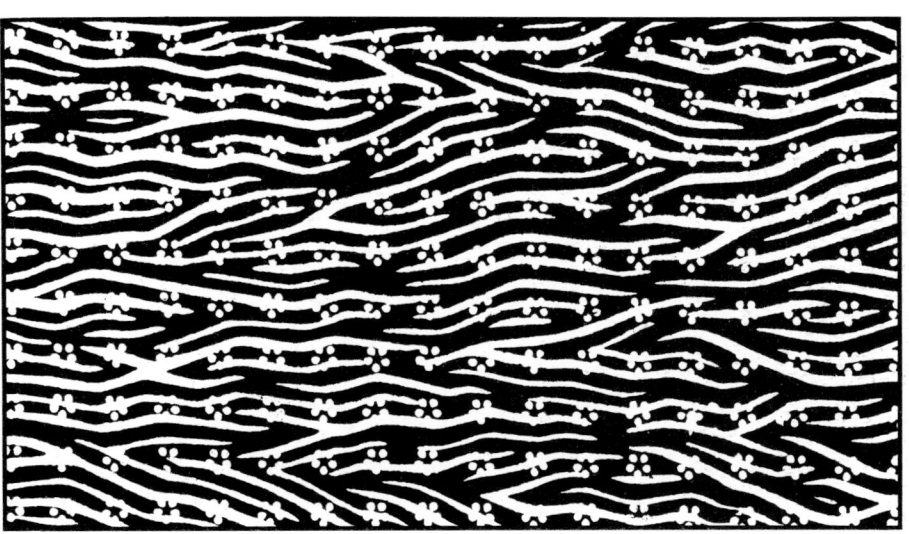
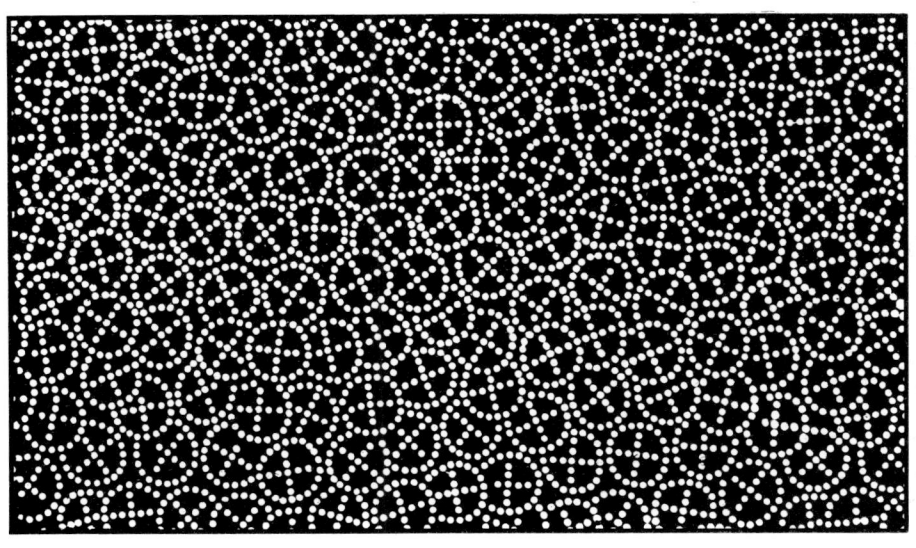

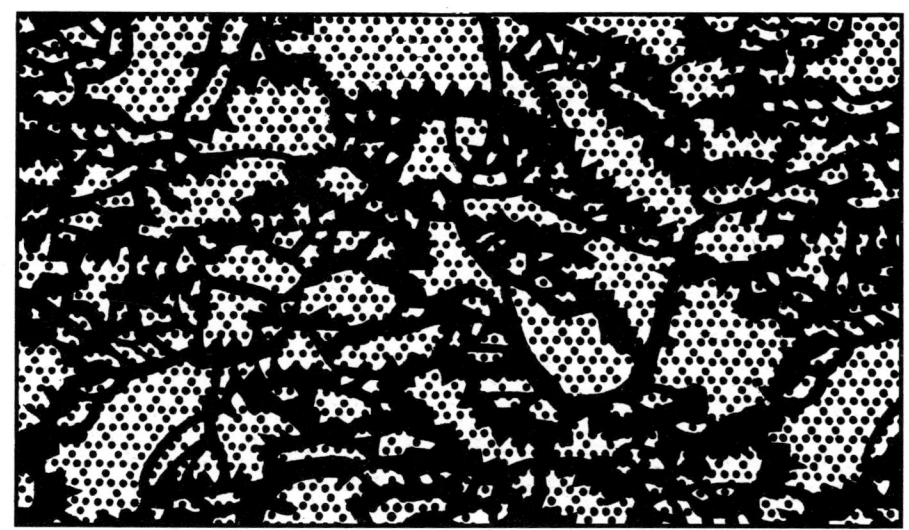

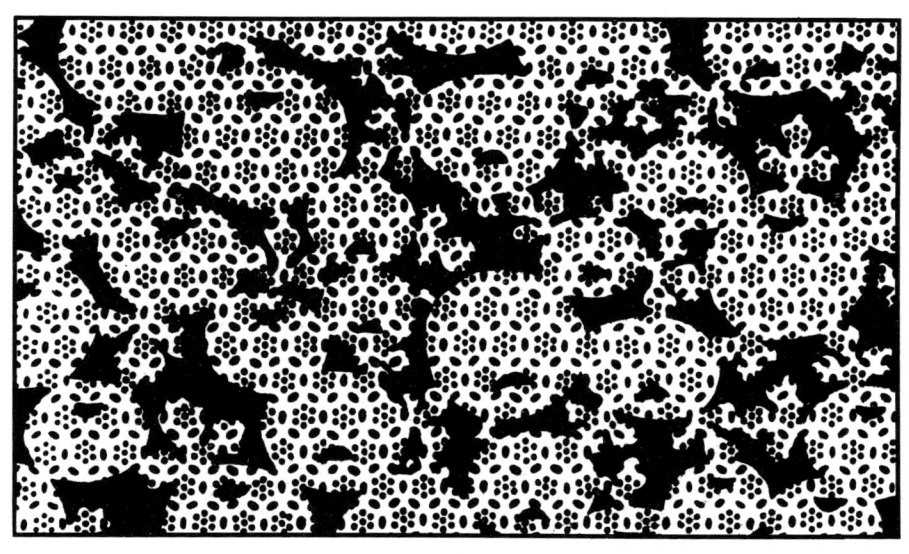

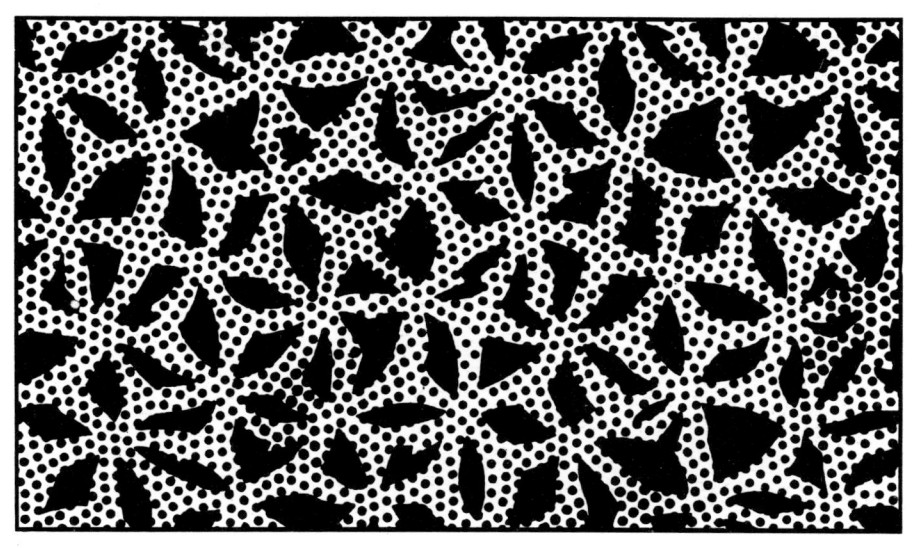

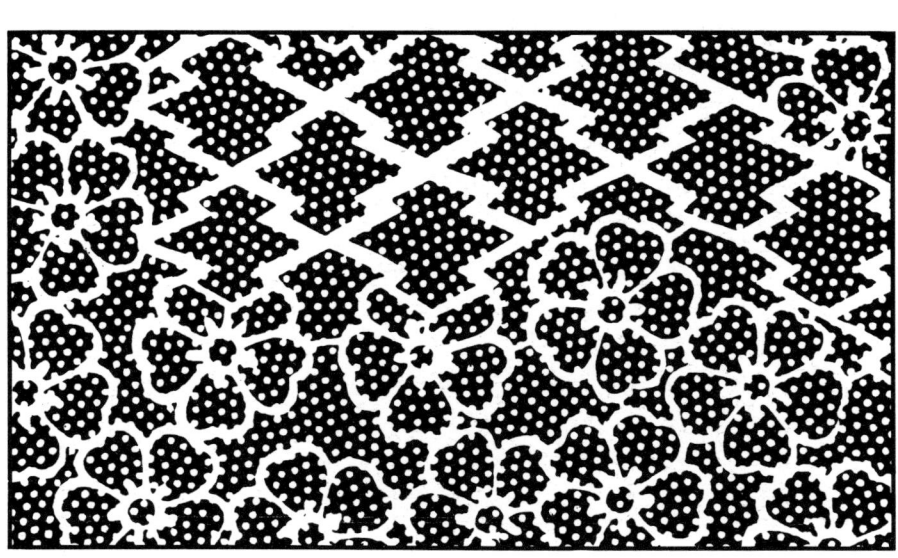

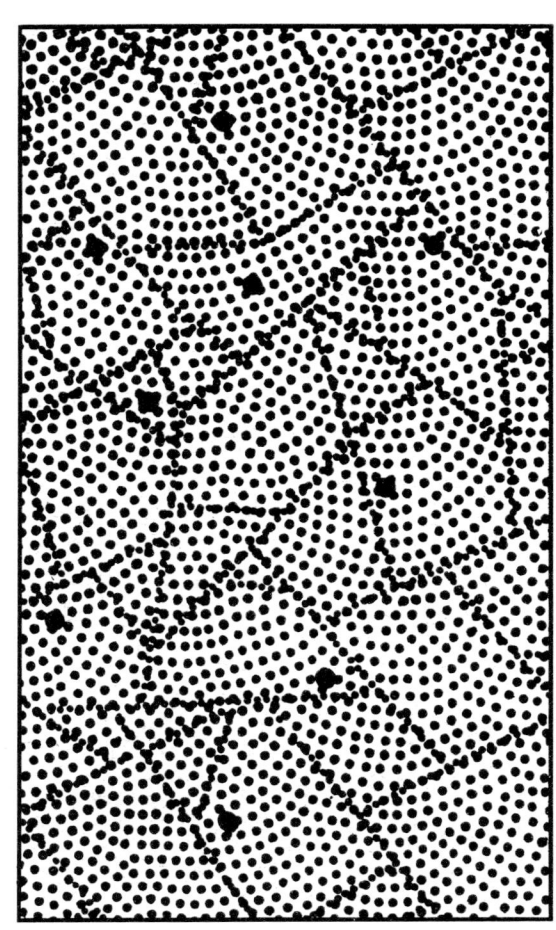

47

48

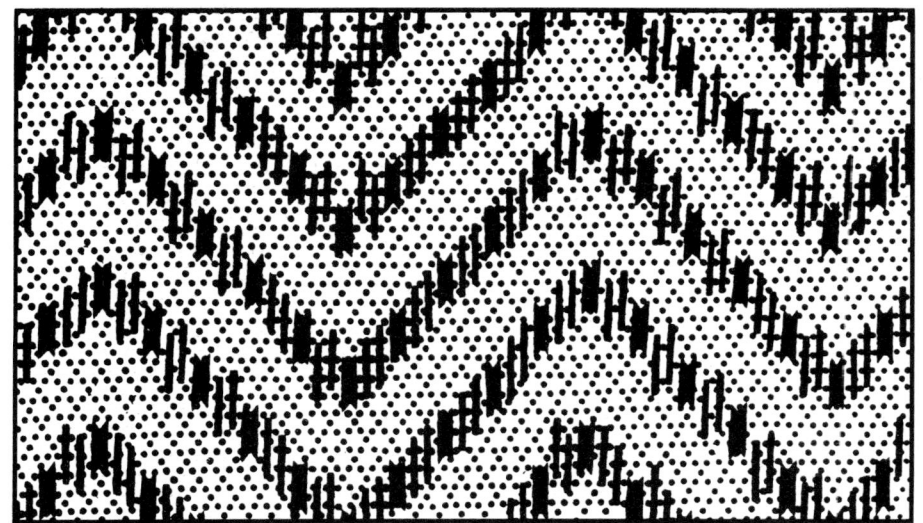

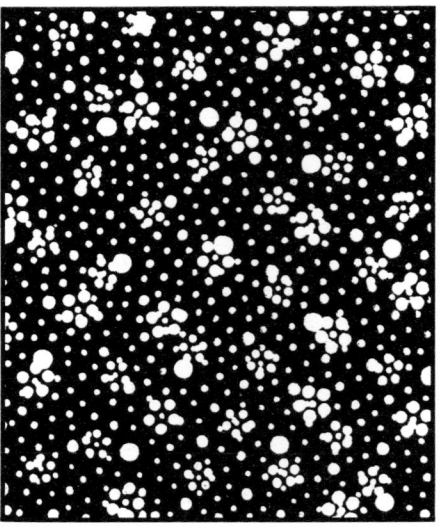

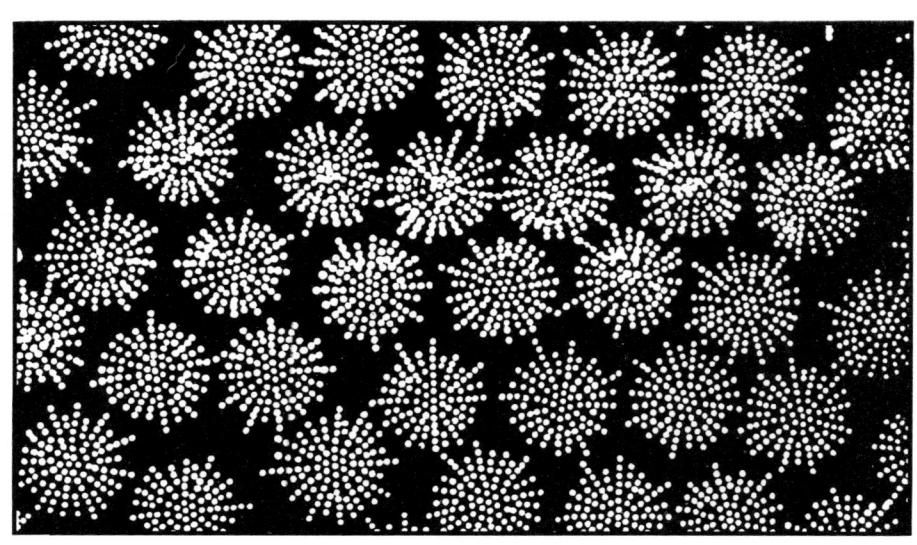

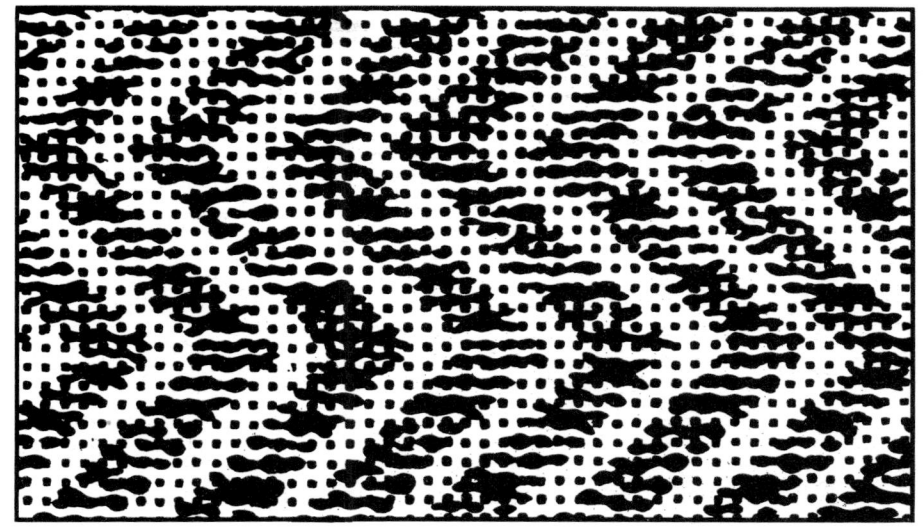
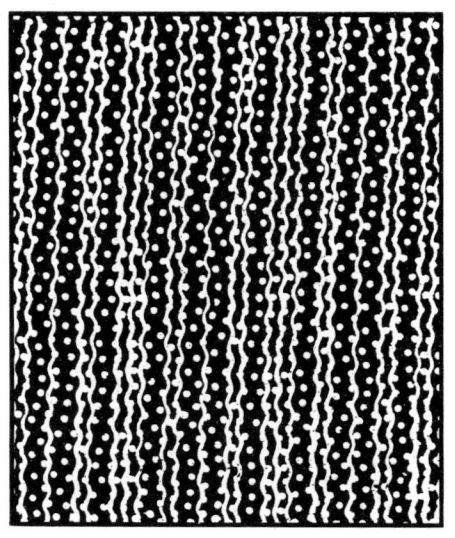
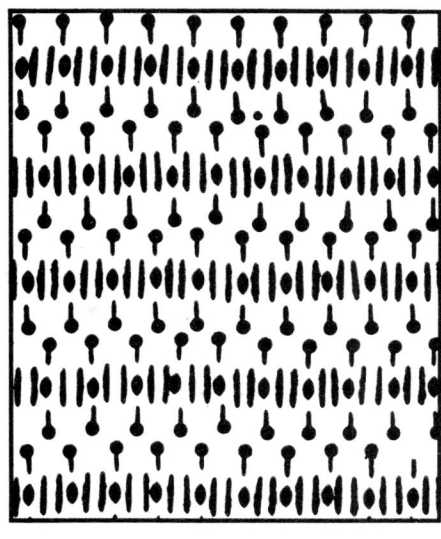
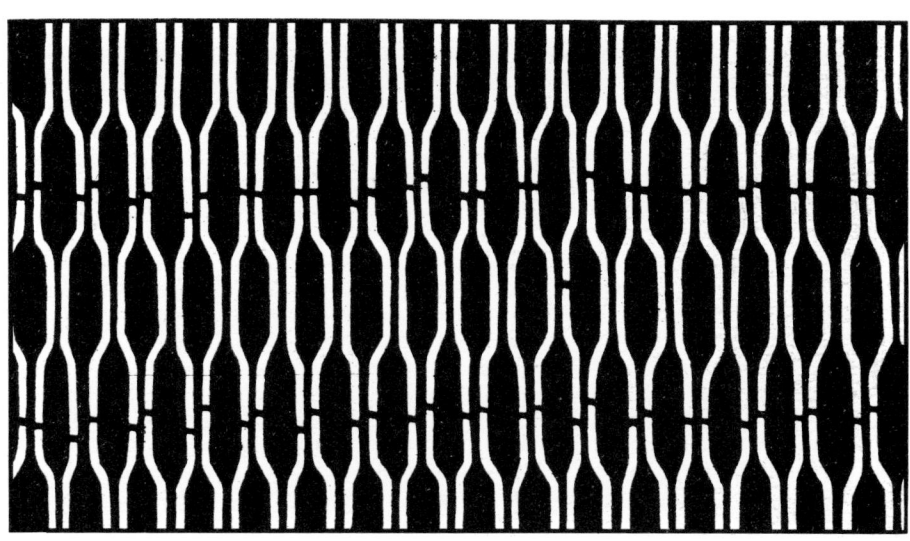
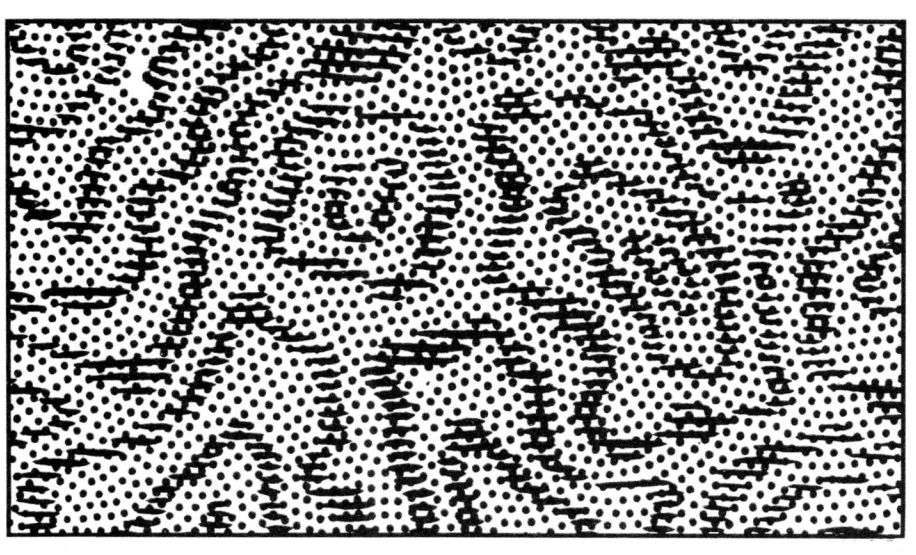

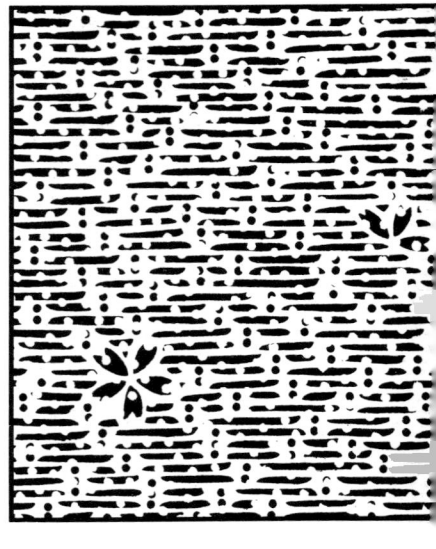
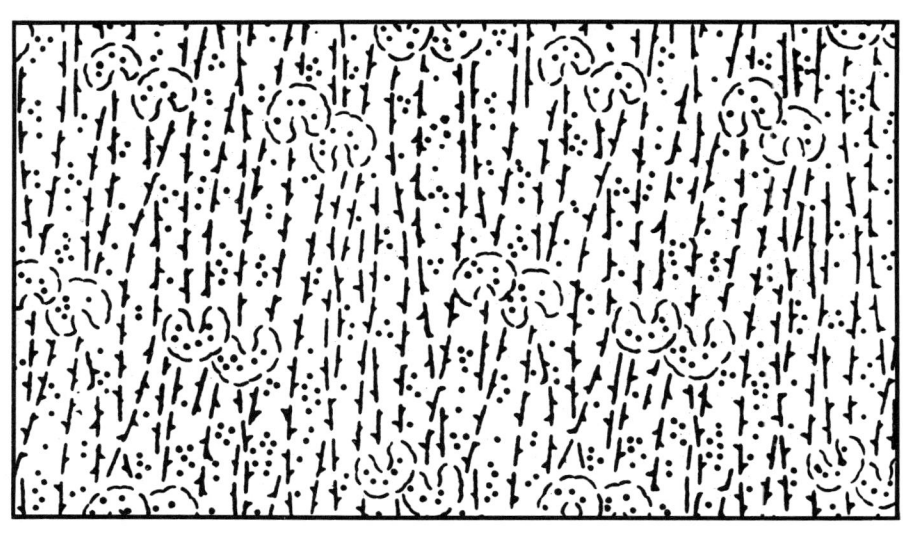

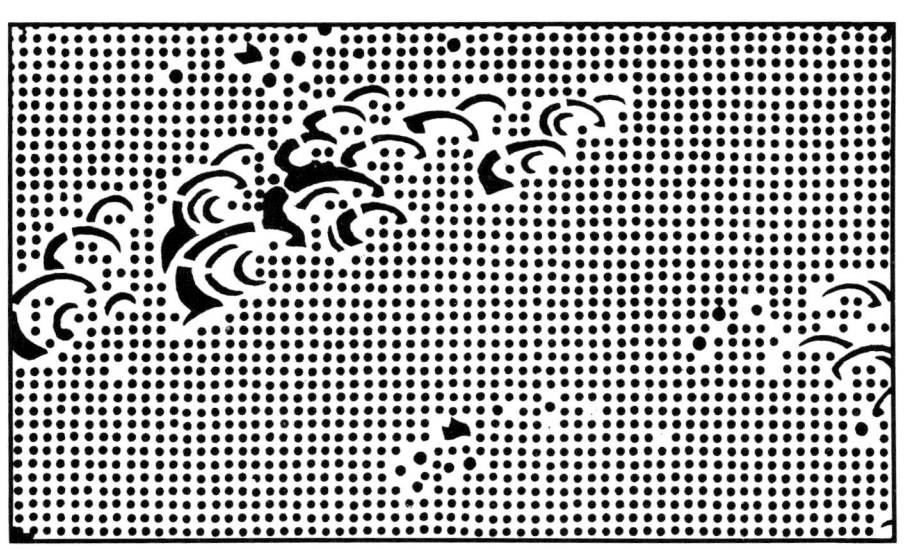
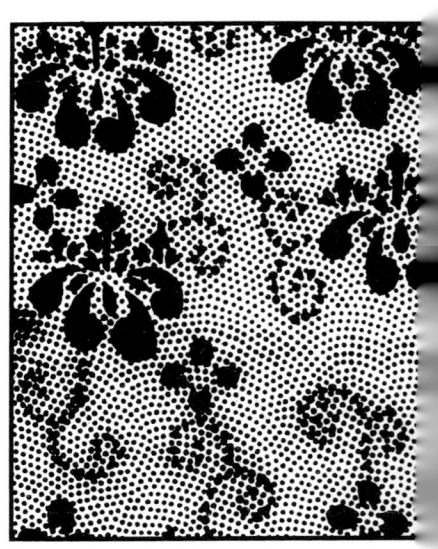

52

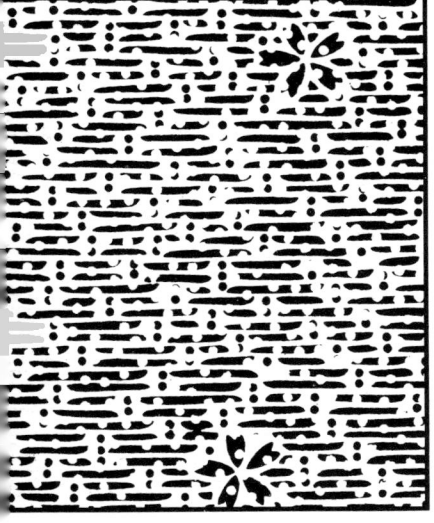

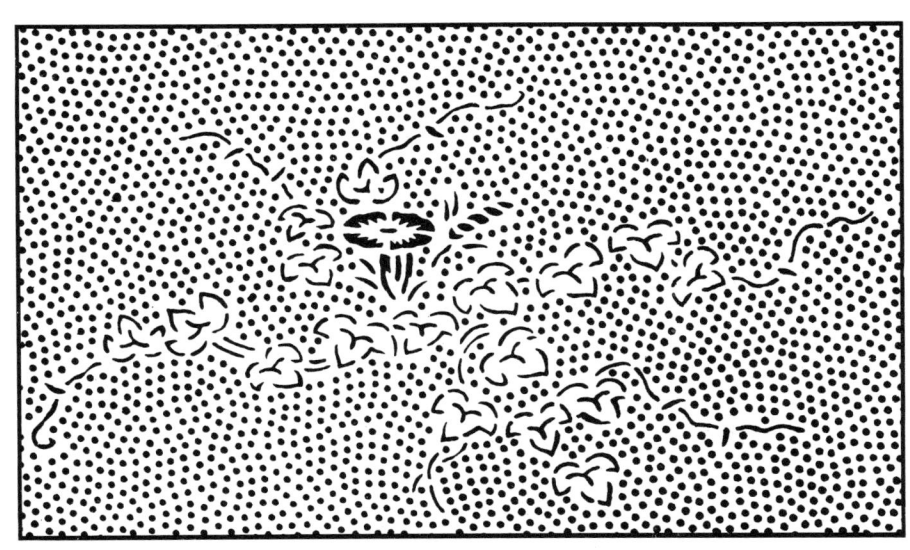

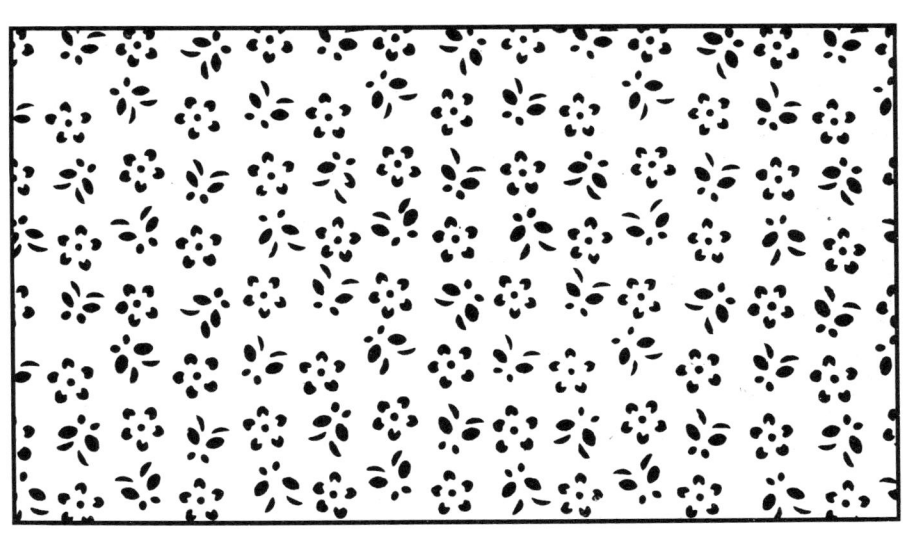

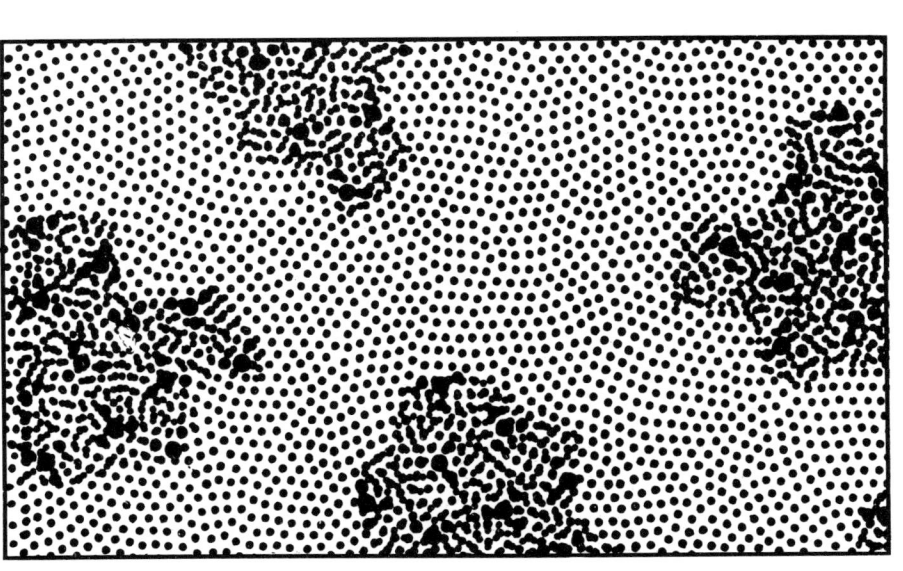

54

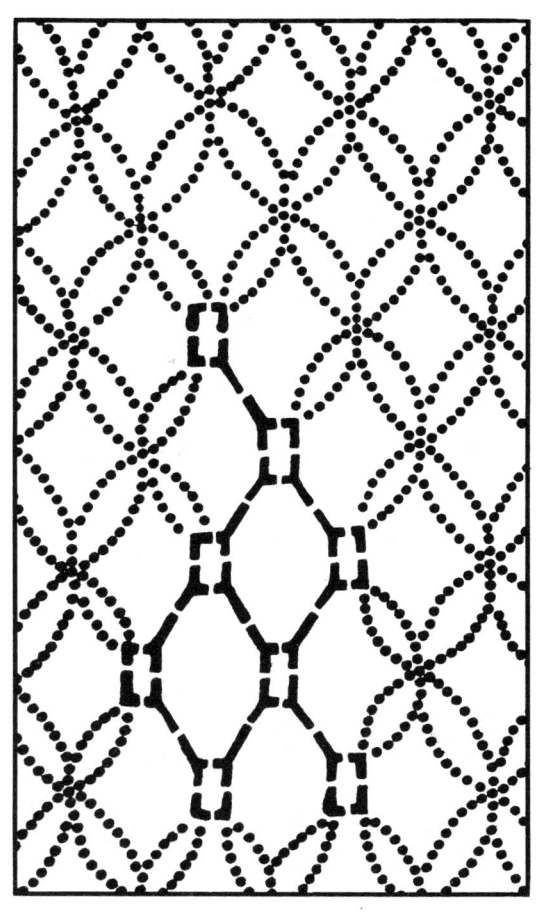

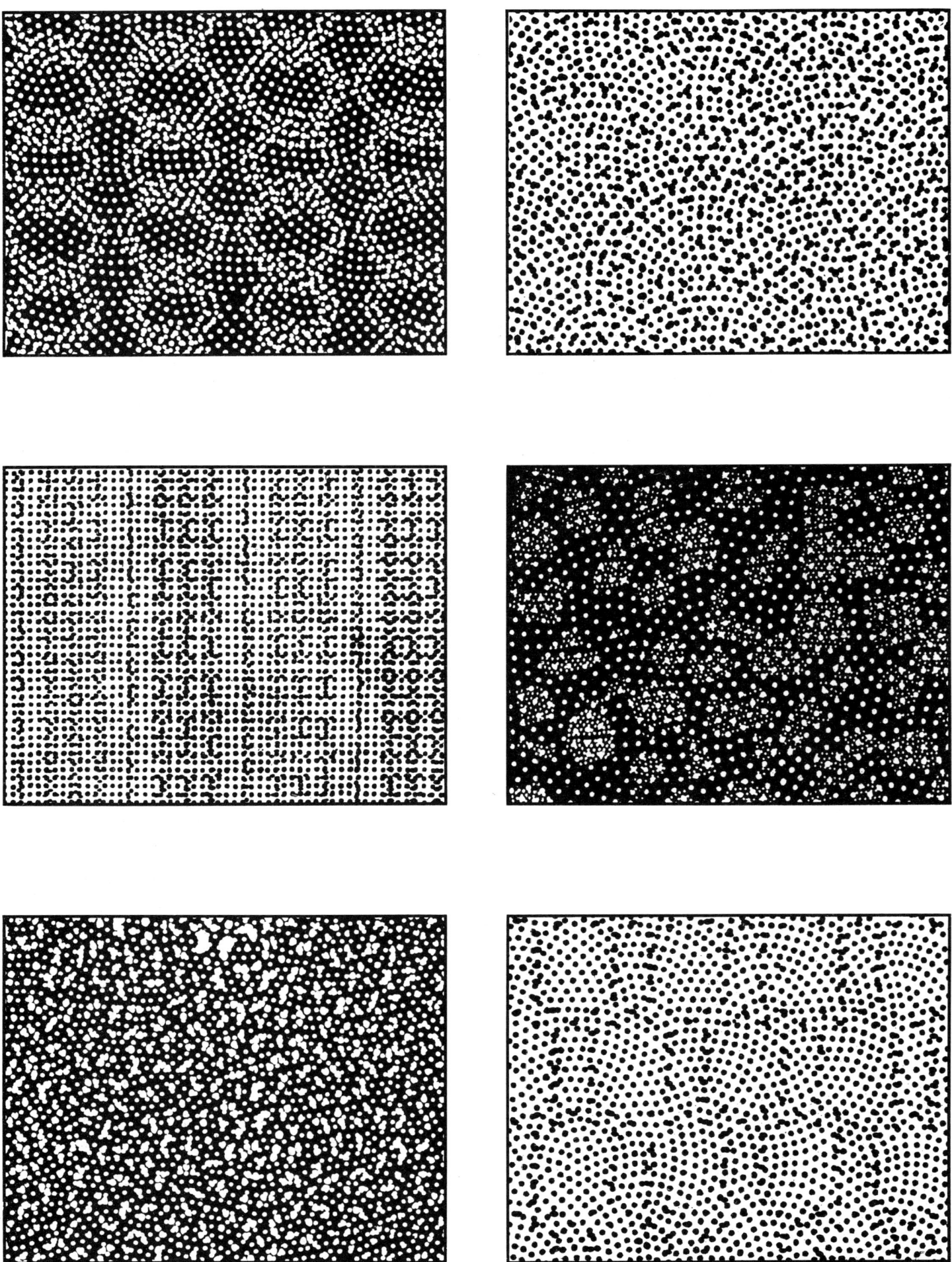

56

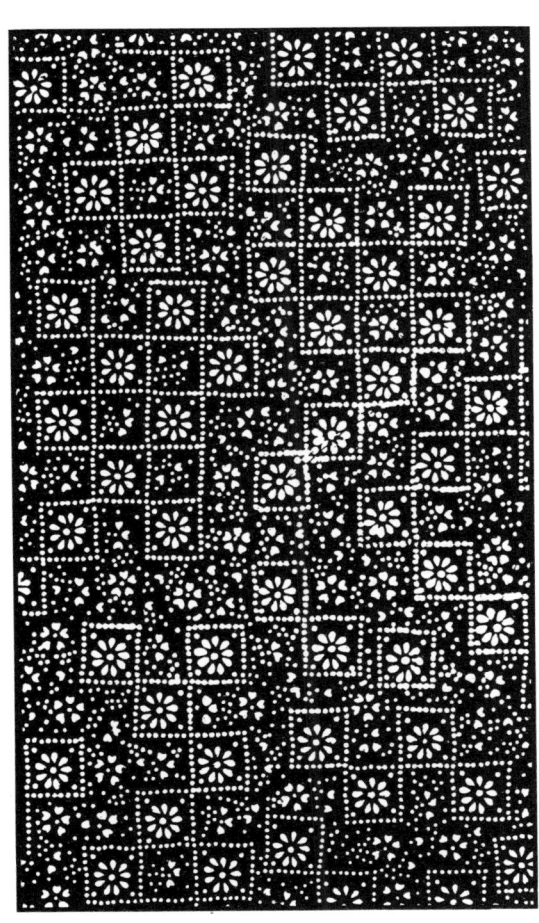

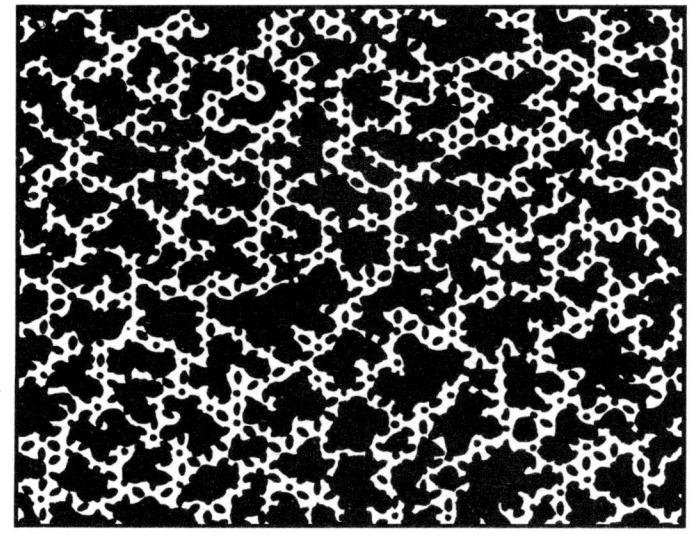
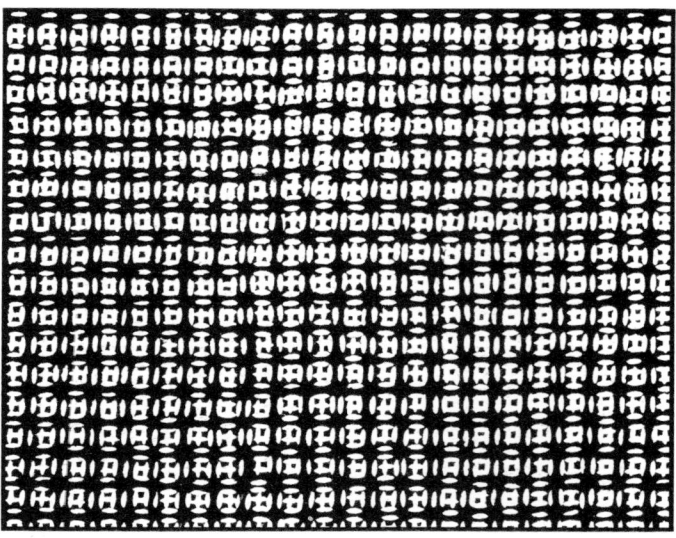

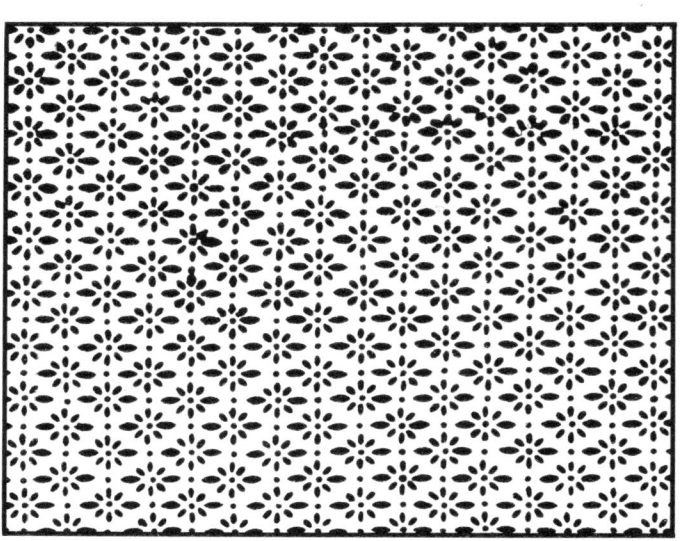
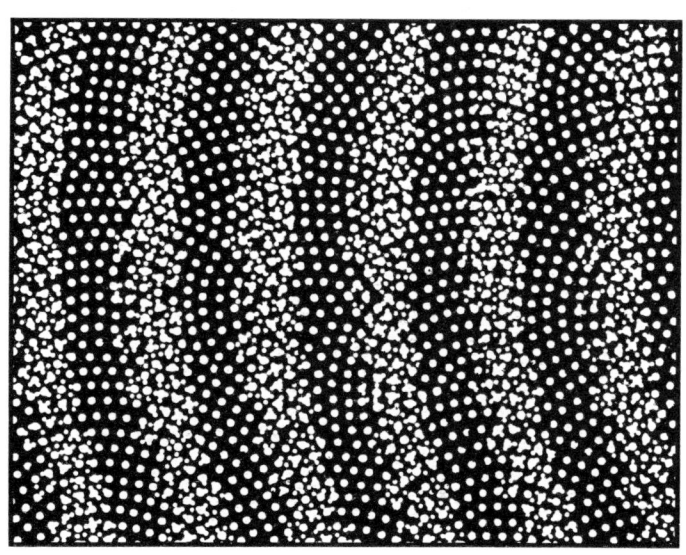
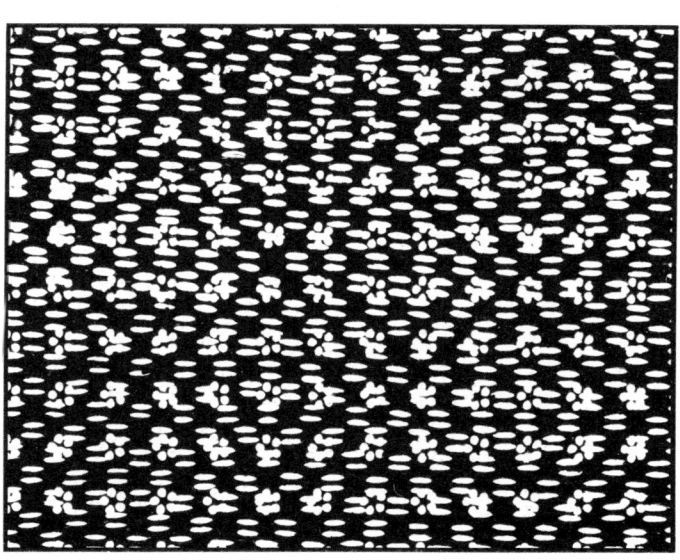

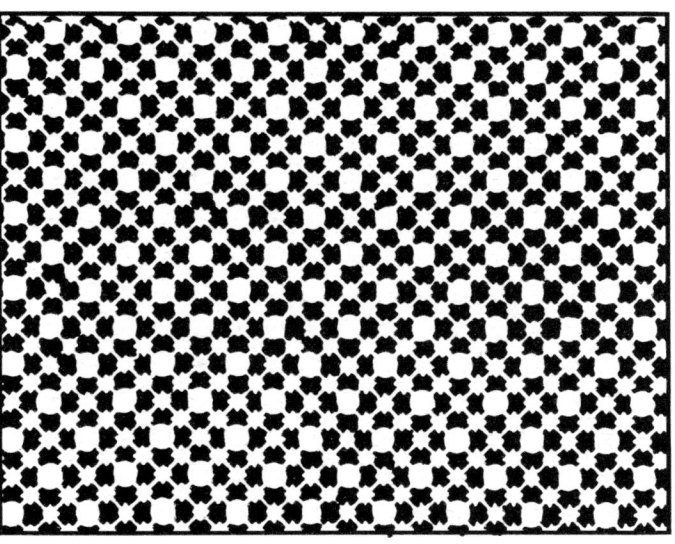

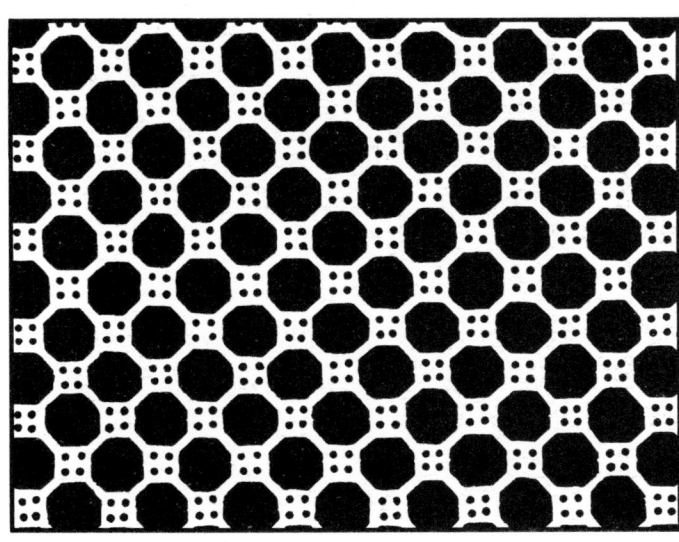

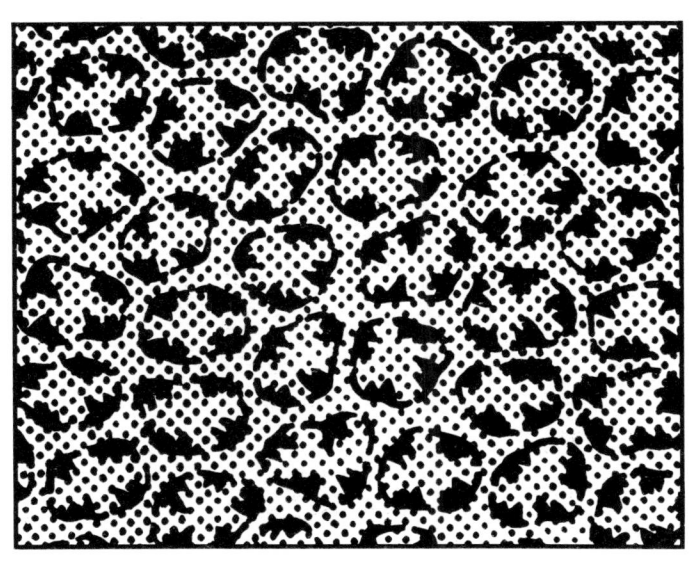

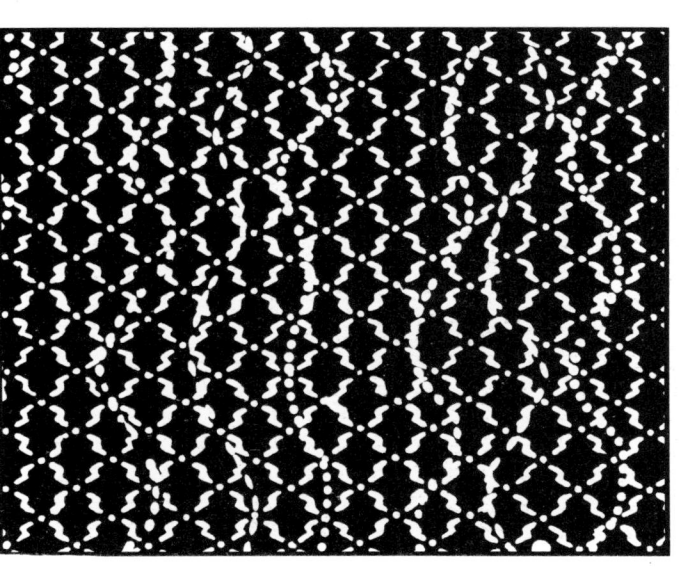

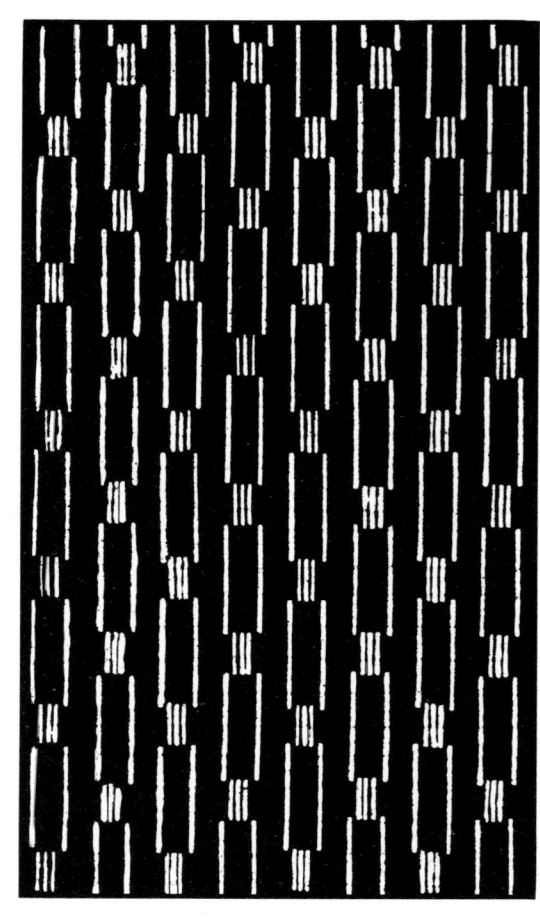

60

61

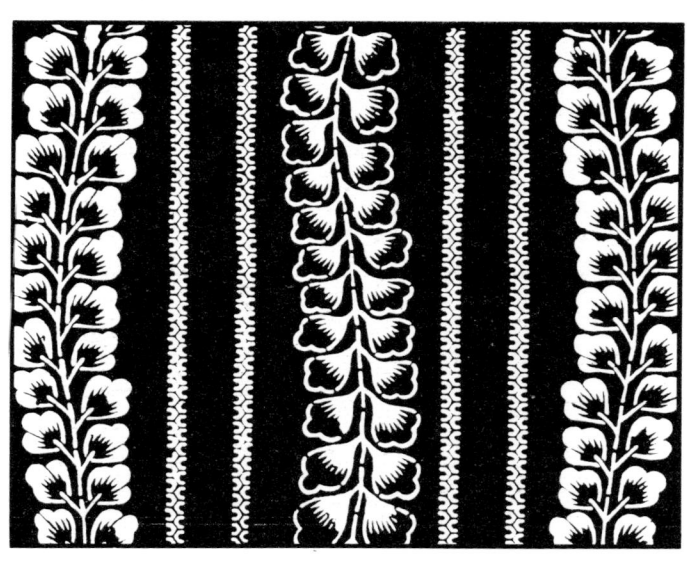

62

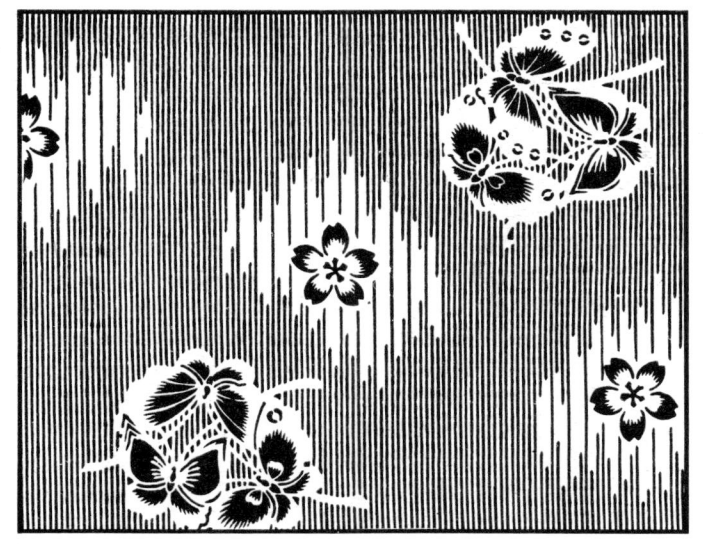

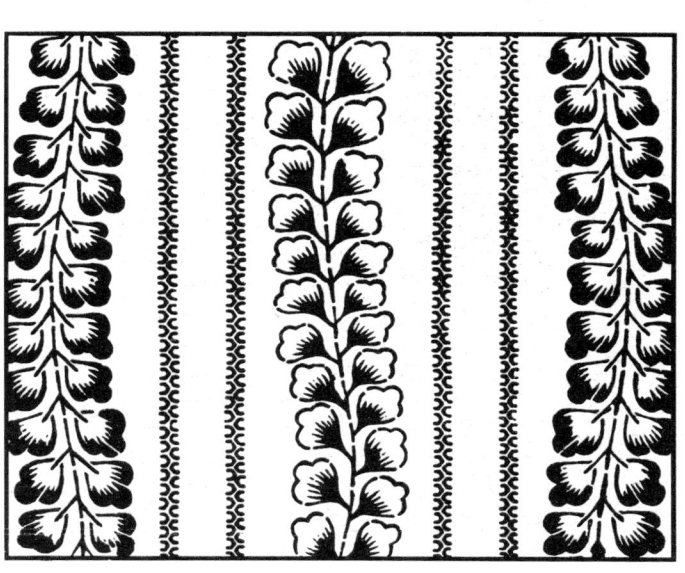

64

65

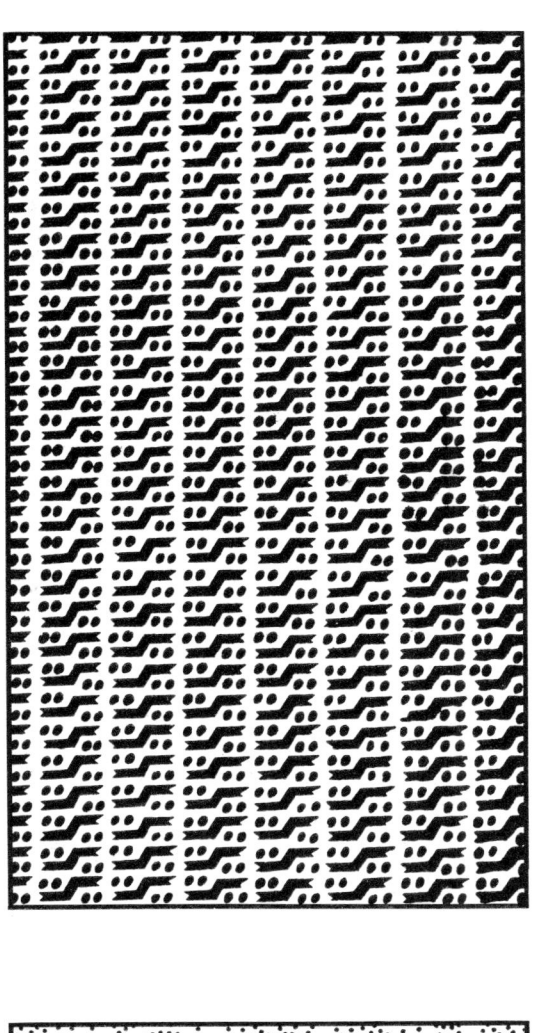

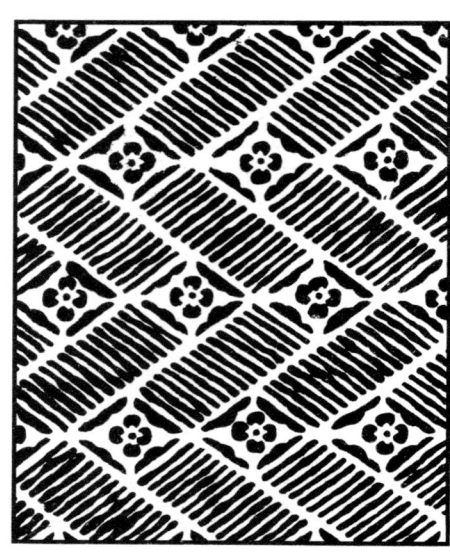

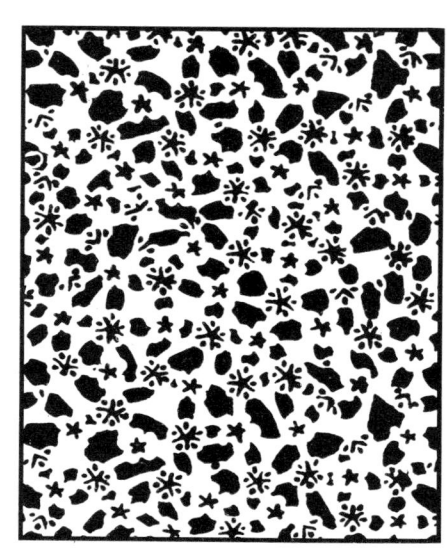

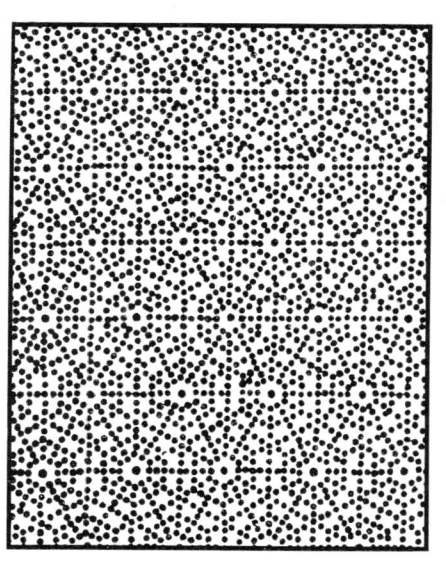
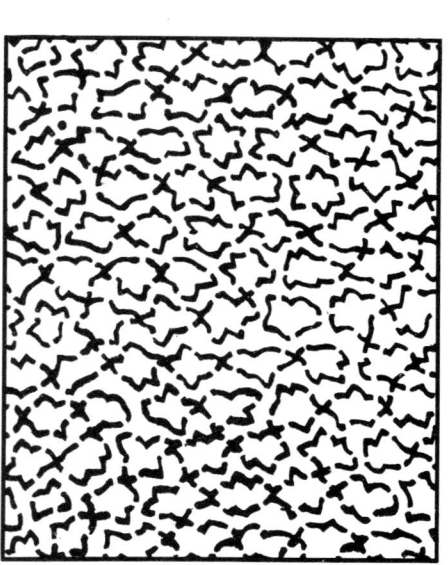

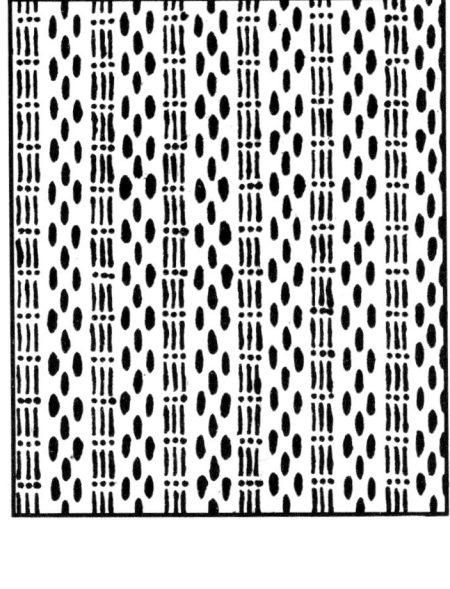
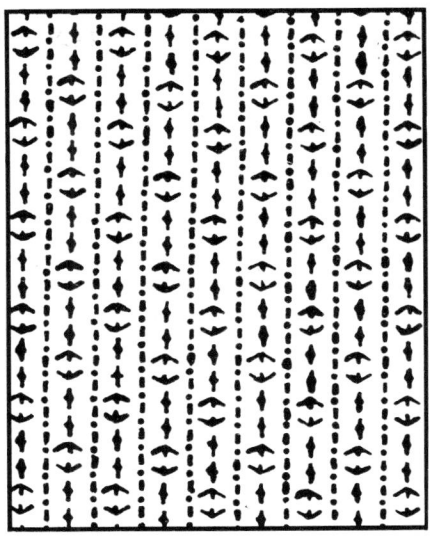

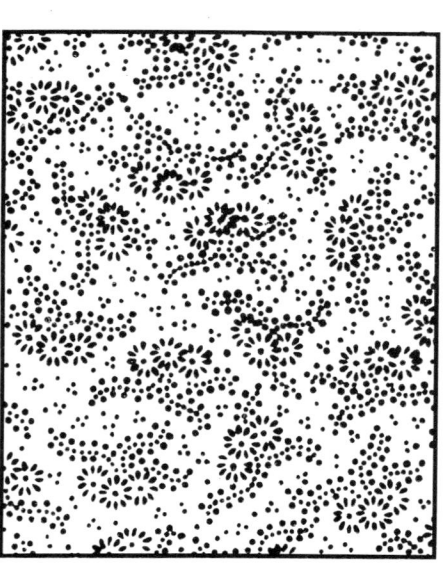

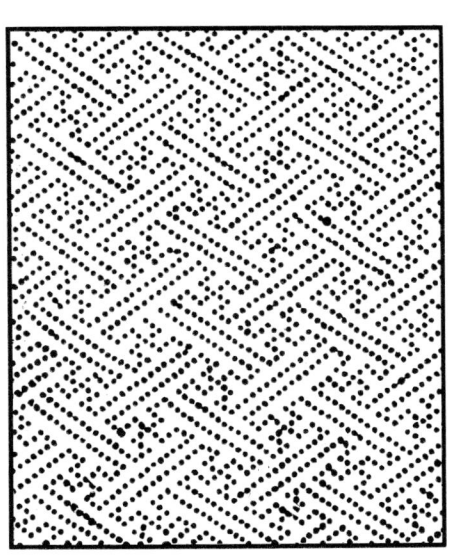

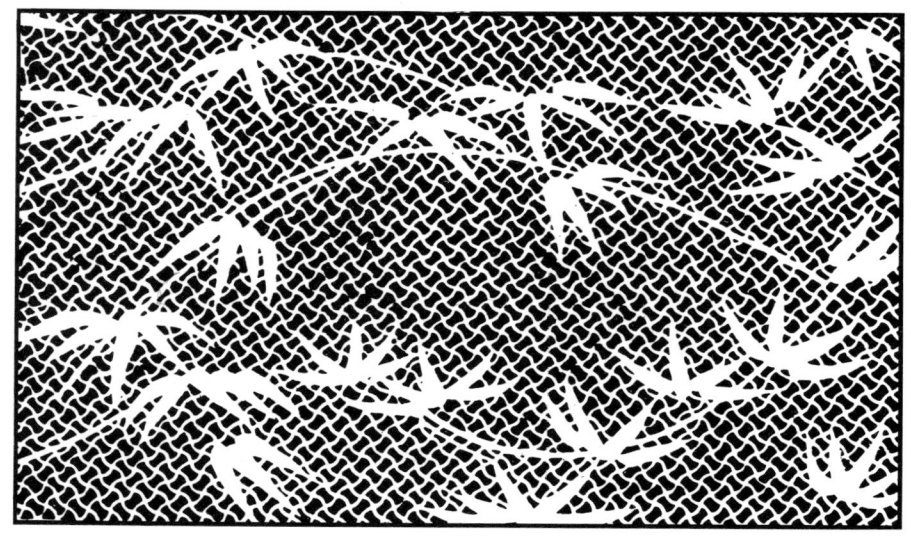

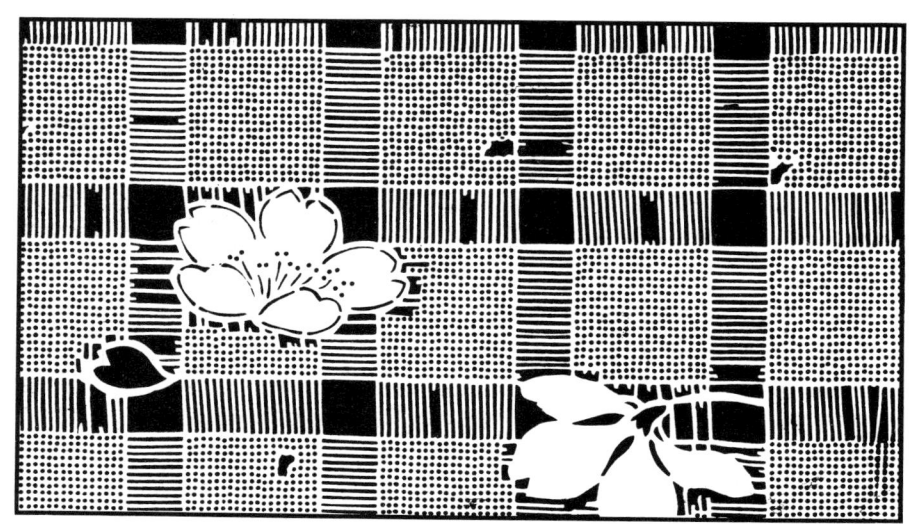

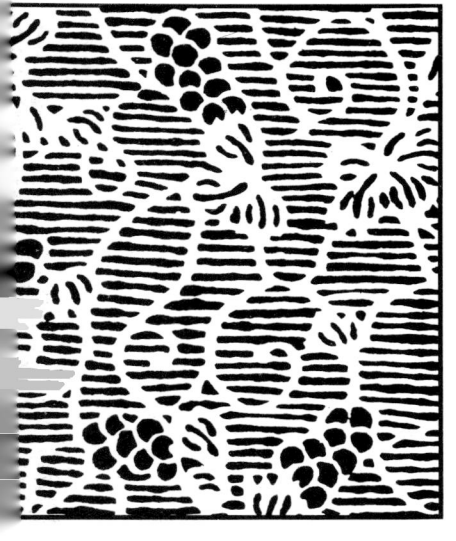

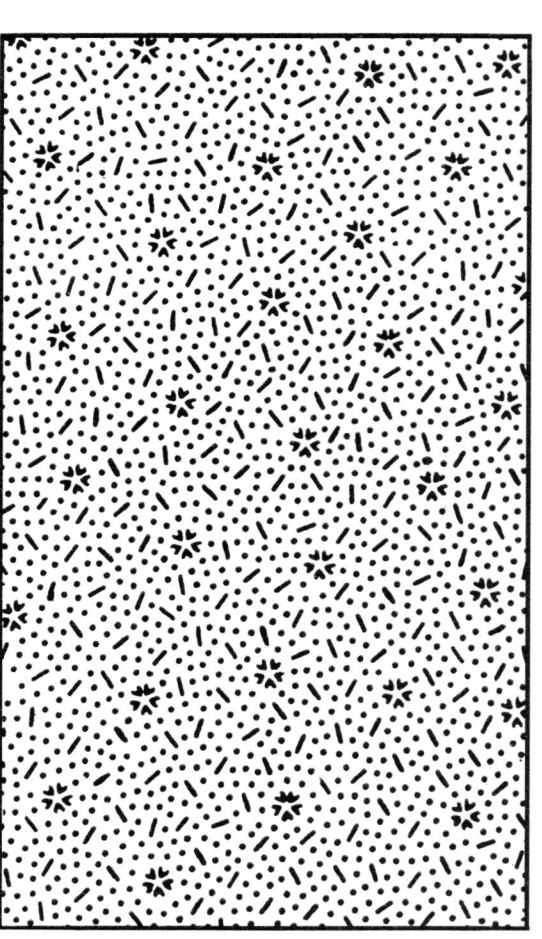

79

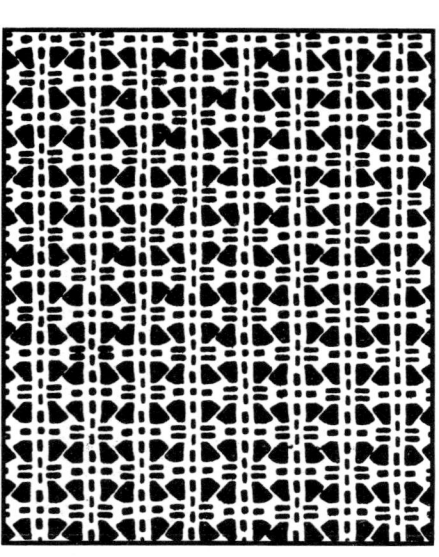

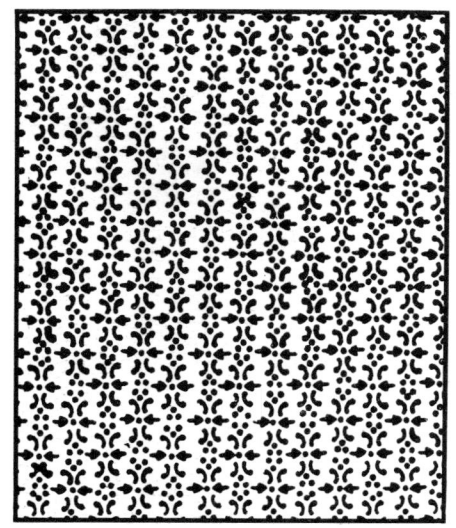

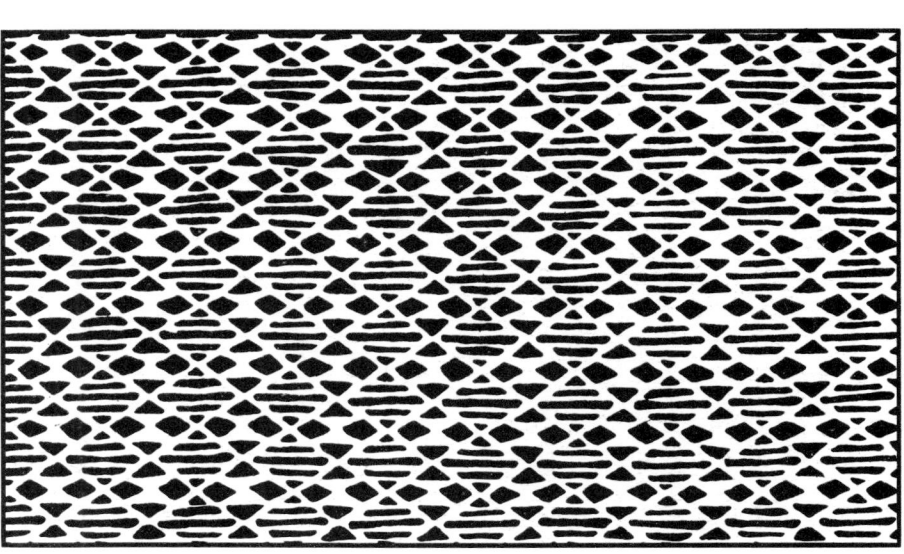

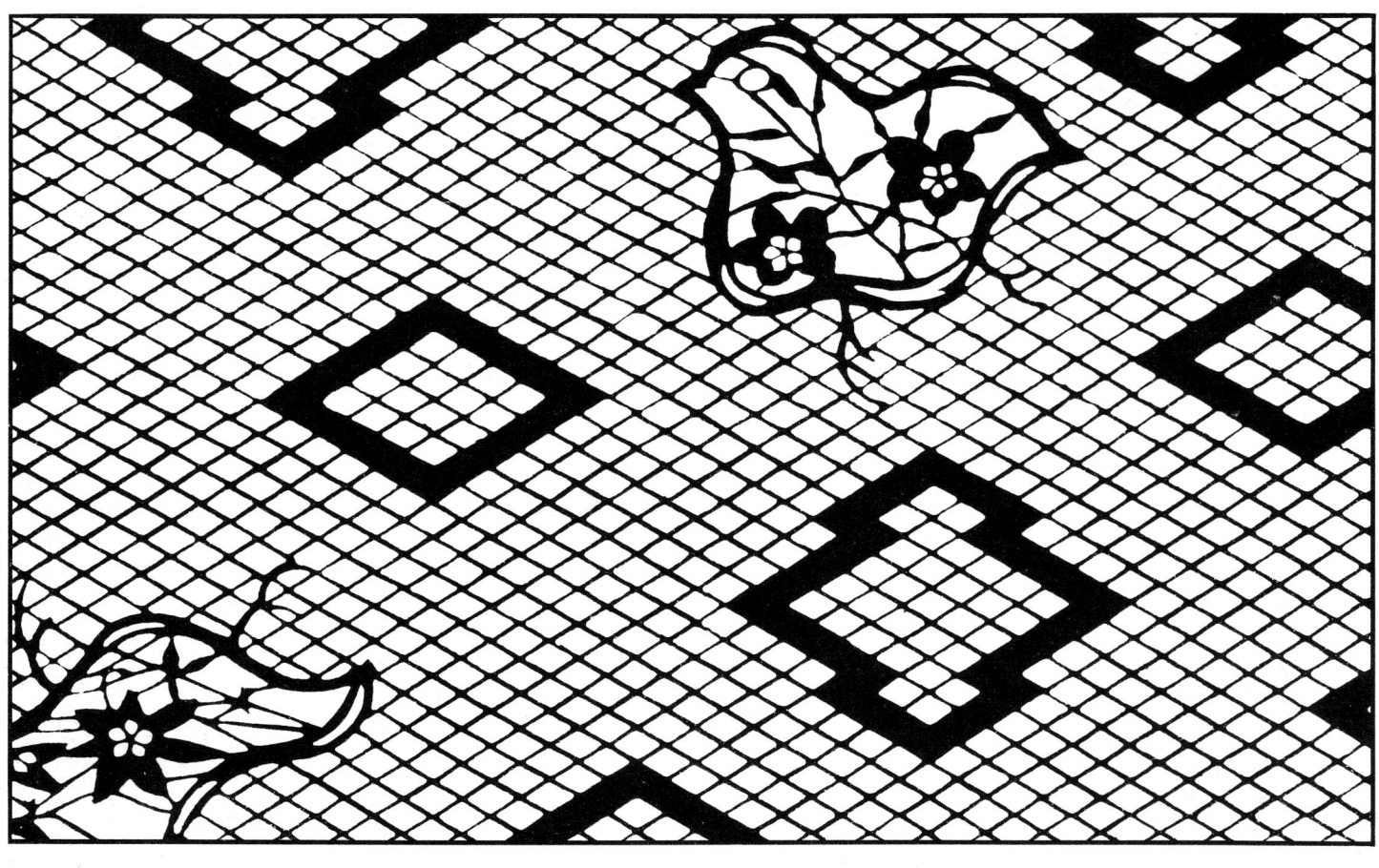

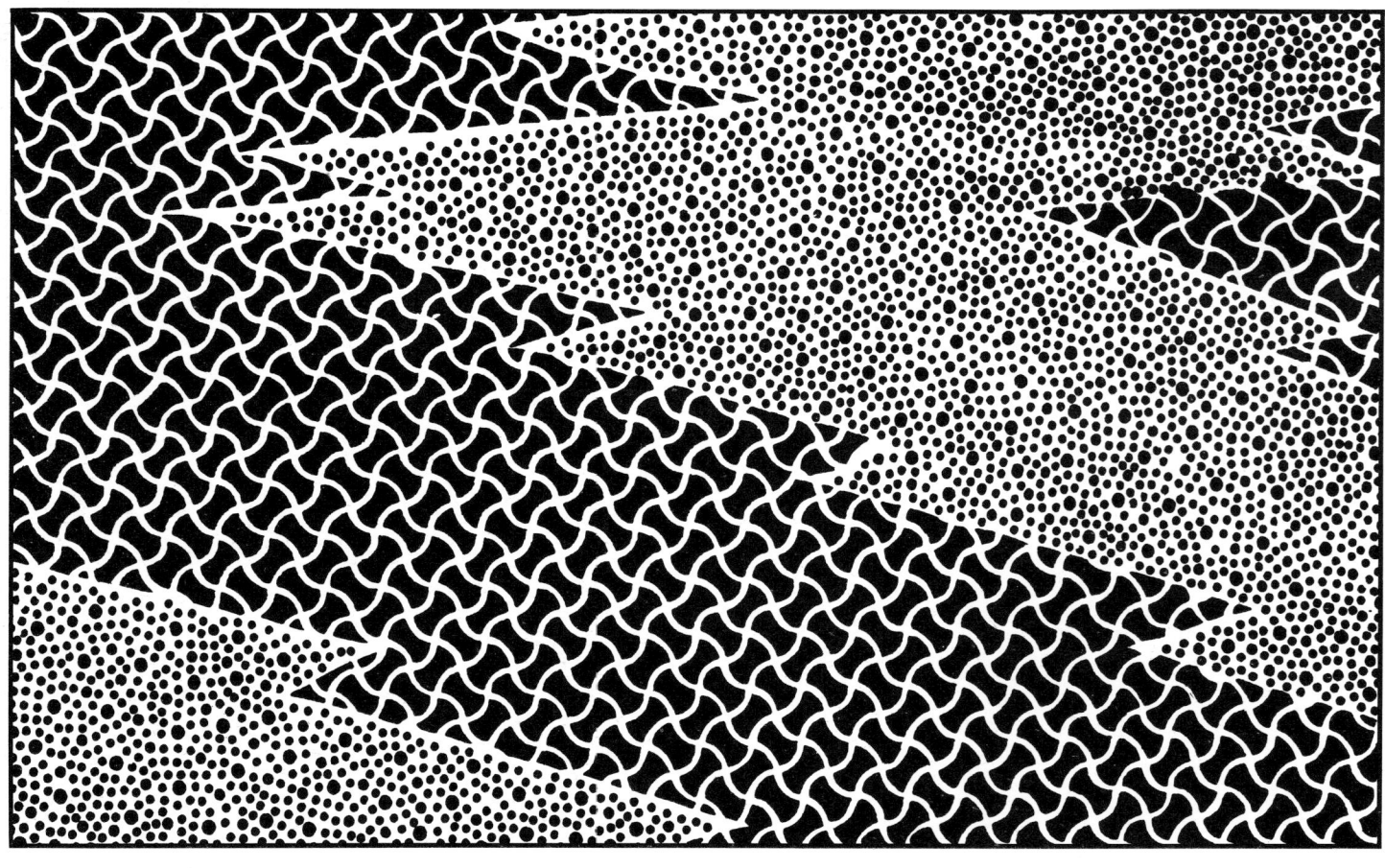

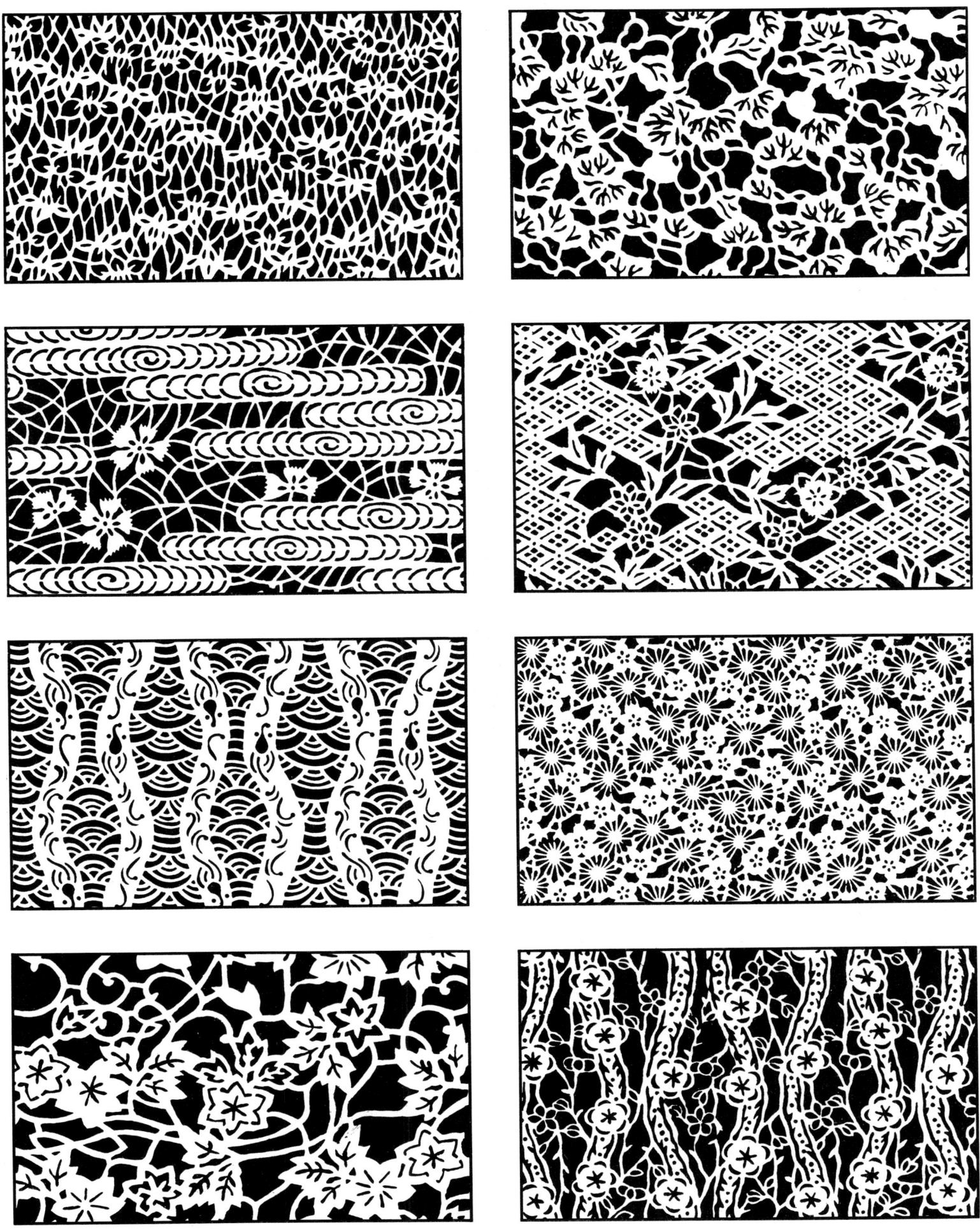

89

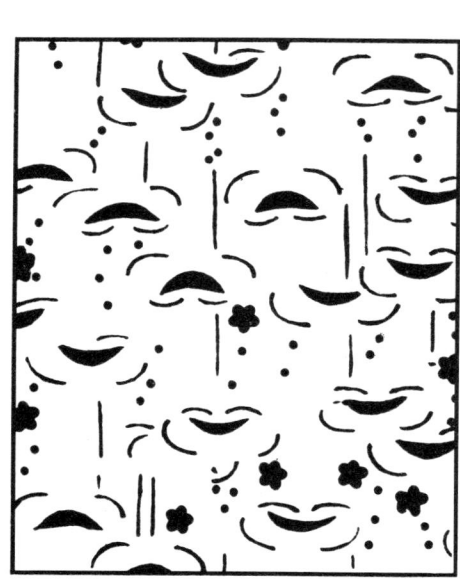

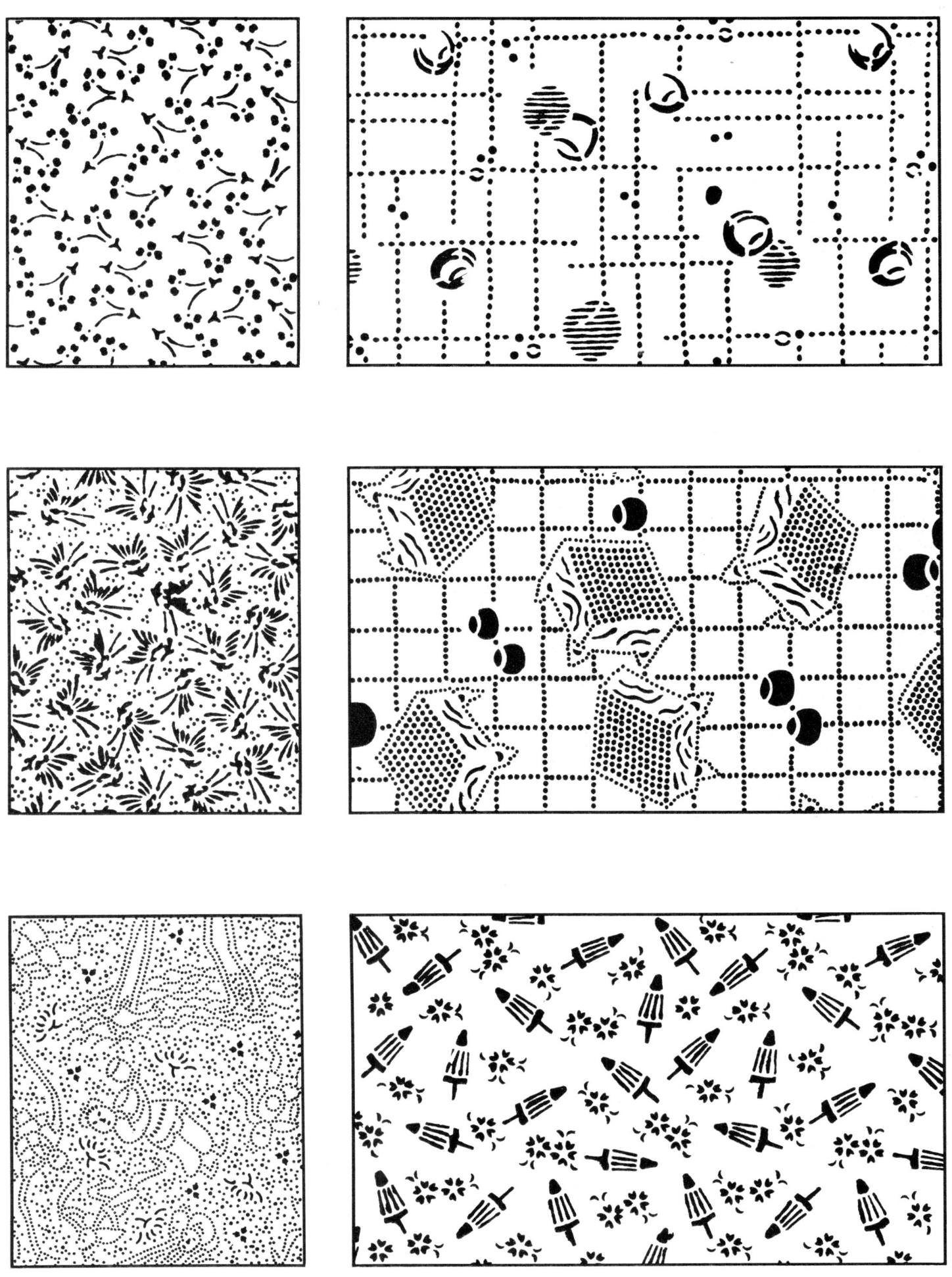

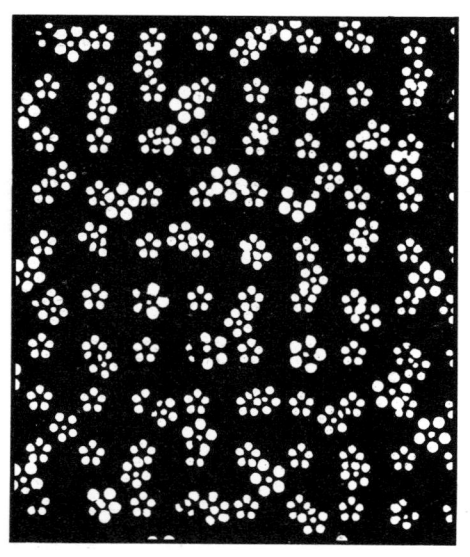

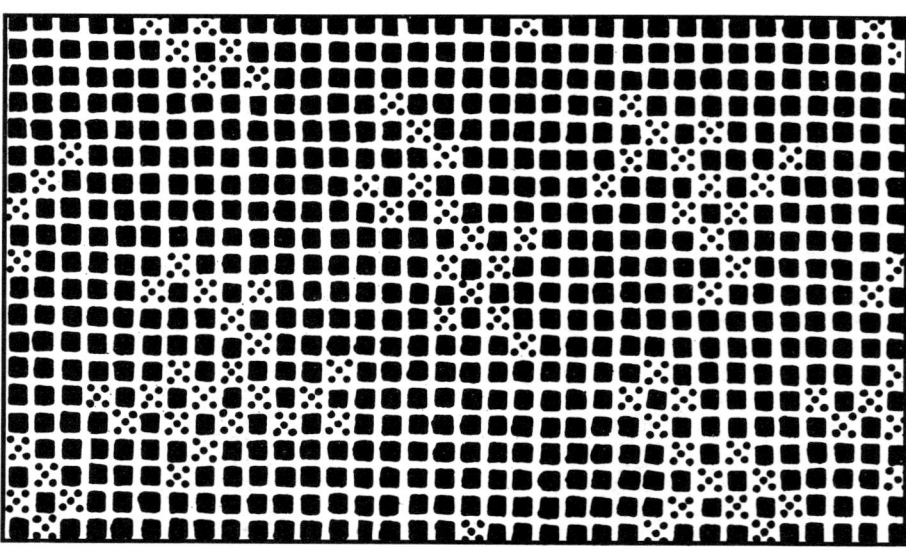

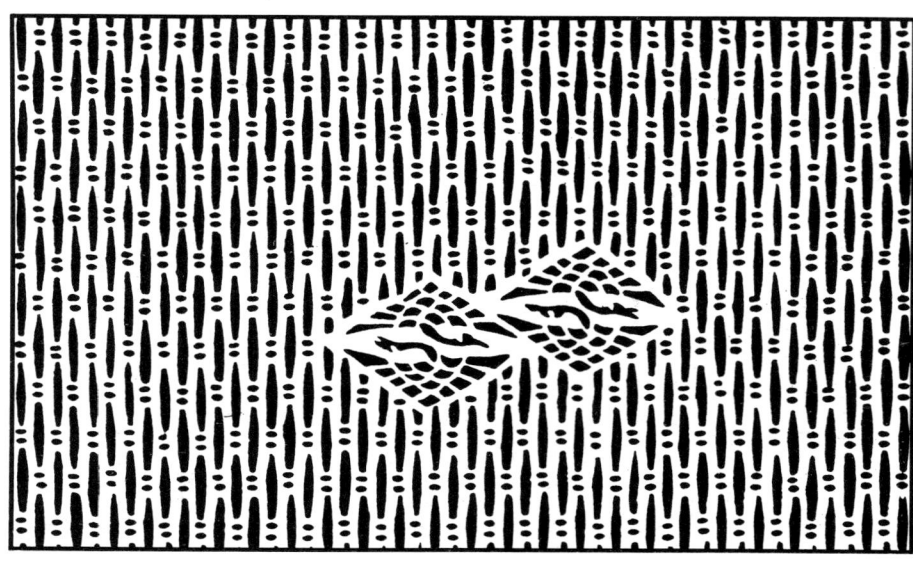

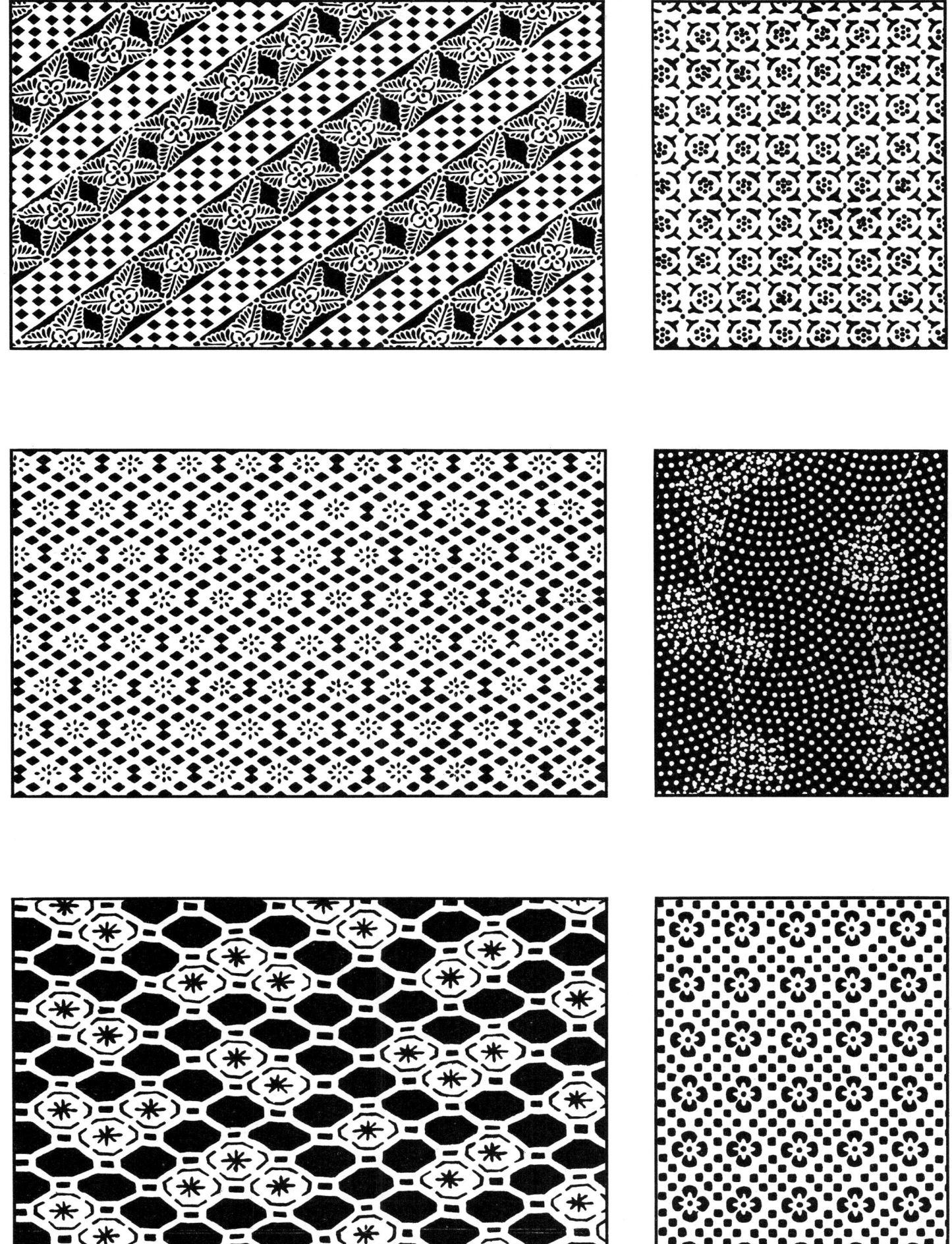

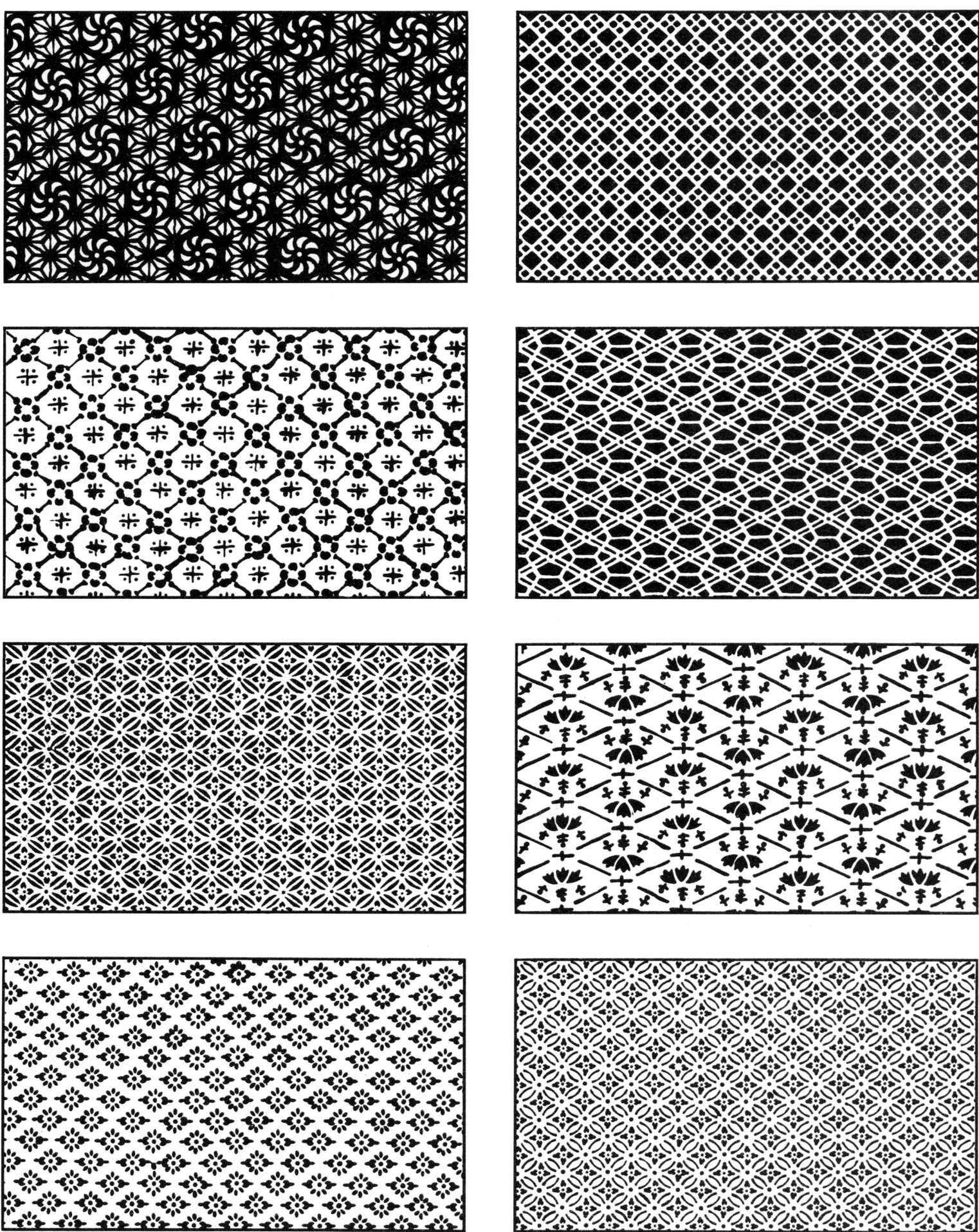

95

JAPAN IDEABOOK
PART III
JAPAN DESIGNS

The present volume shows about 350 designs with floral and graphic motifs, produced in the majority of cases for decorative purposes, mainly by the traditional crafts, out of the most intimate interrelation with Japanese art.

Flower, animal designs and decorative ornamentation found application in, among other things, fabrics and textiles, kimonos, gift wrapping paper, rice paper, book and print decoration, as well as in the adornment of the most varied kinds of commercial products. Motifs such as these are typical of the Isegata technique, one of the oldest Japanese methods of multiple printing.

A decor reduced to the essential elements and thus enriched by this basic, yet very effective graphic quality. It reflects, in its ordering, the high sensitivity to form of the Japanese ornamental style.

The simple simbolism, the graphic clarity and the signal character of the motifs, their arrangement in rows, reiteration, duplication or mirroring, their repeat or their symmetry, bear unmistakably the hallmarks of stamp or wood block printing, which suggests that they came into use very early.

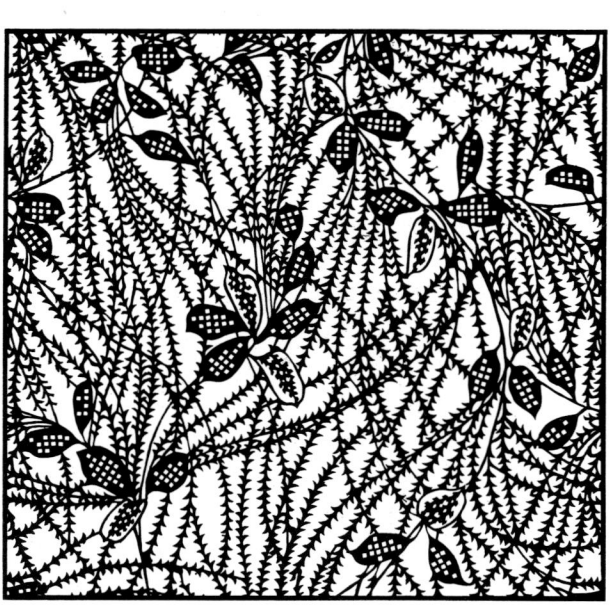

8

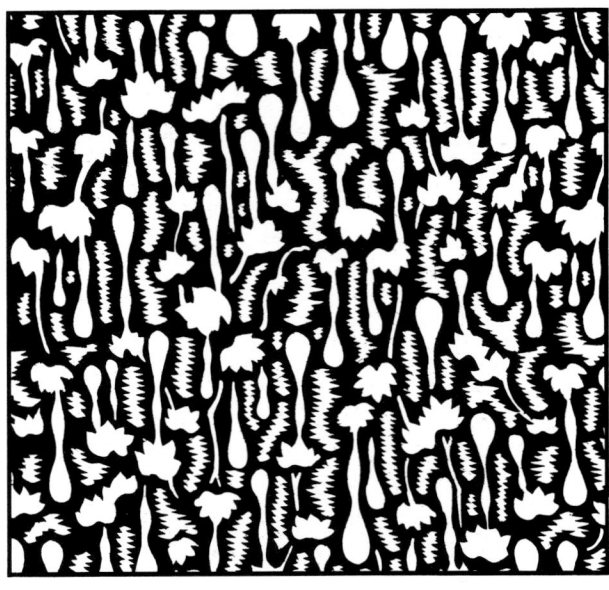

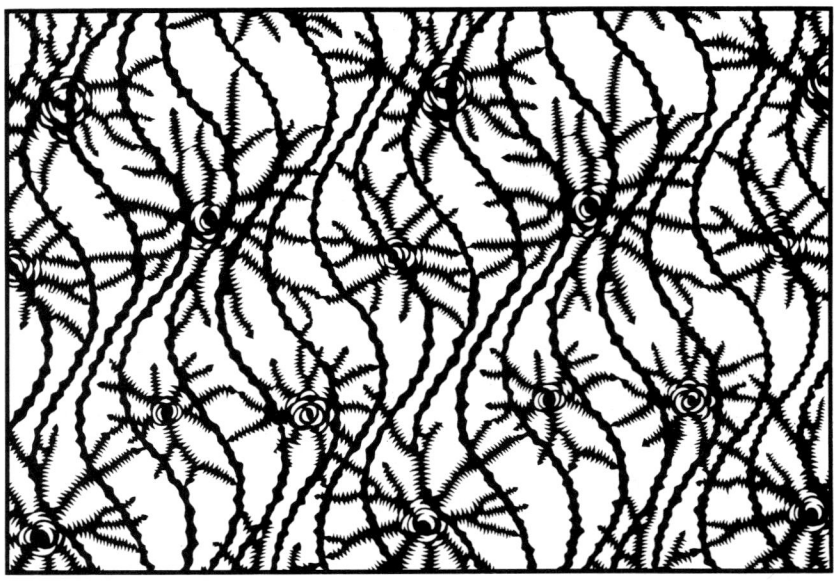
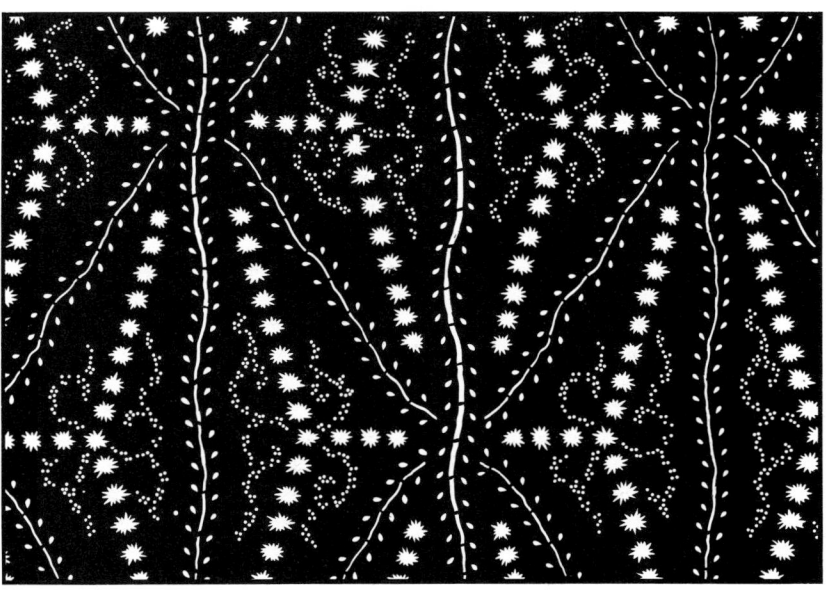

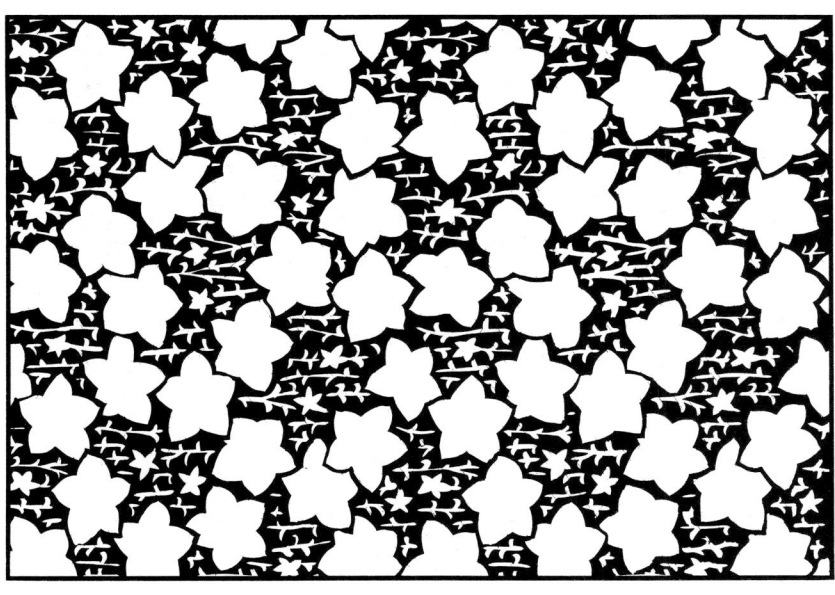

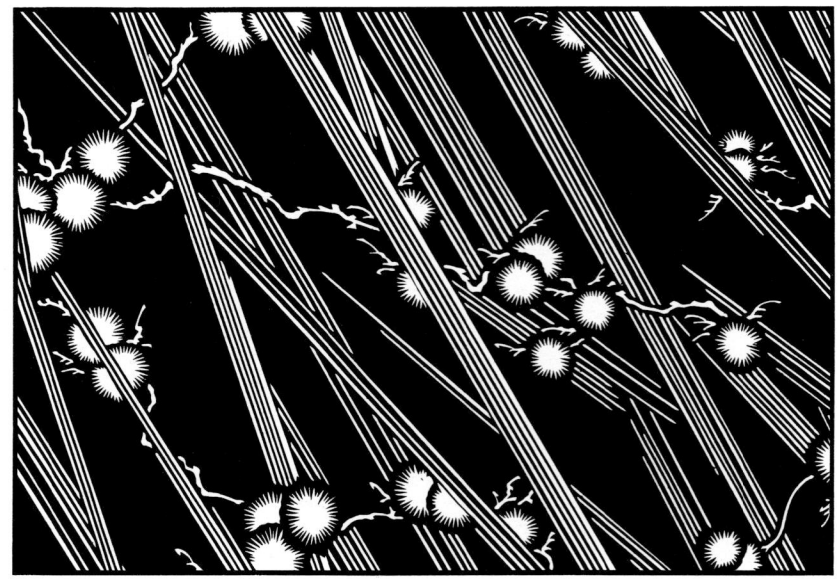

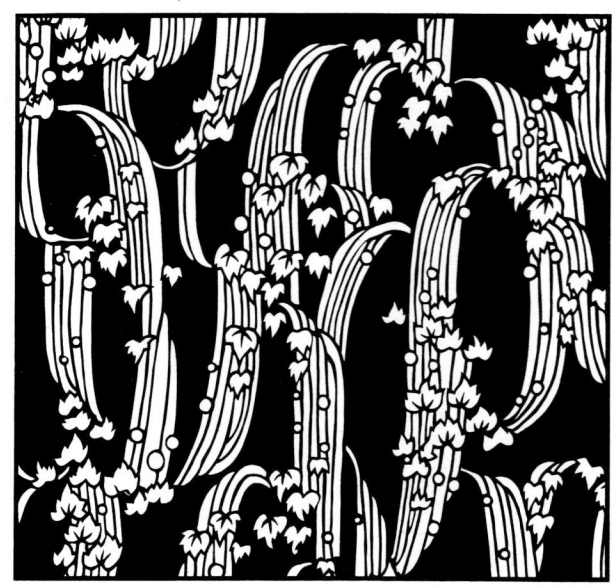

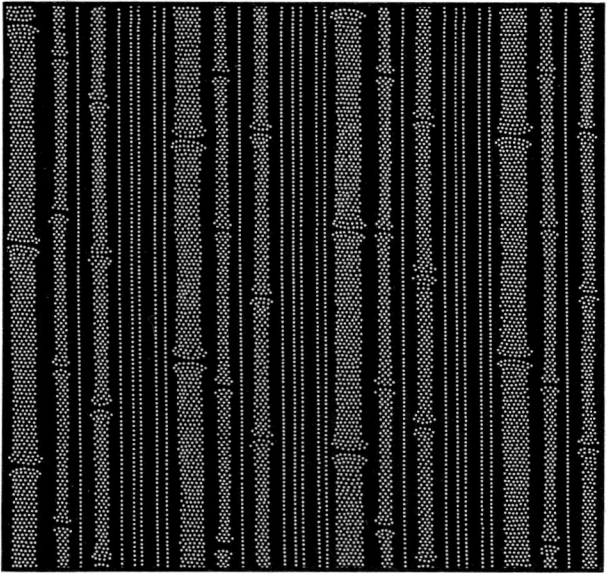

18

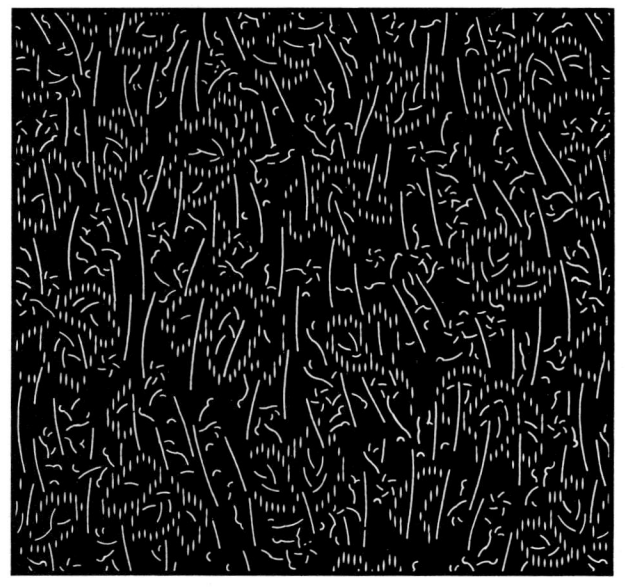

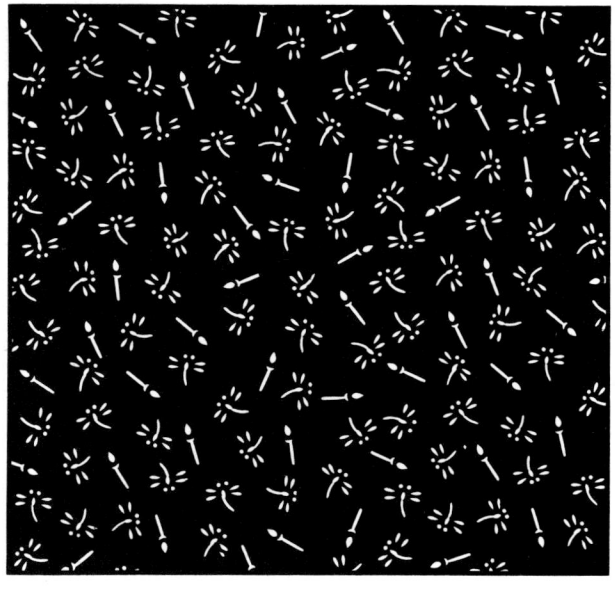

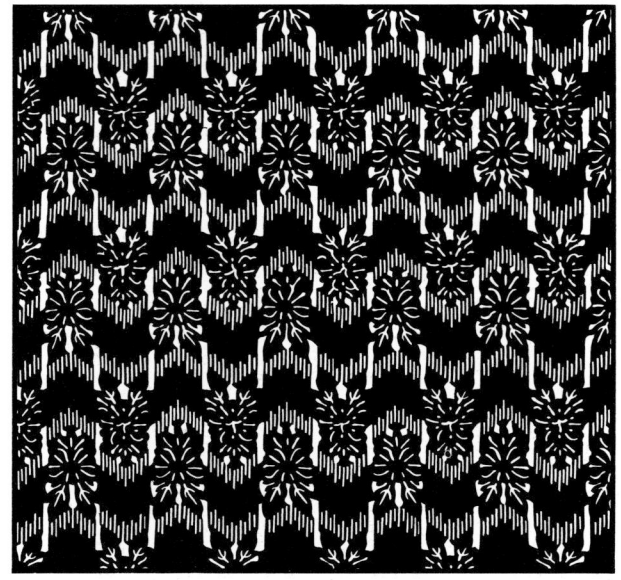
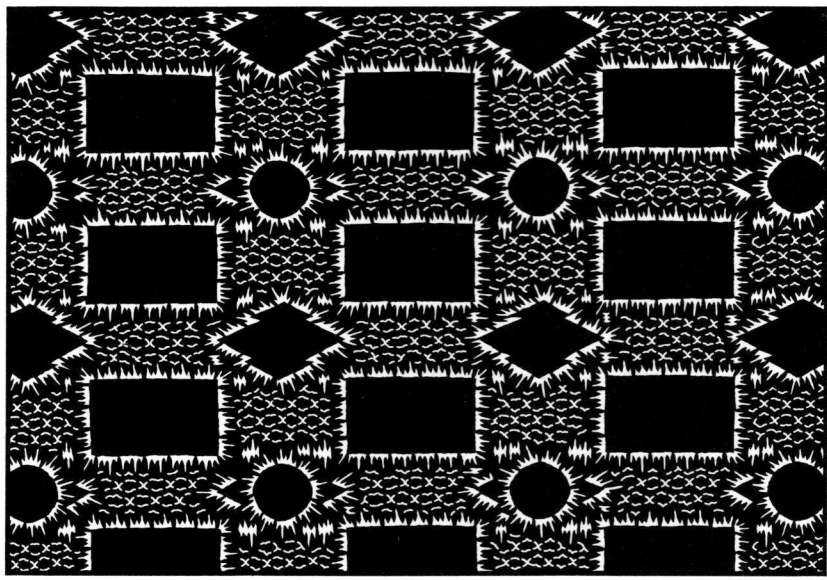

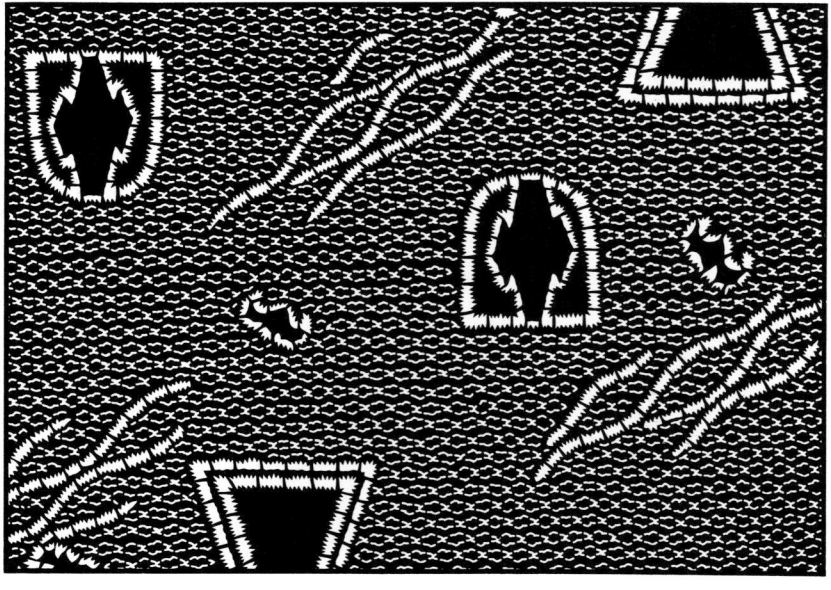

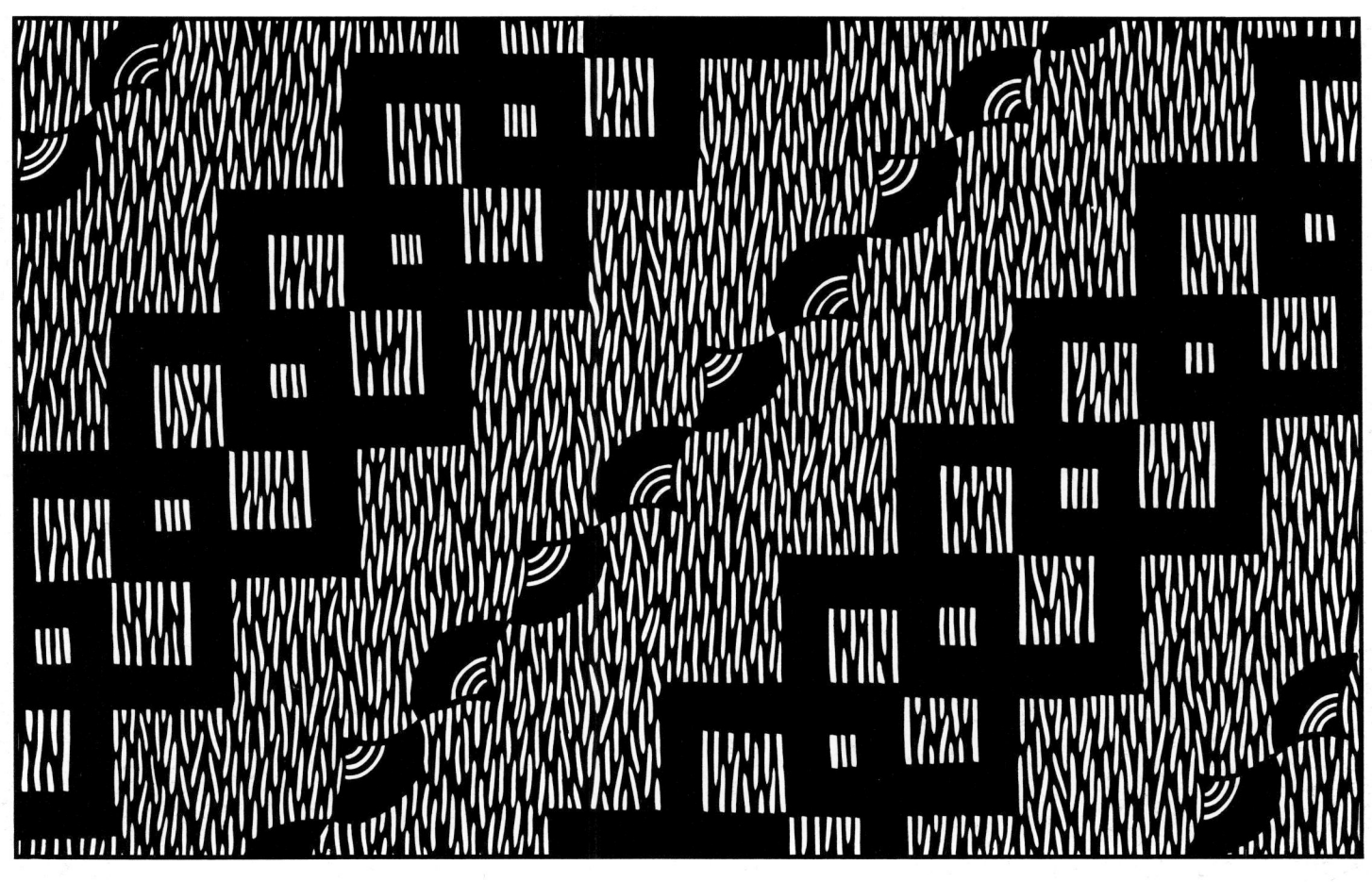

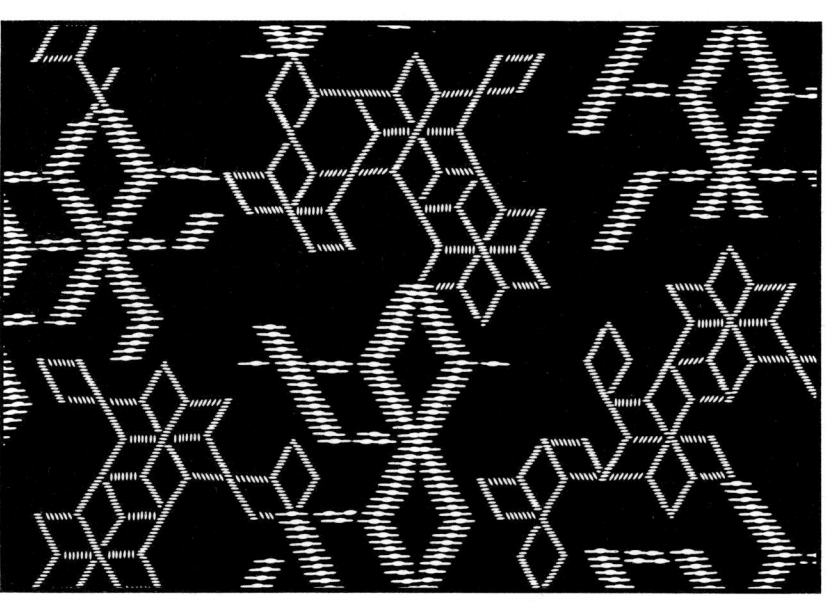

31

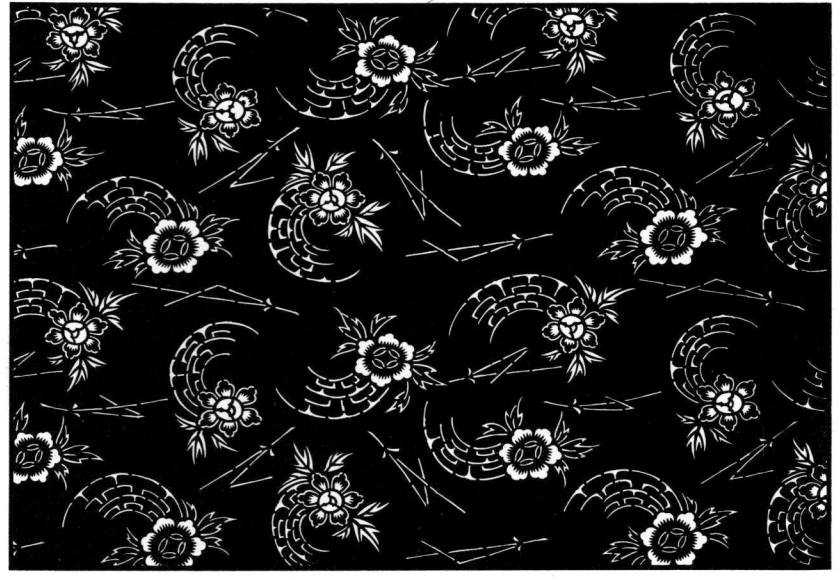
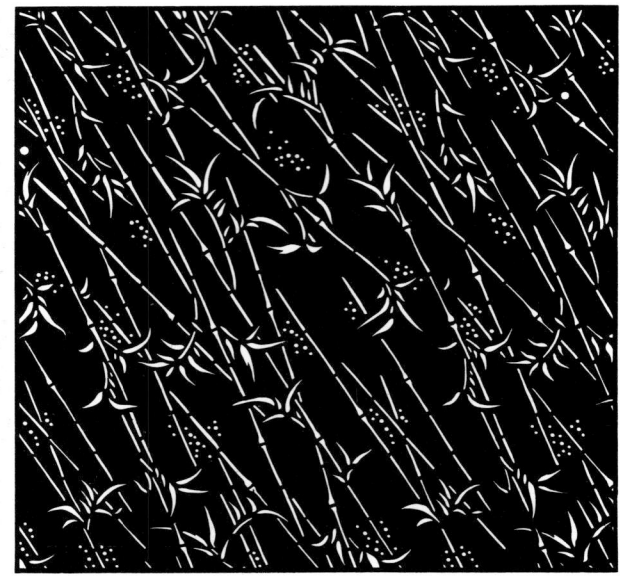

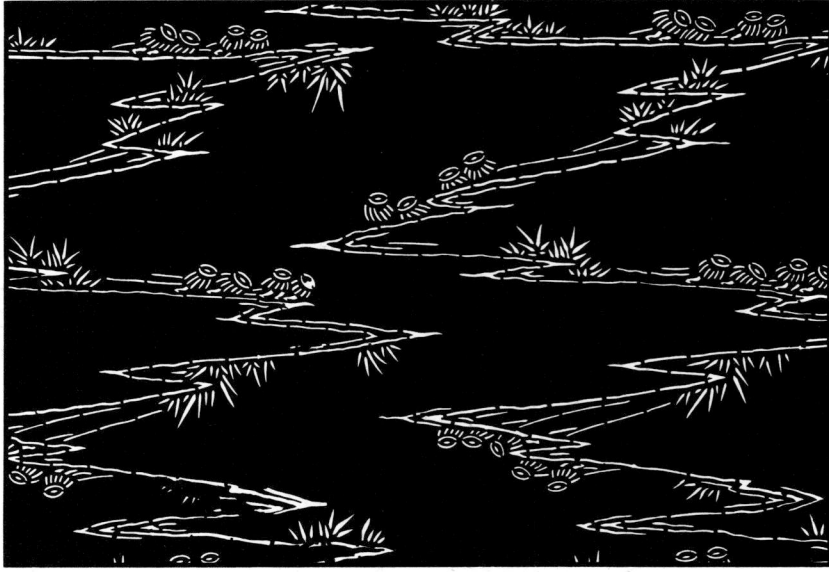

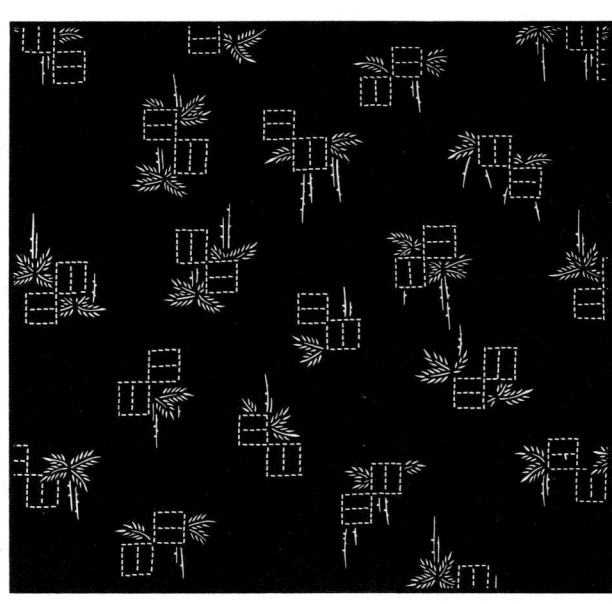

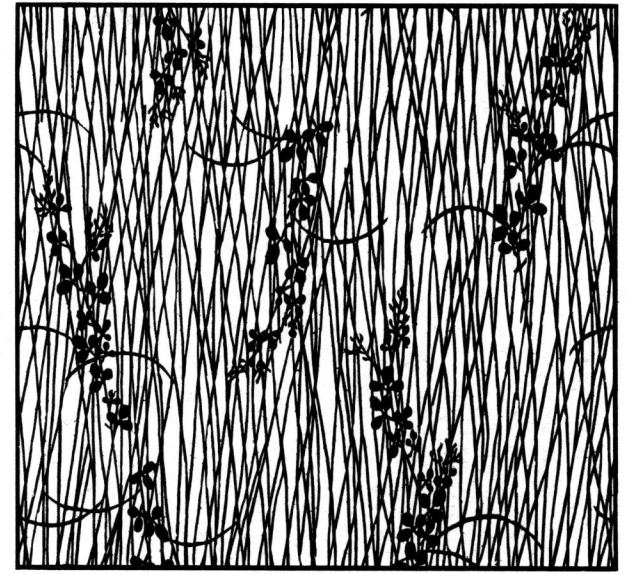

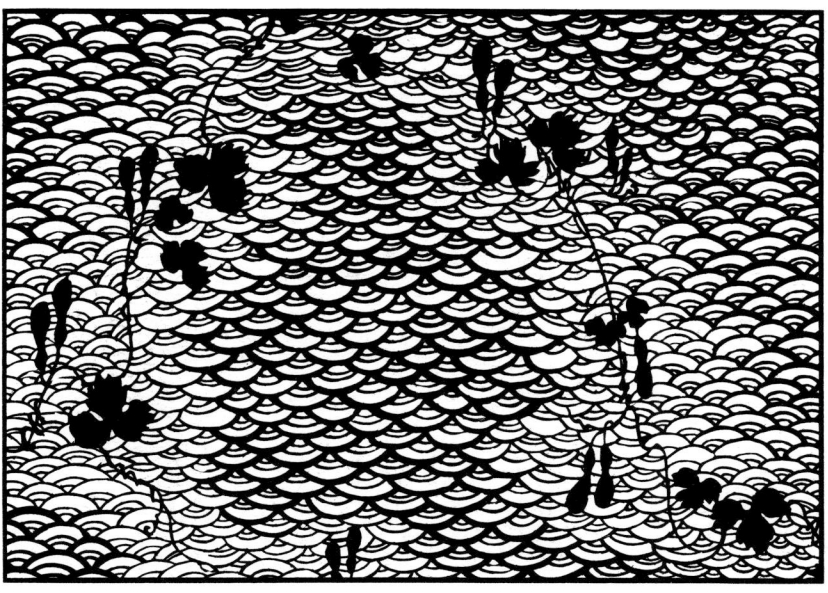

40

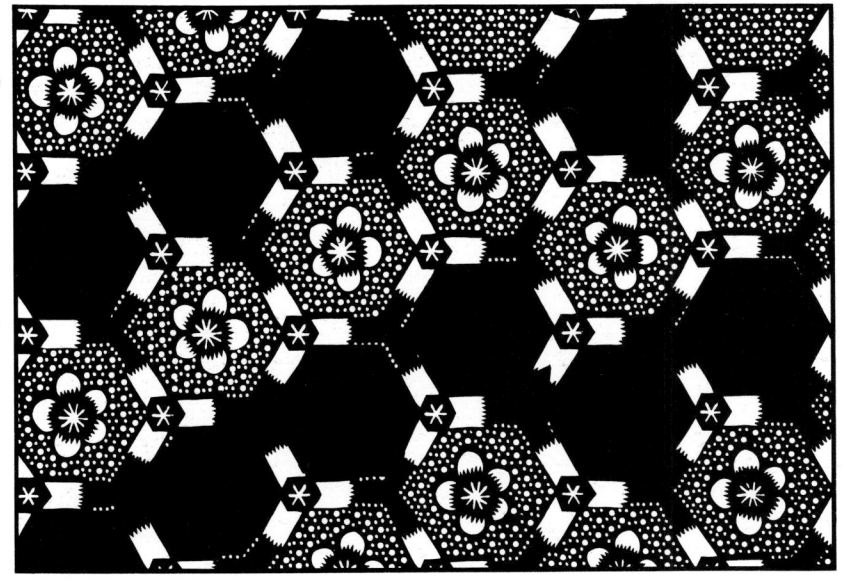

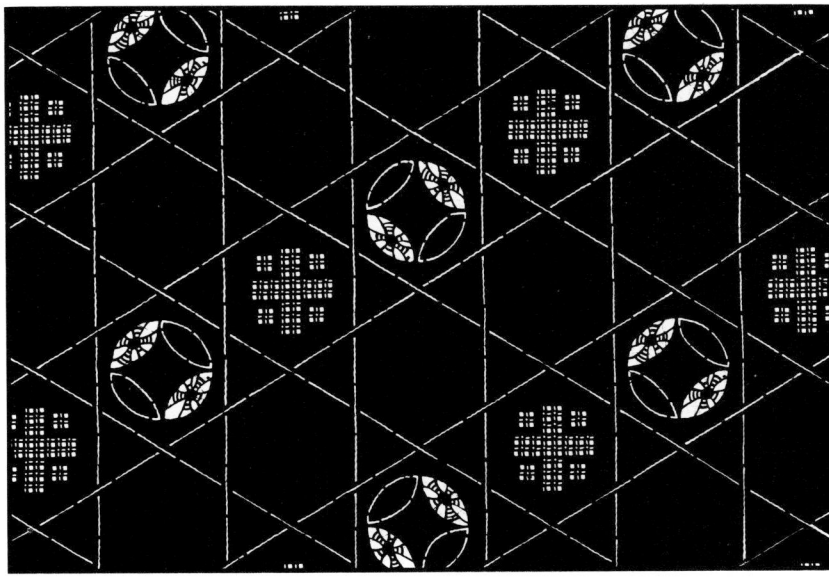

41

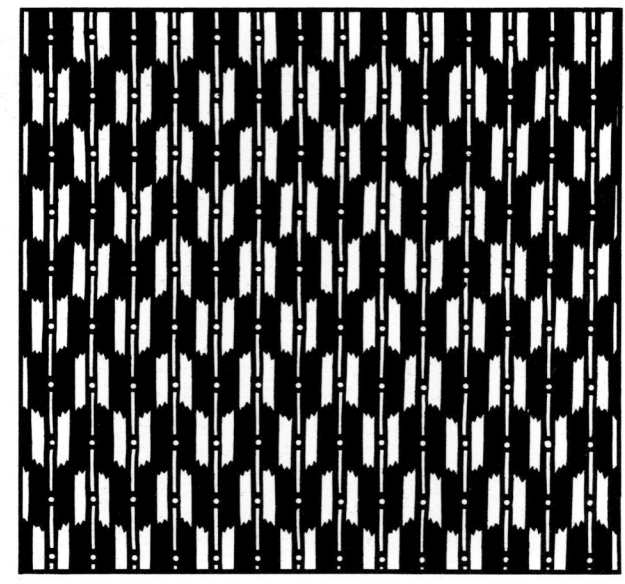

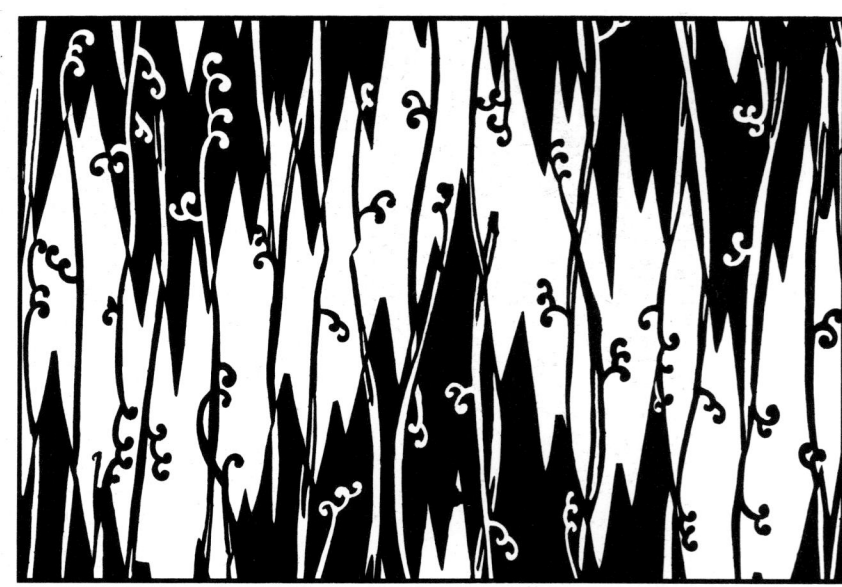

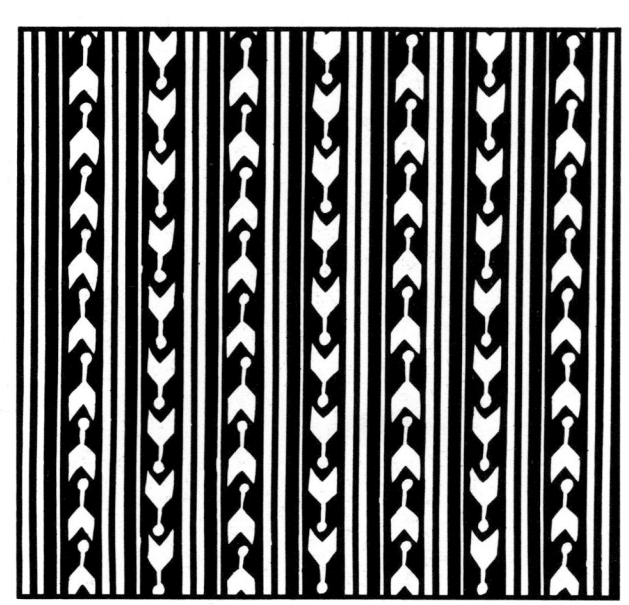

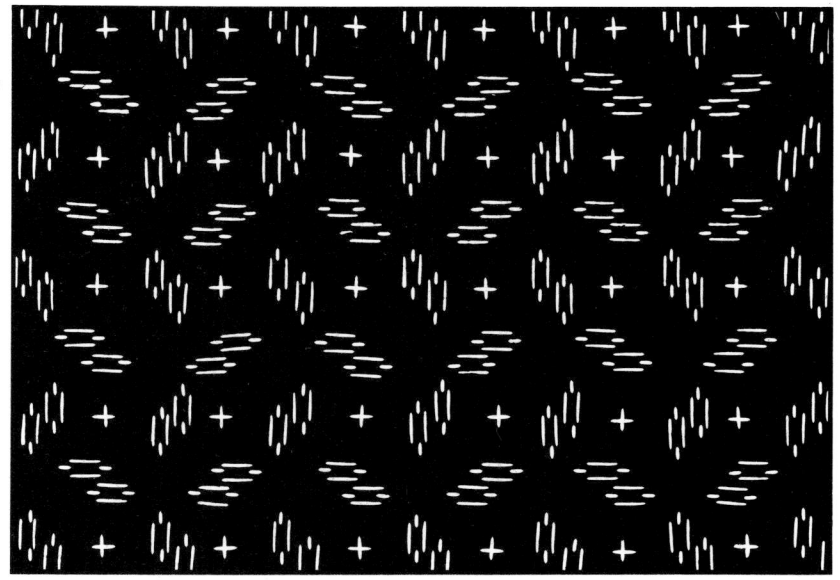

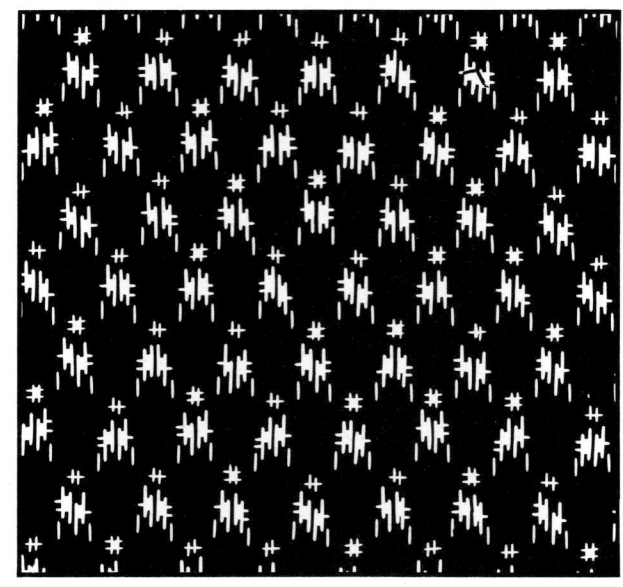

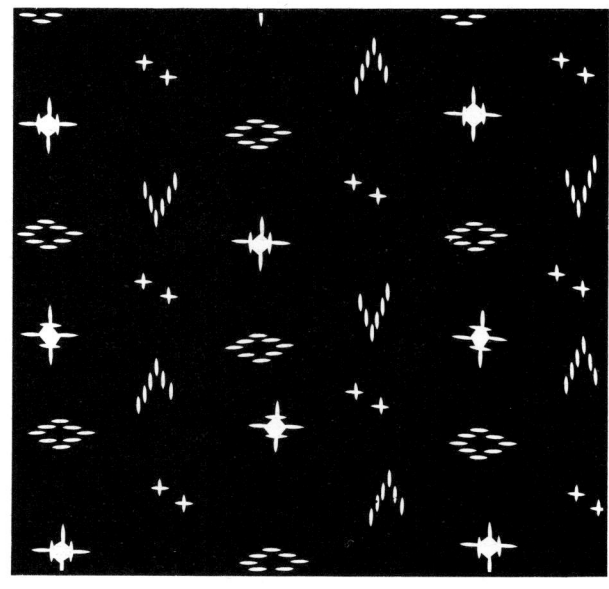

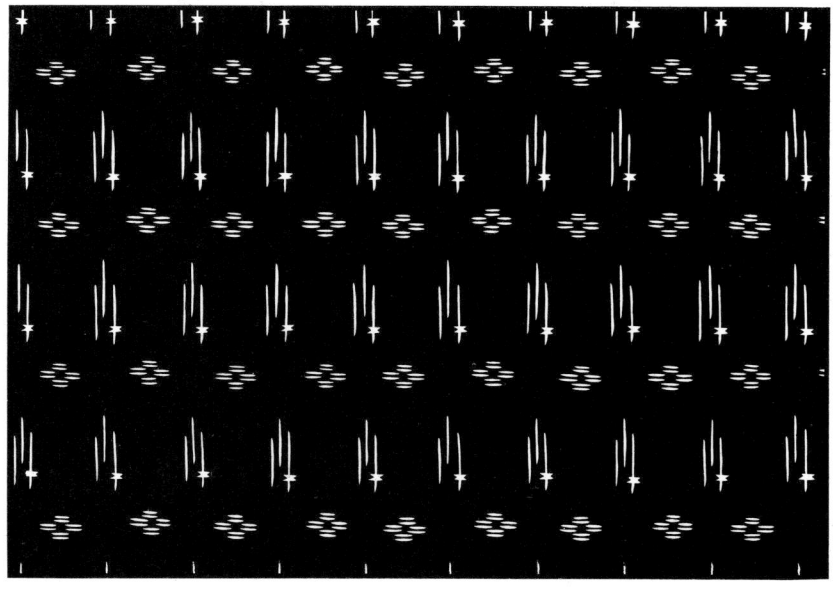

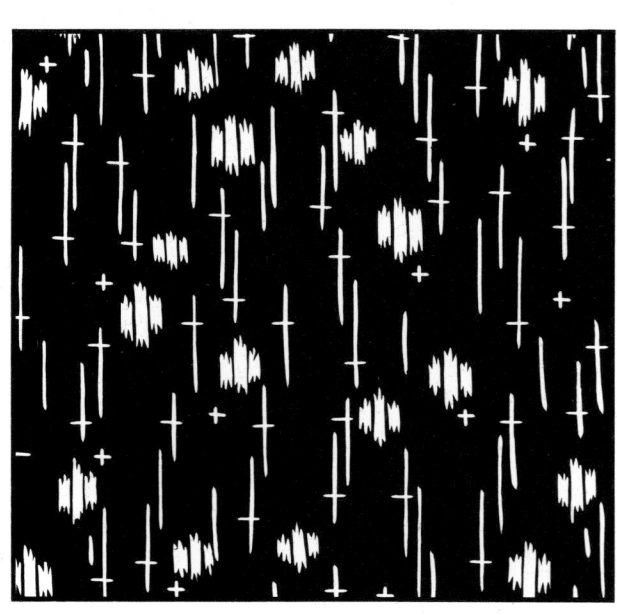

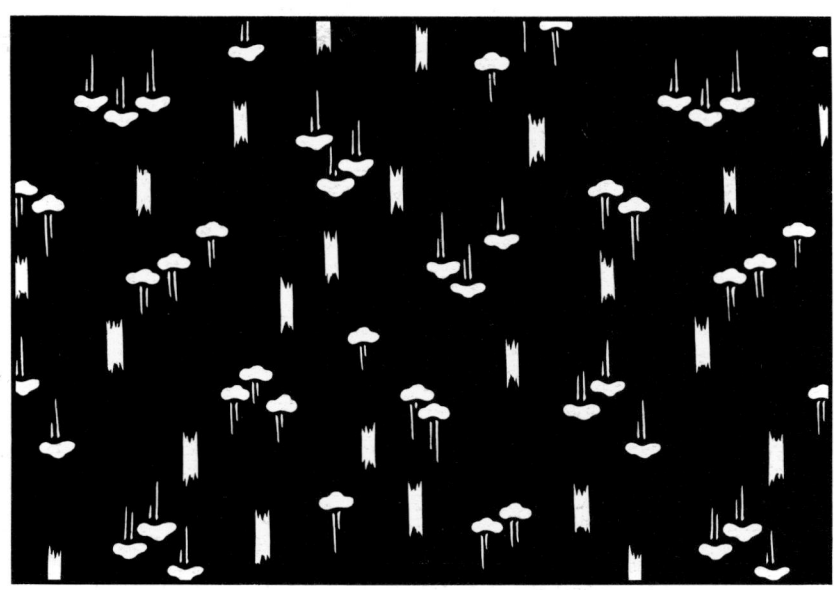
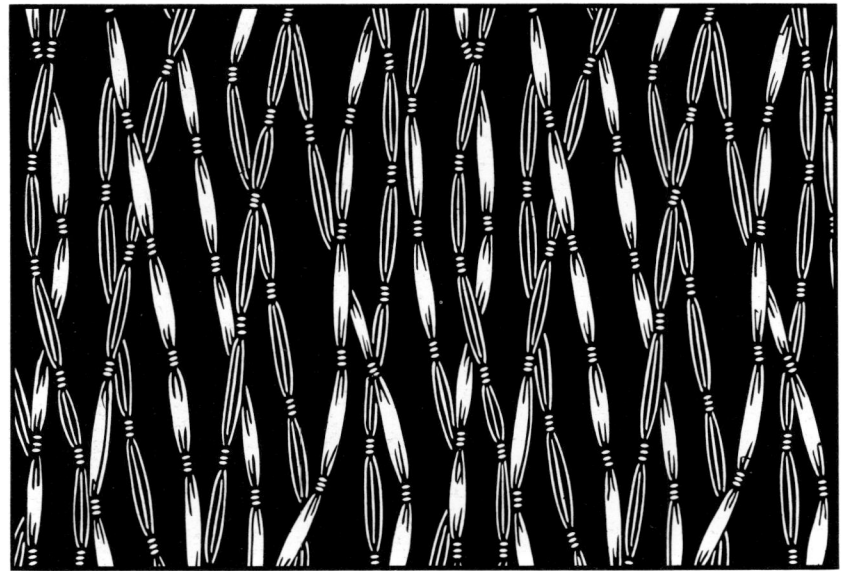
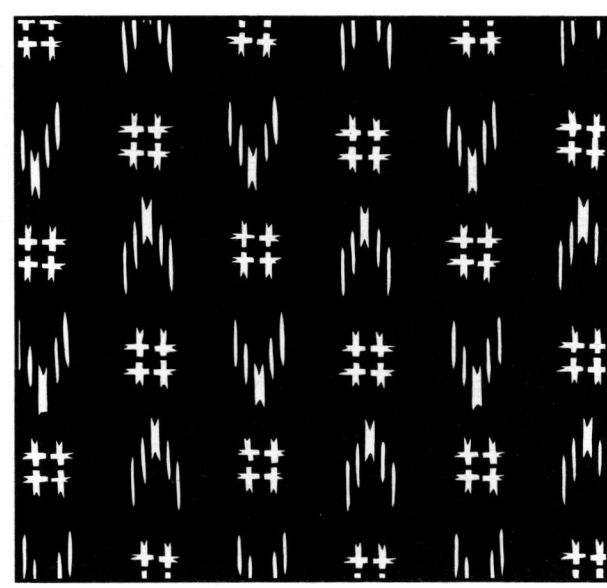
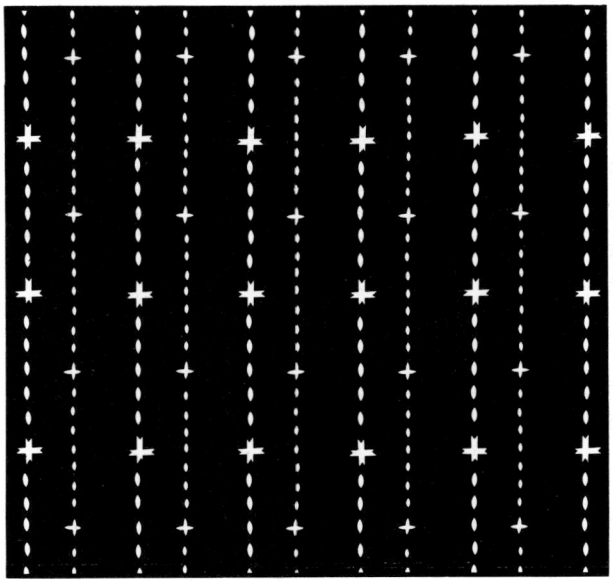

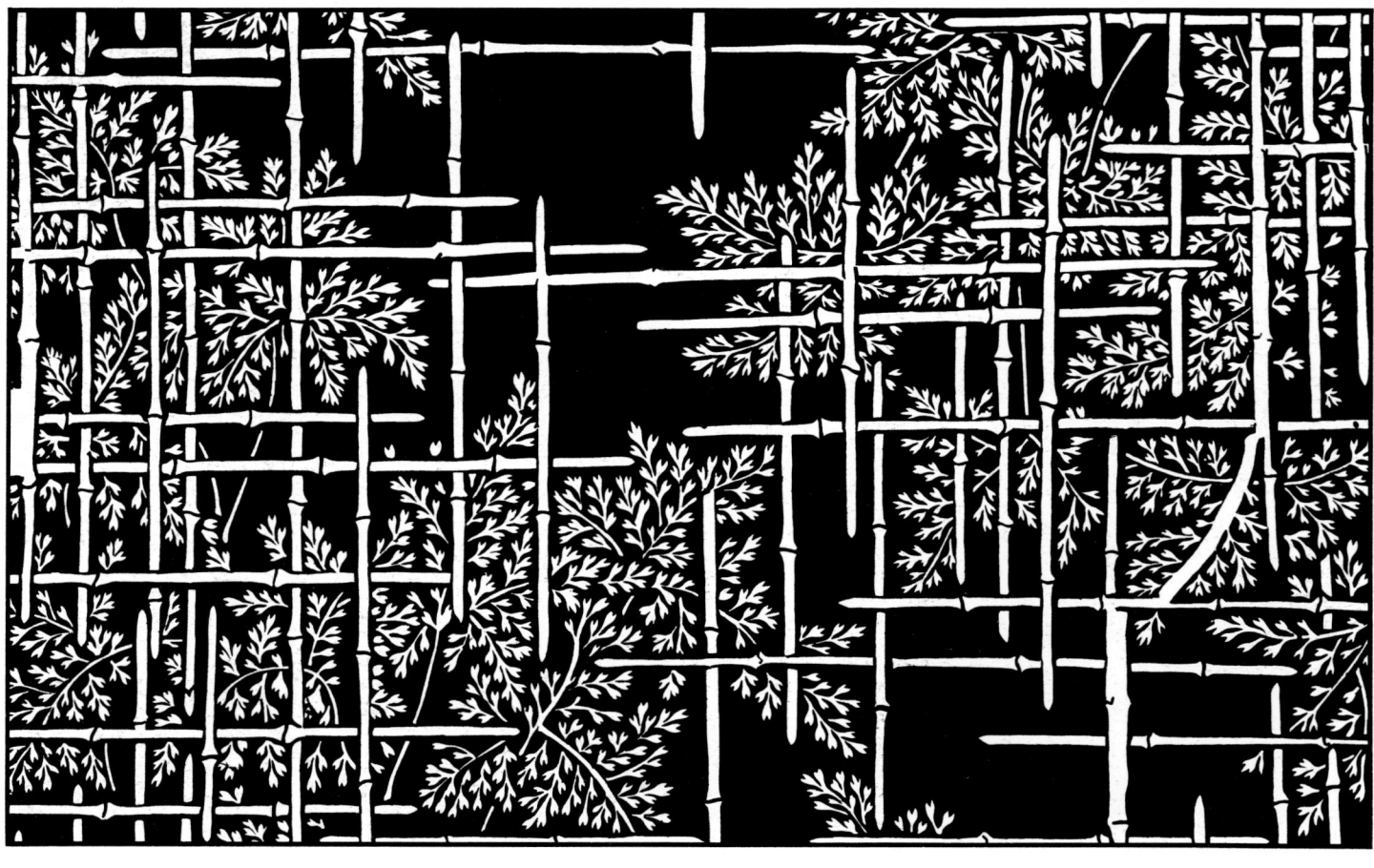

47

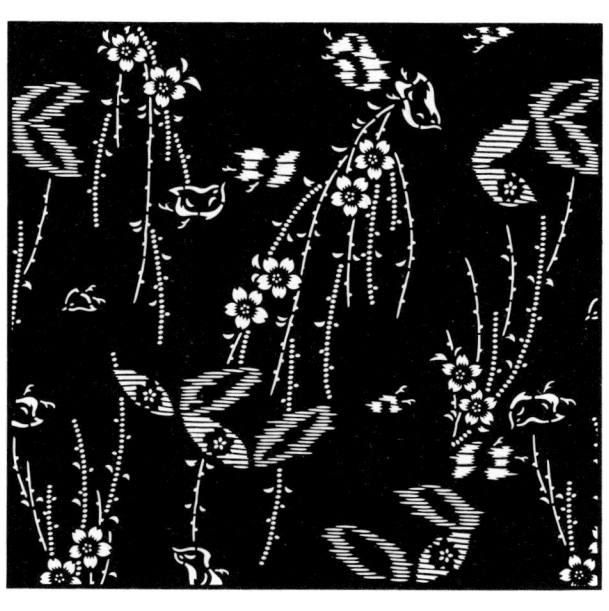

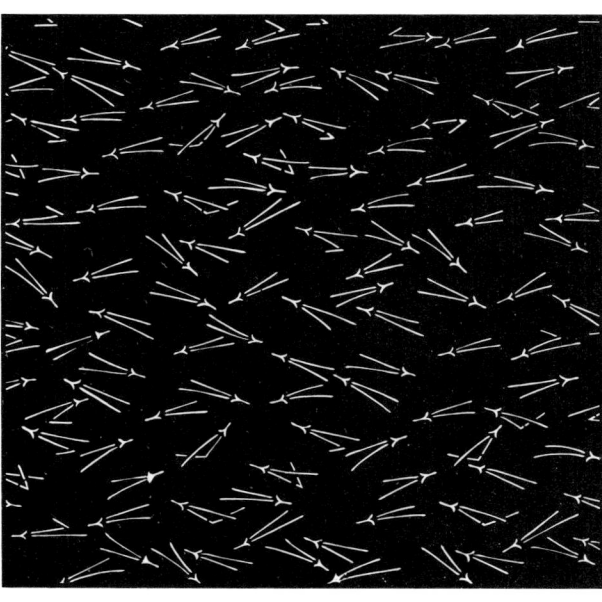

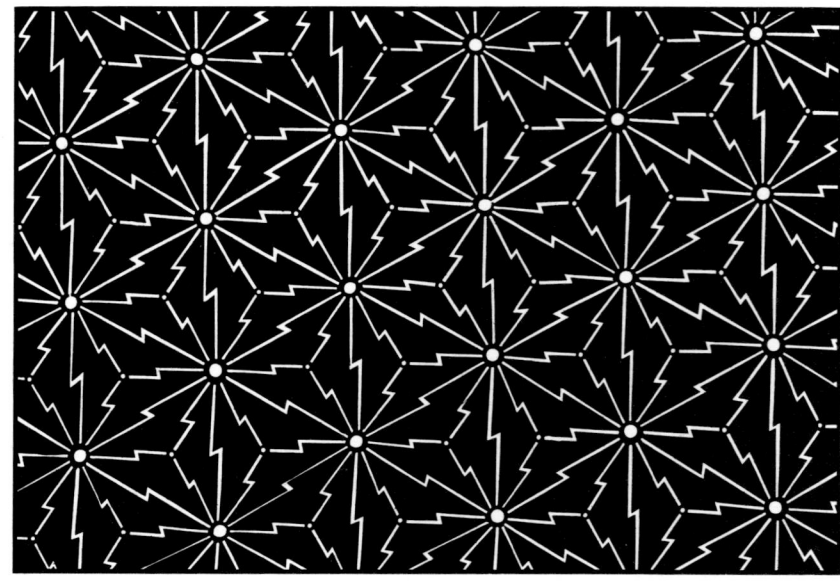

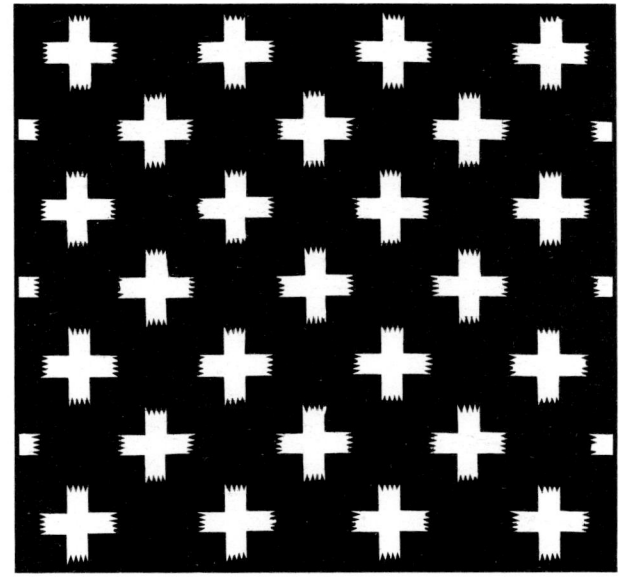

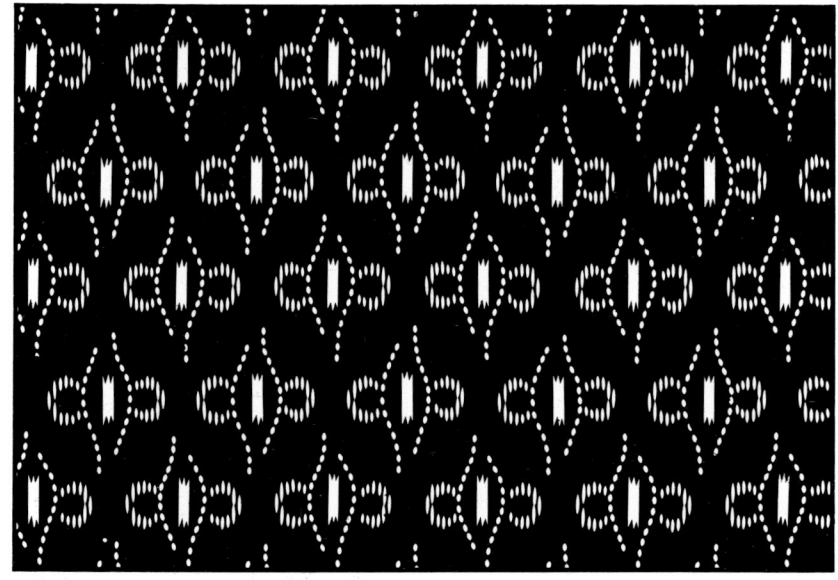

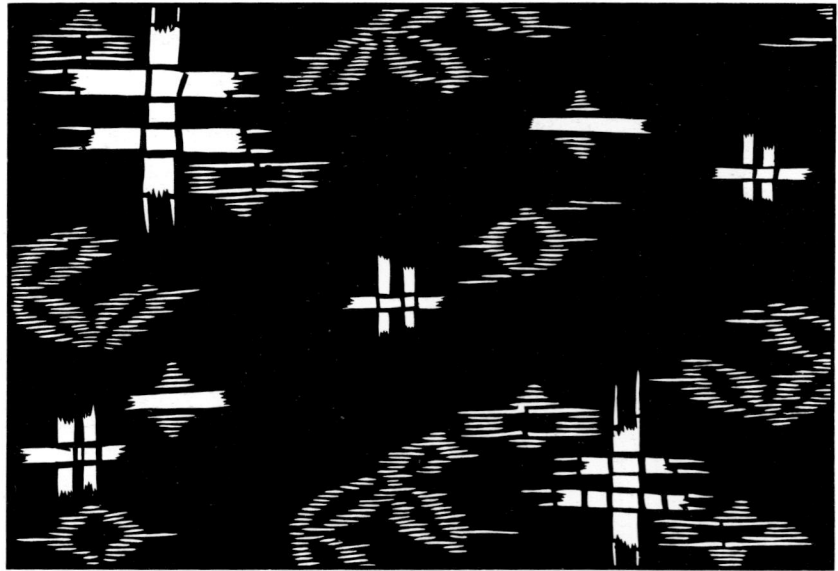
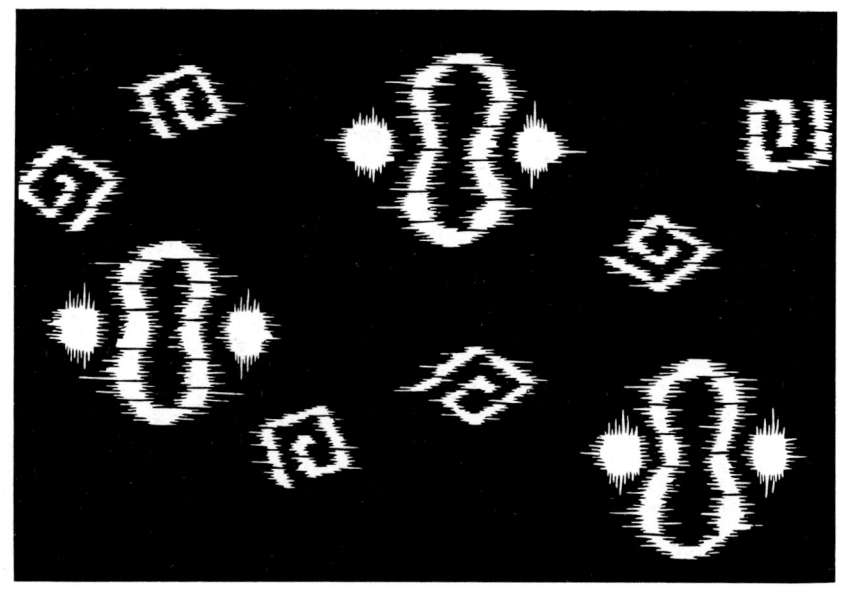

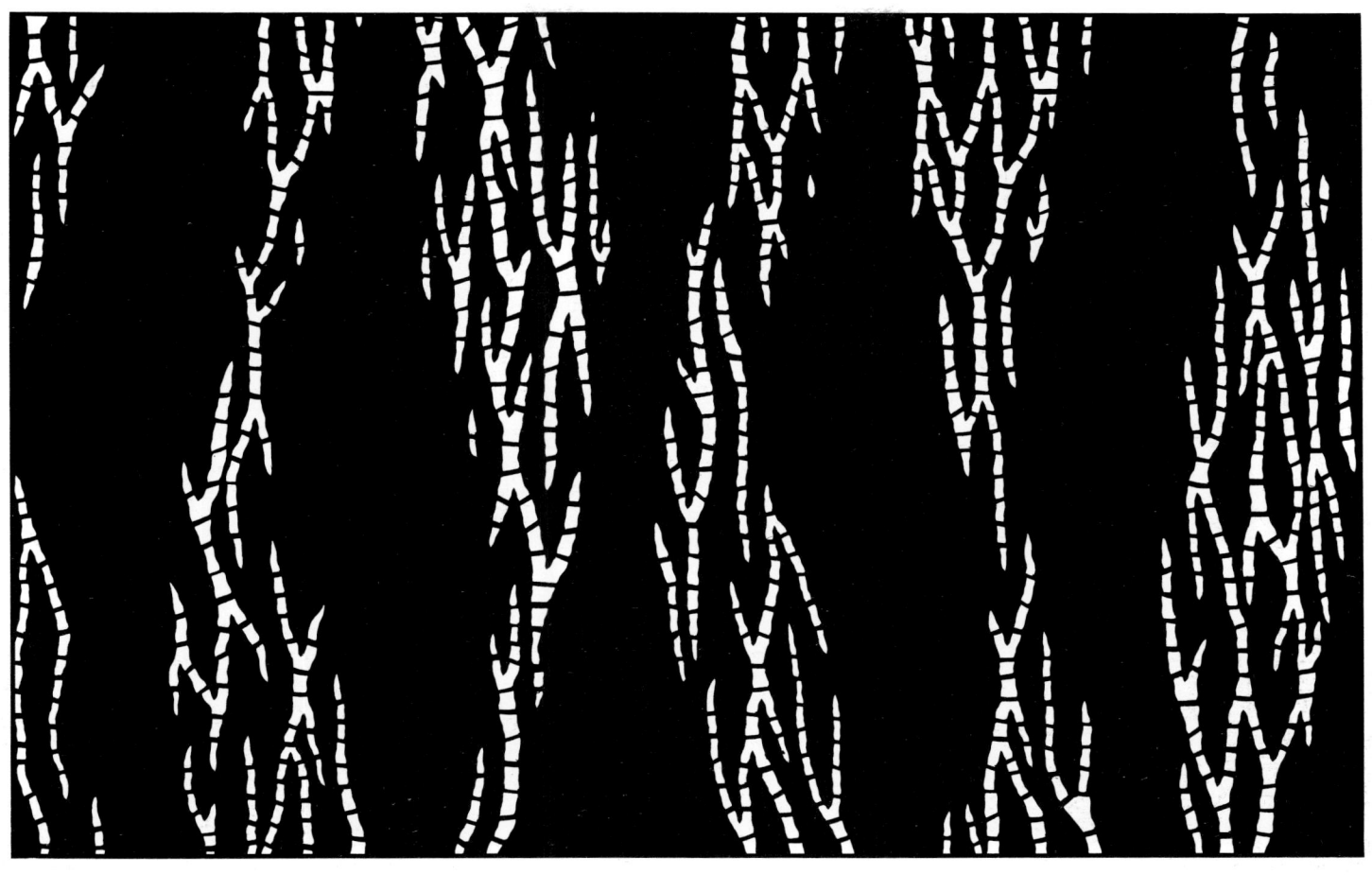

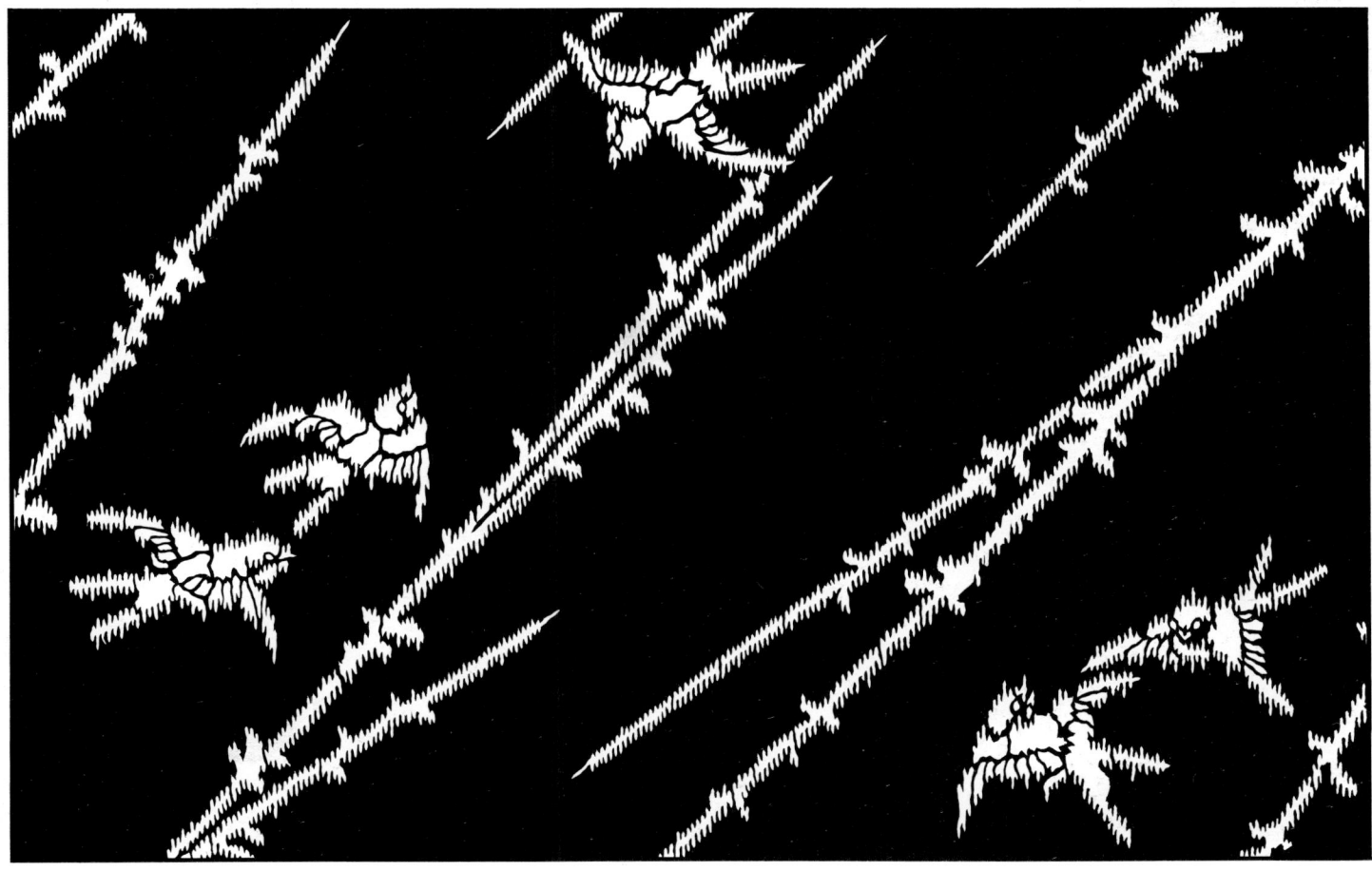

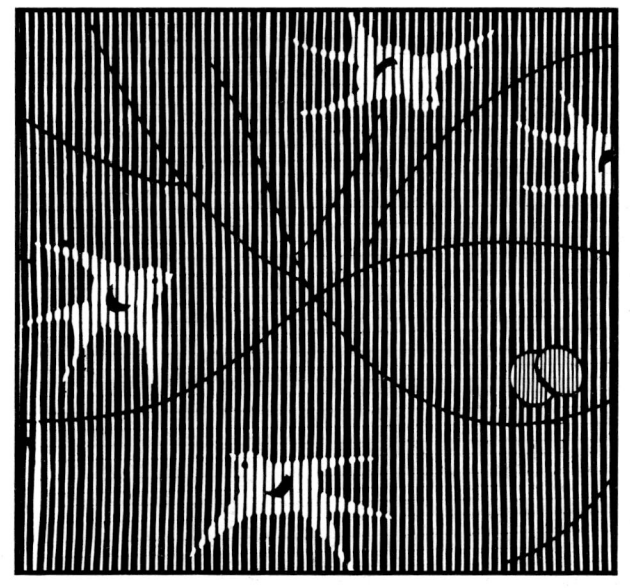

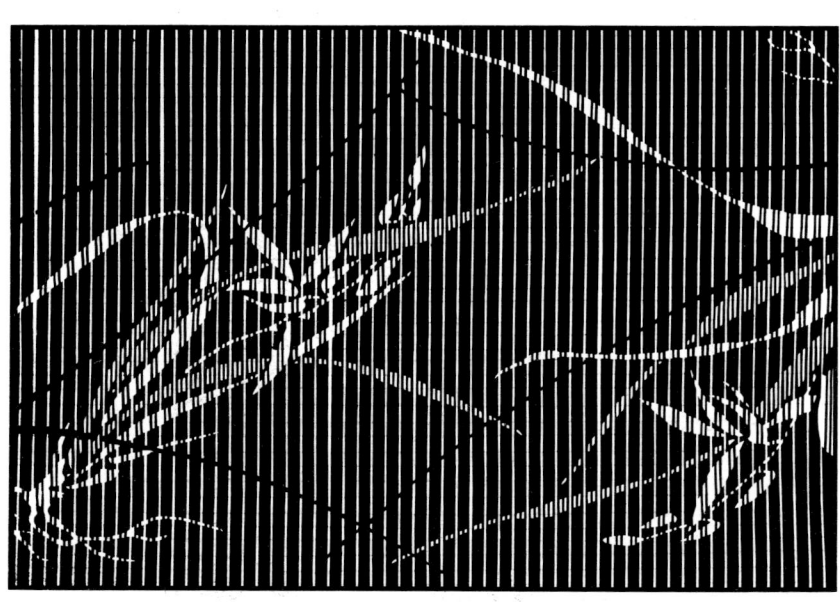

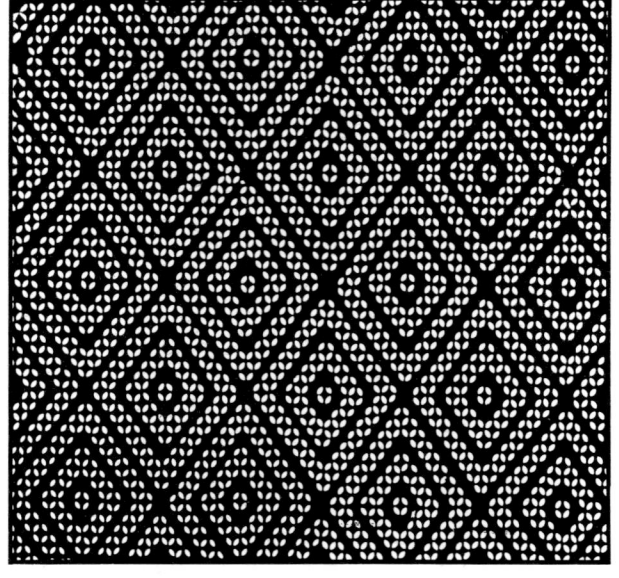

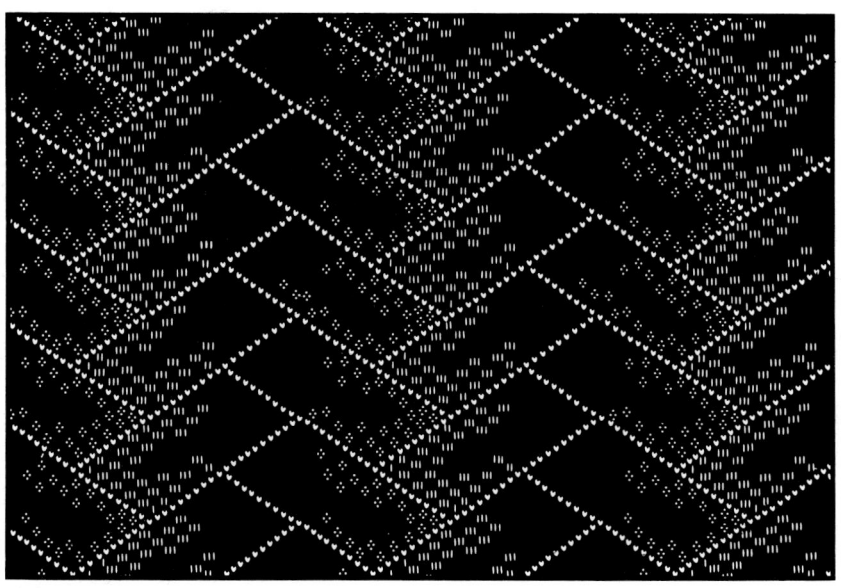
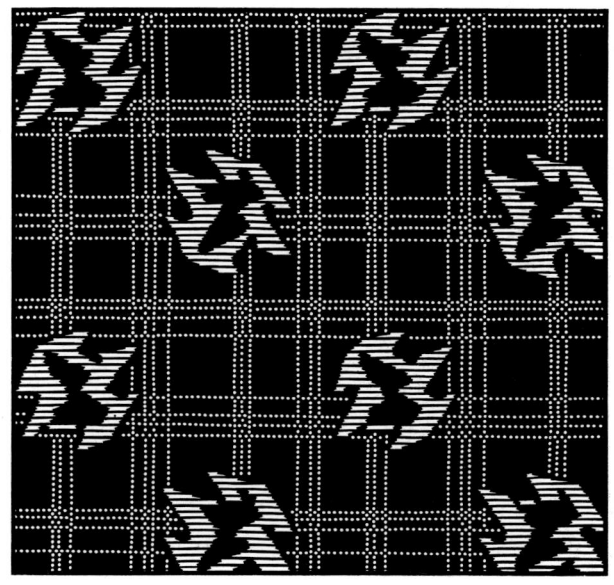
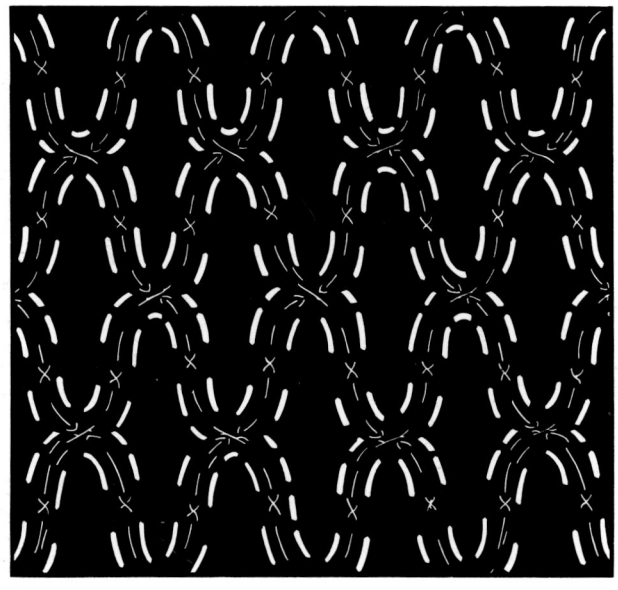
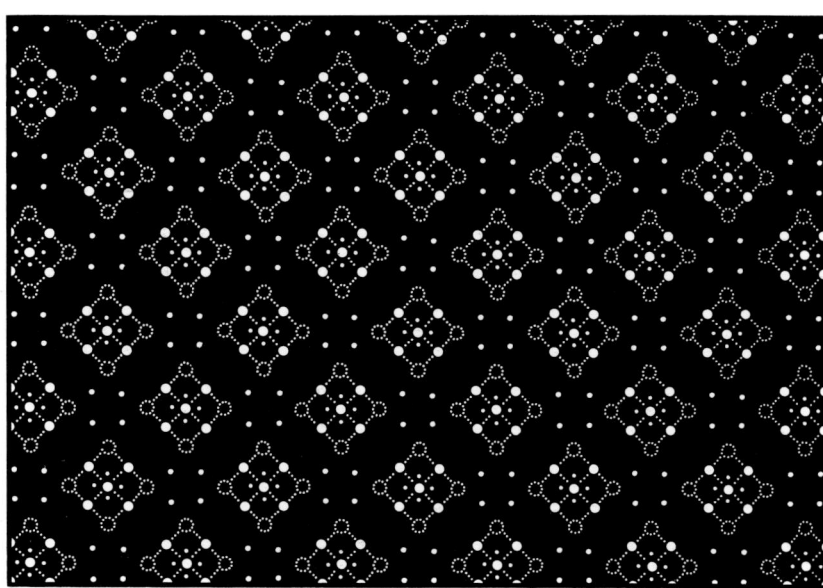

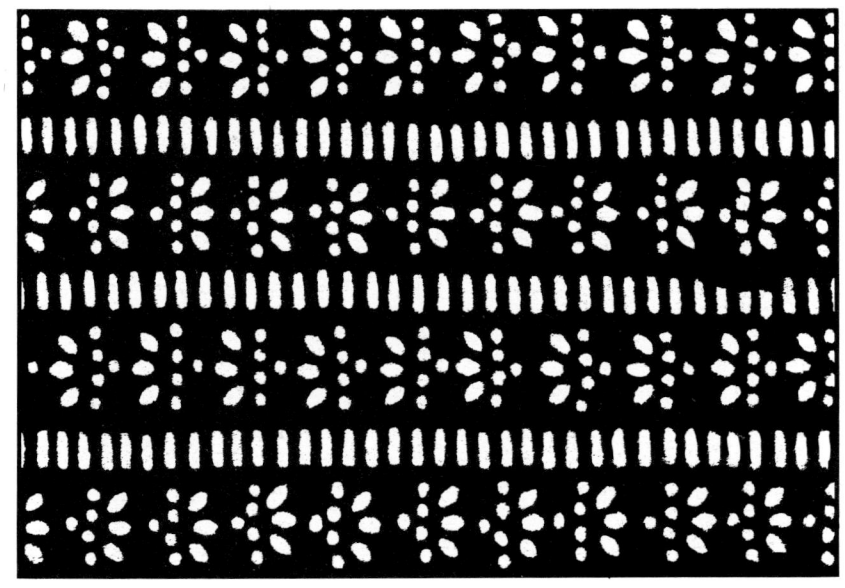

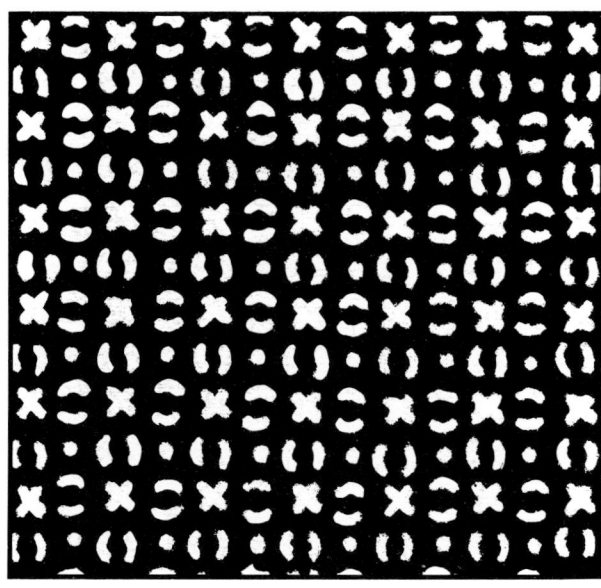

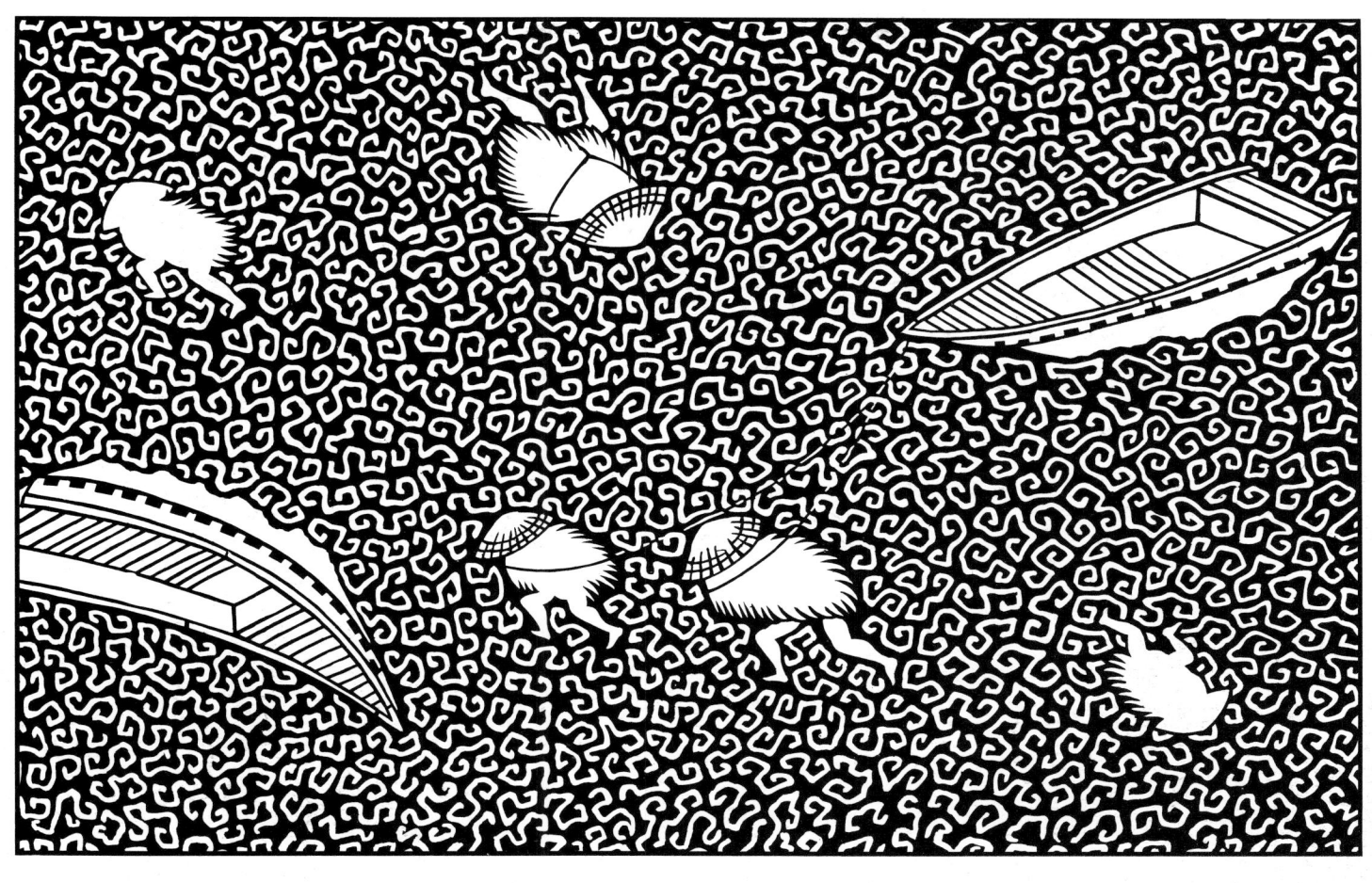

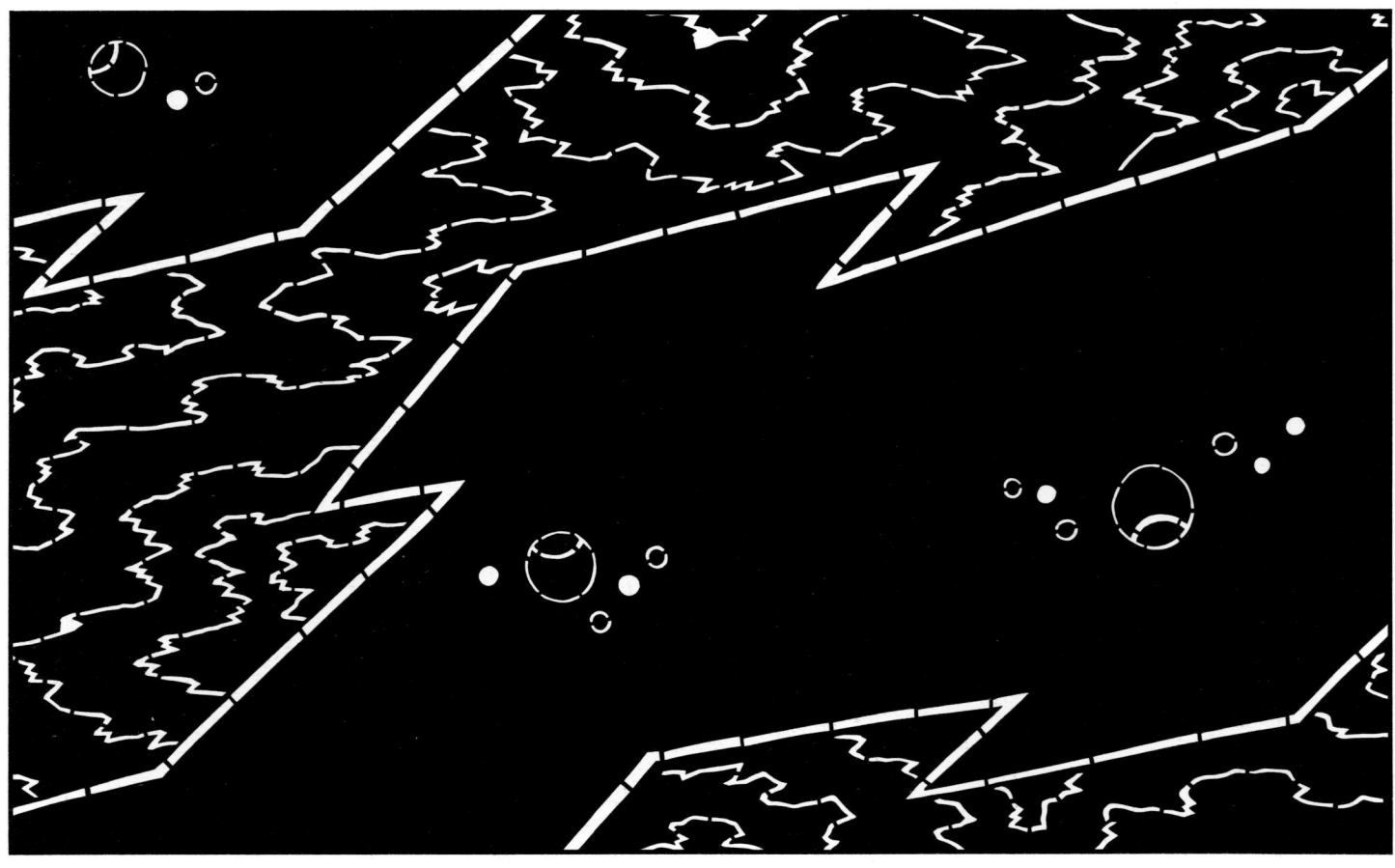

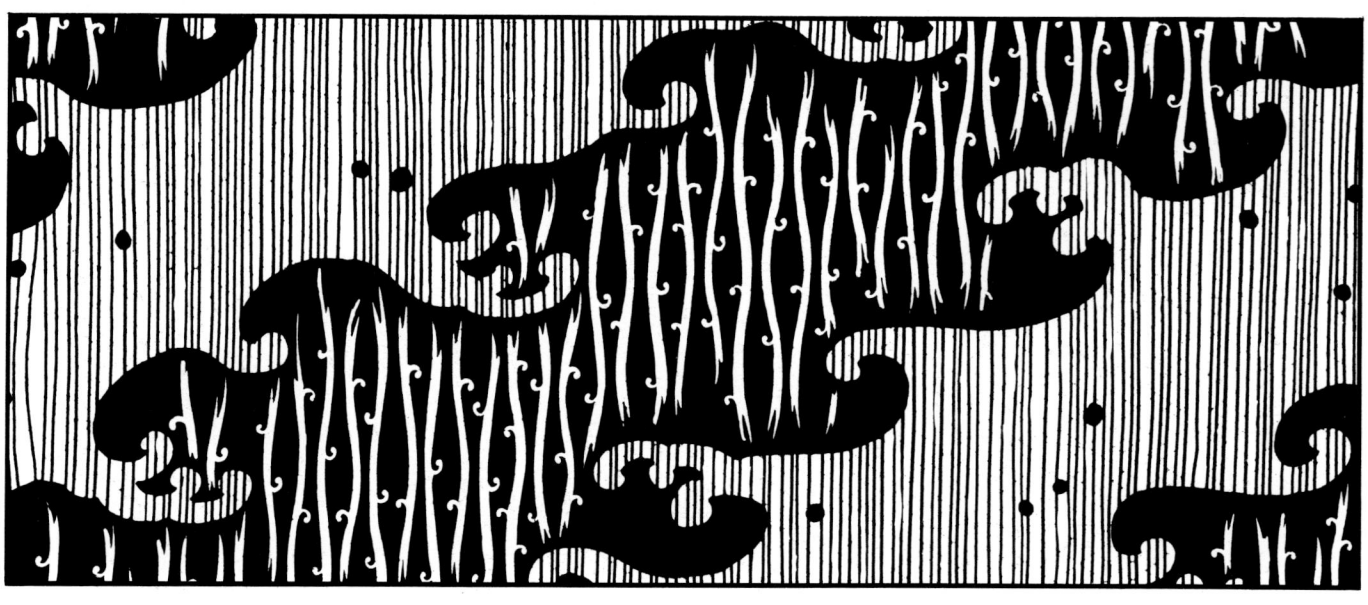

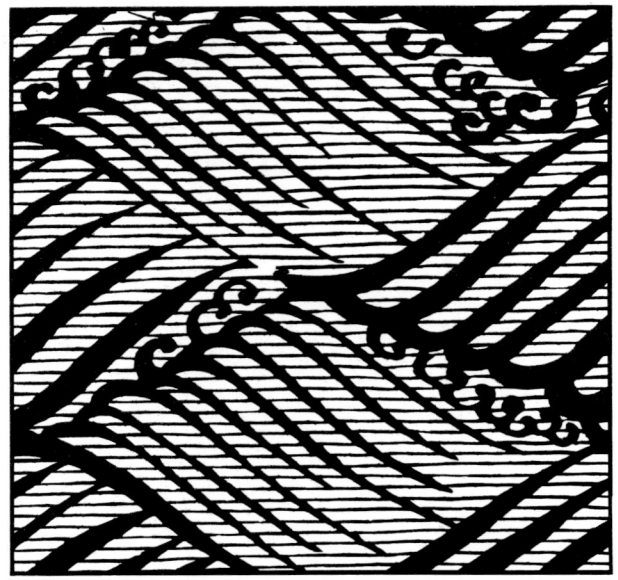

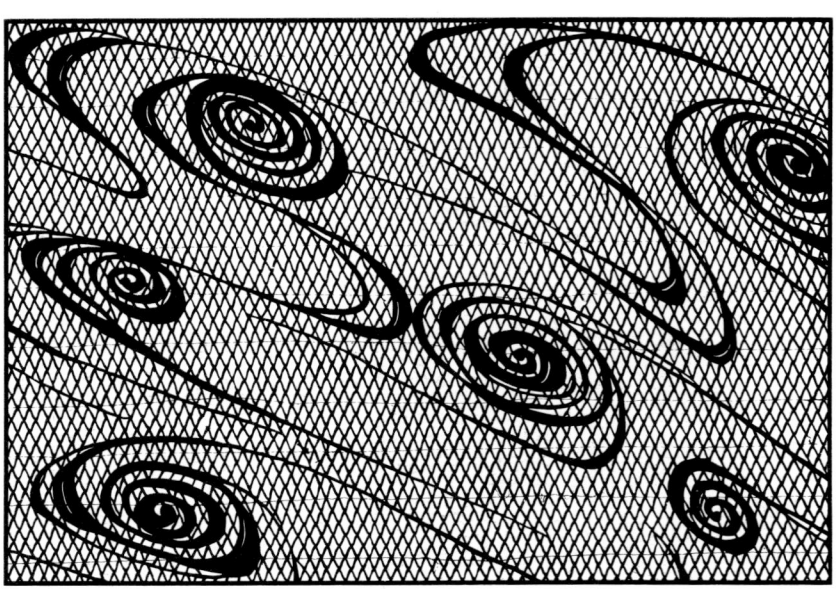

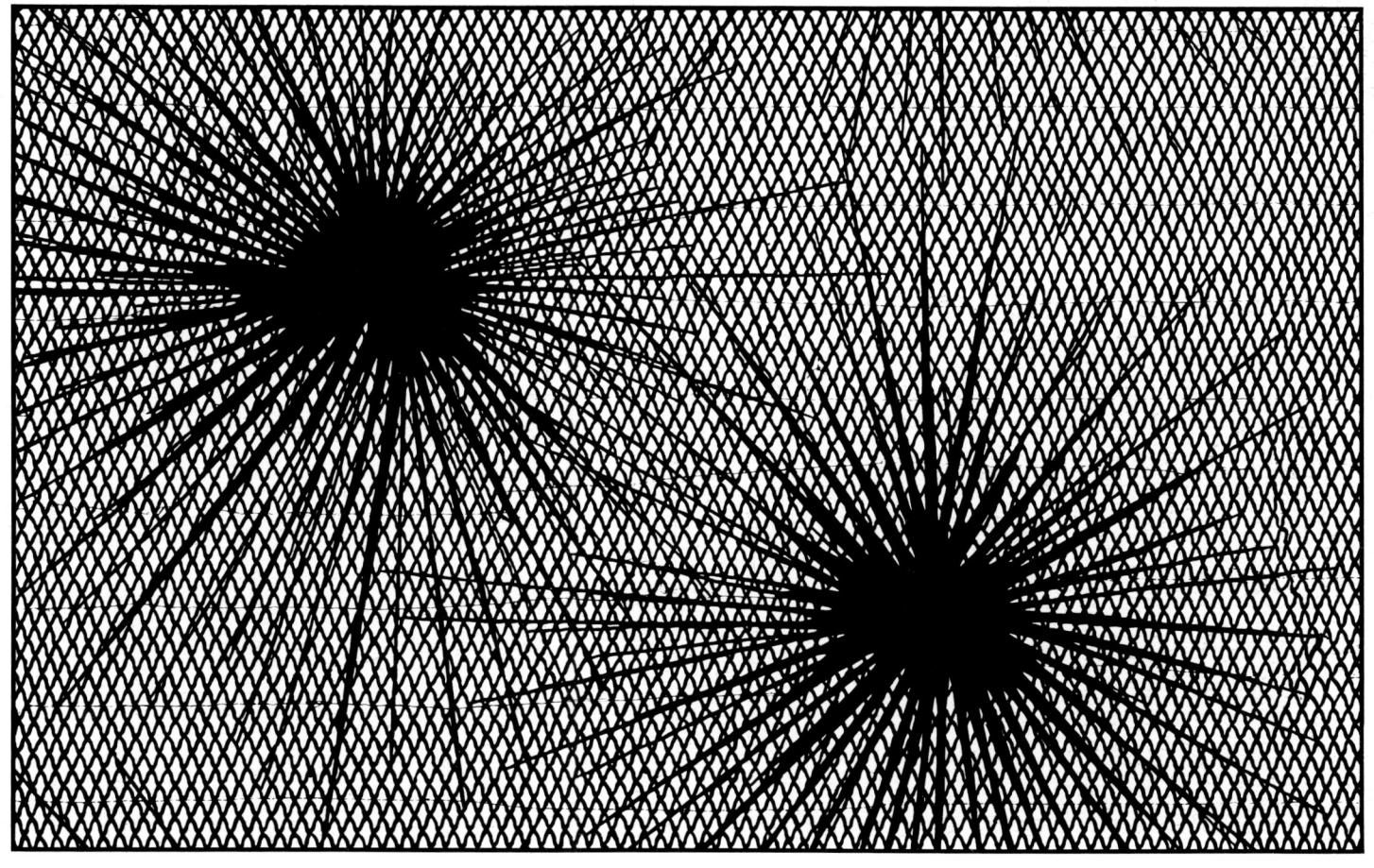

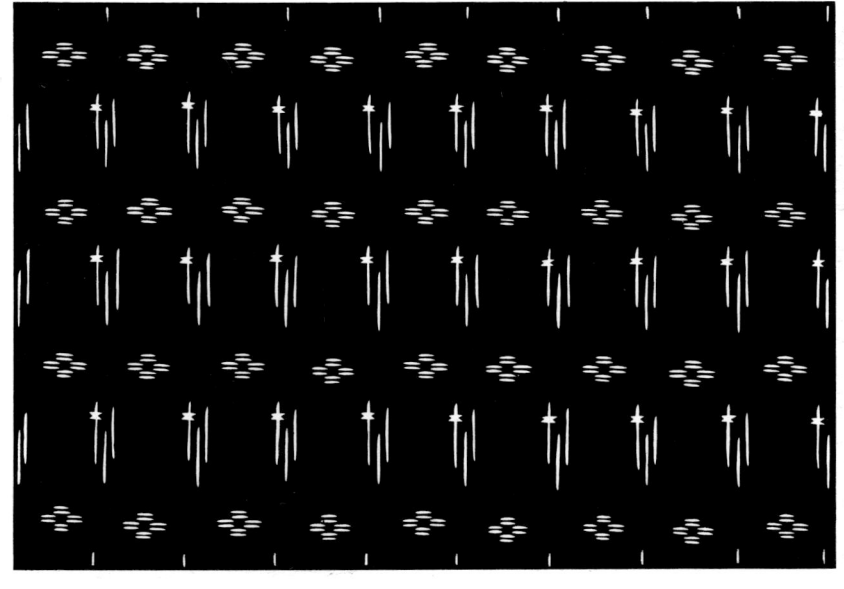

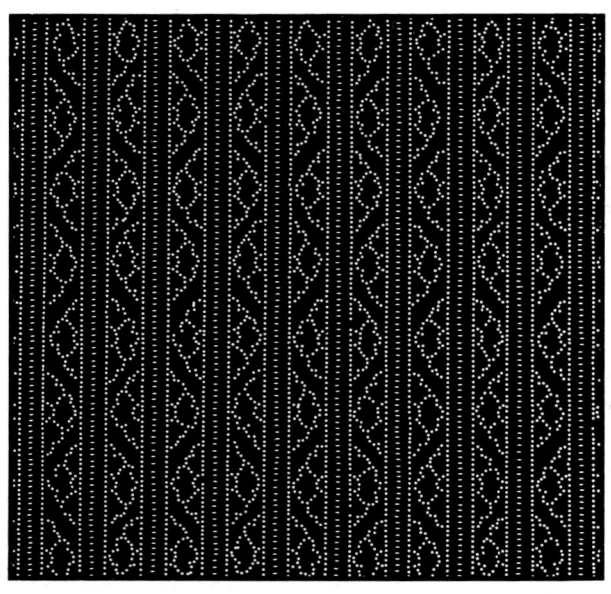
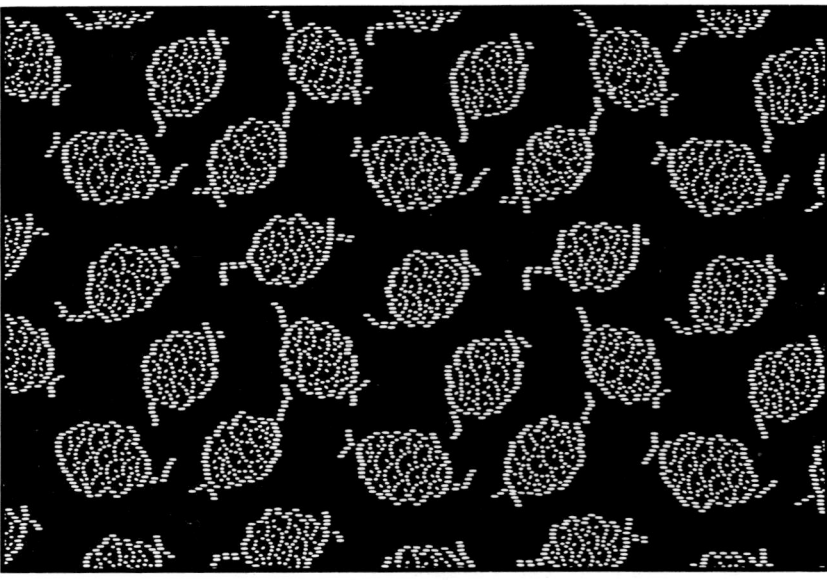
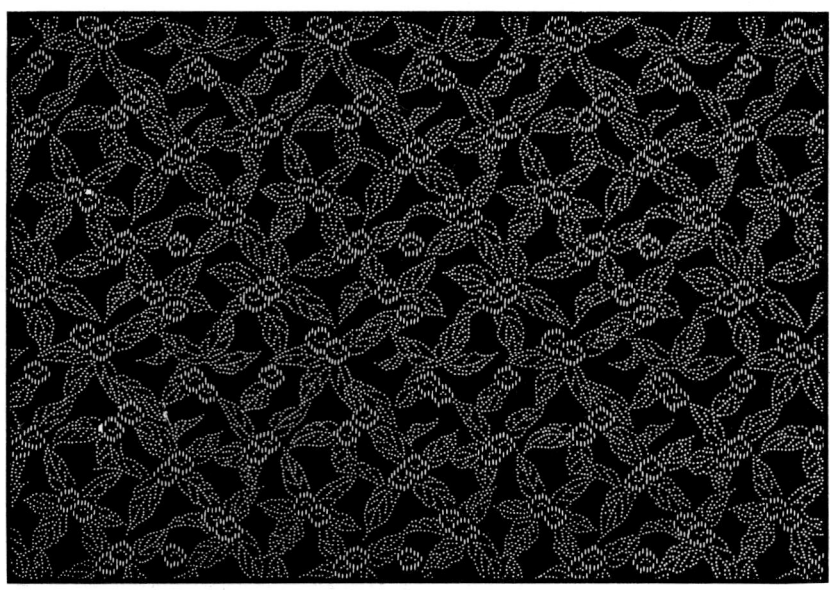
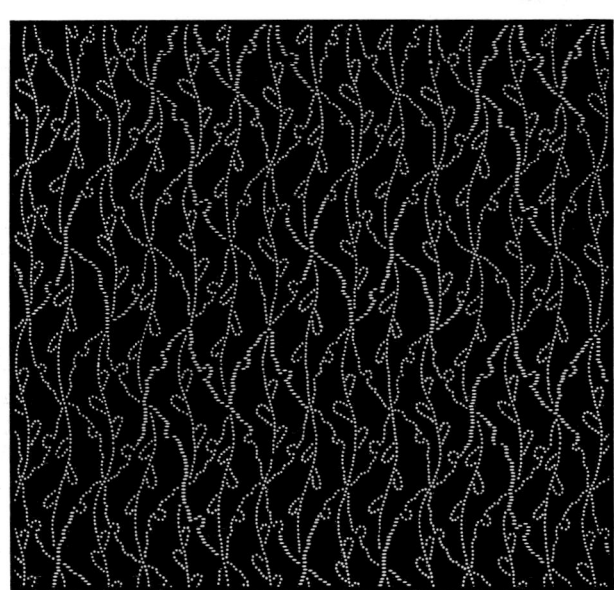

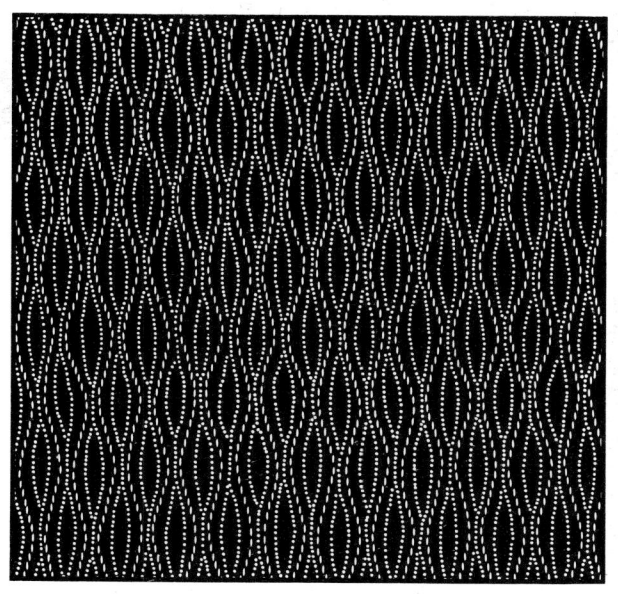
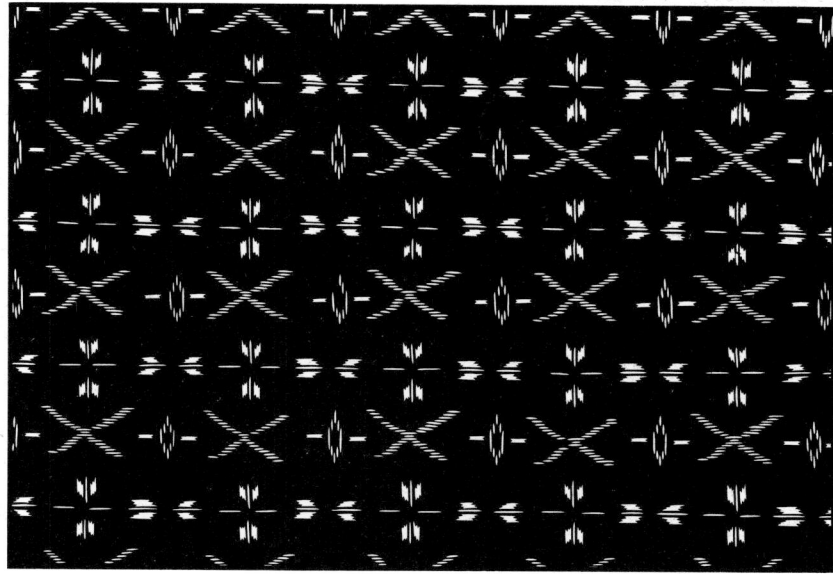
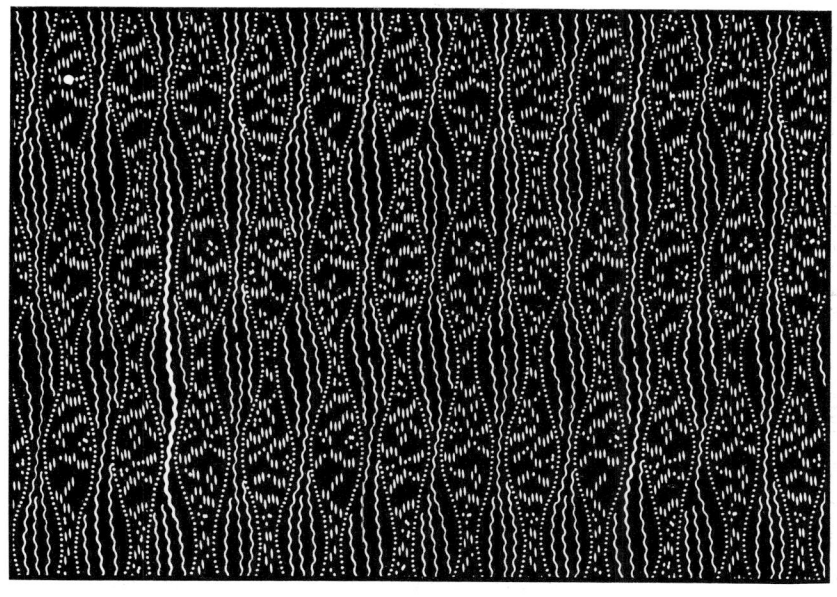
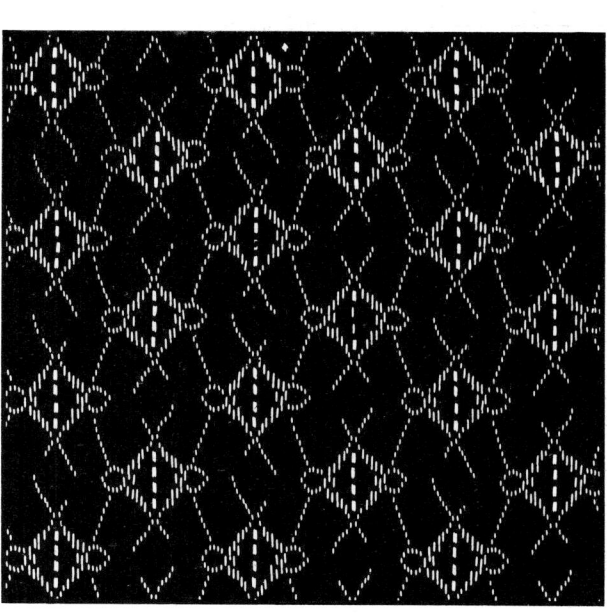

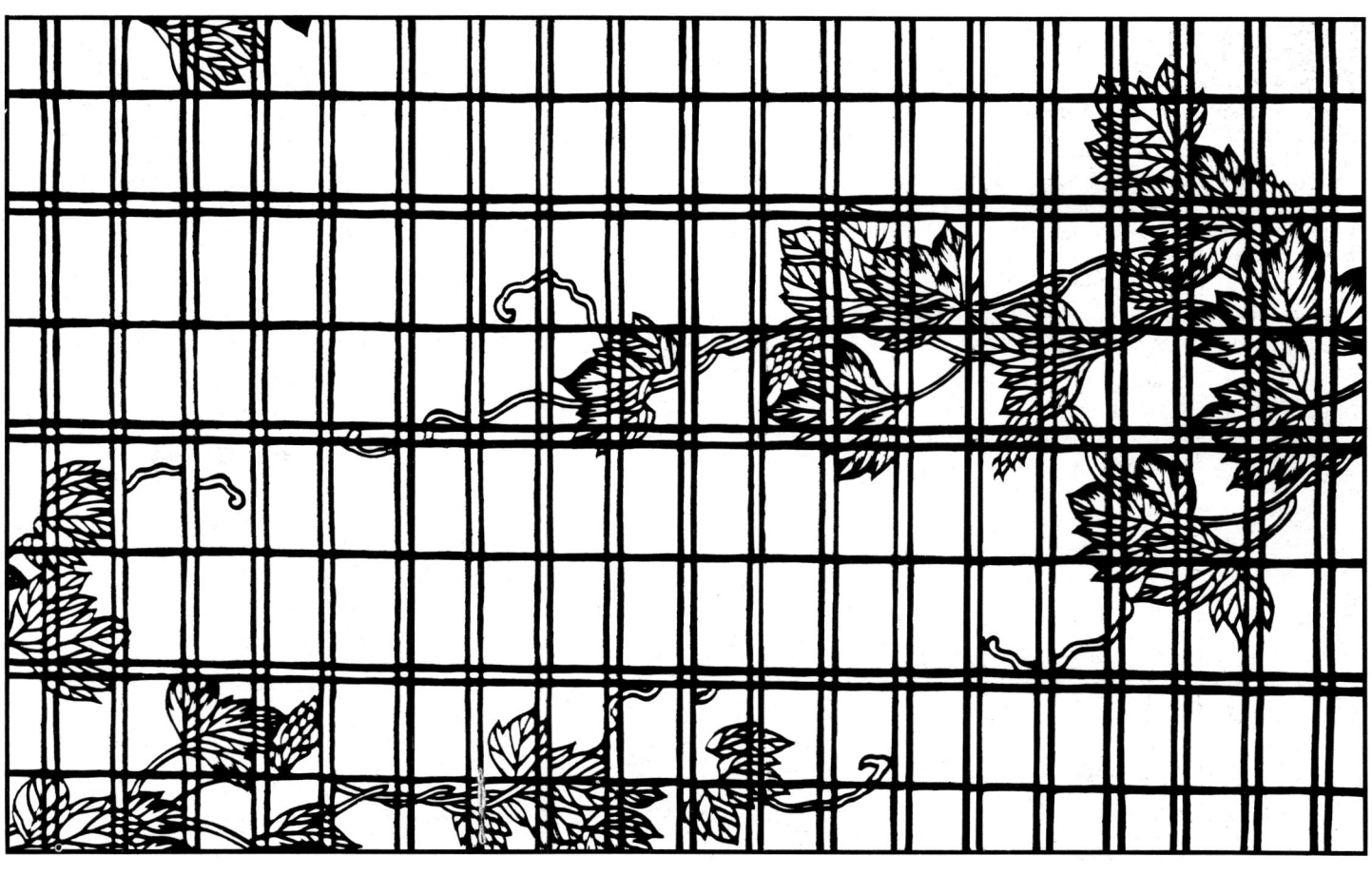

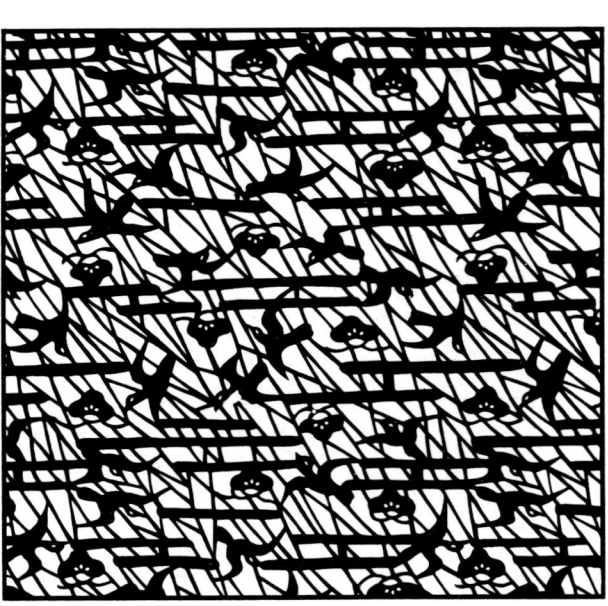

85

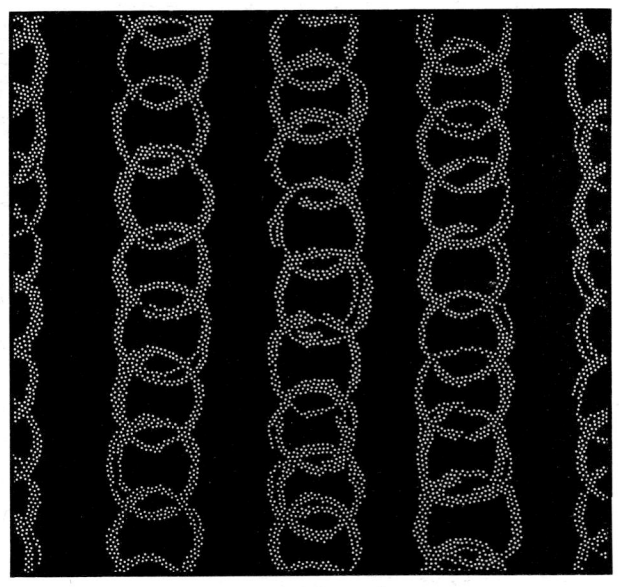
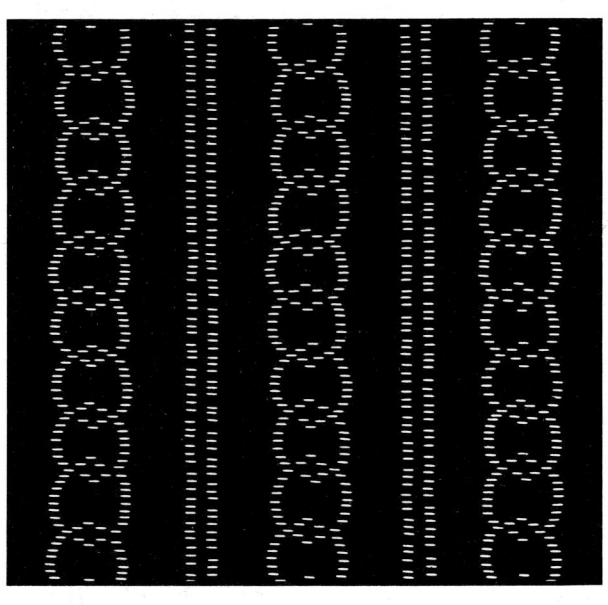

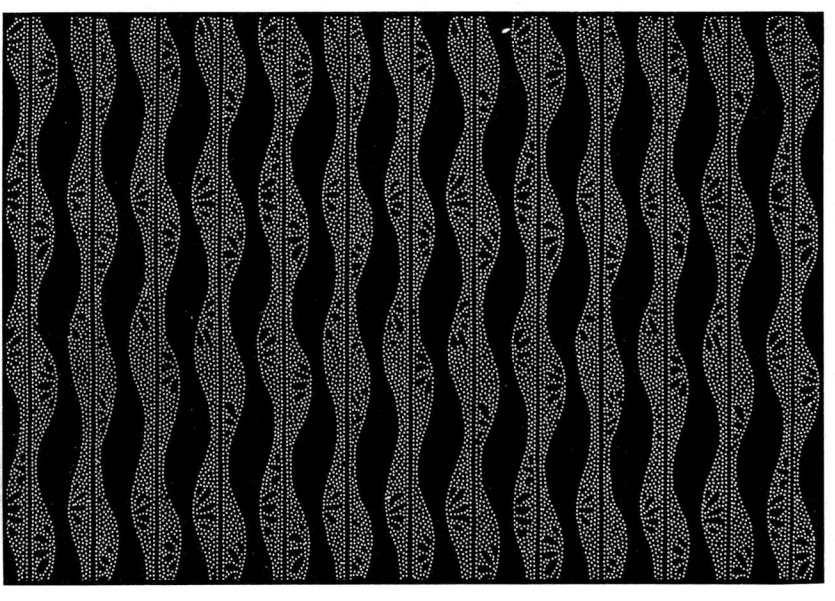

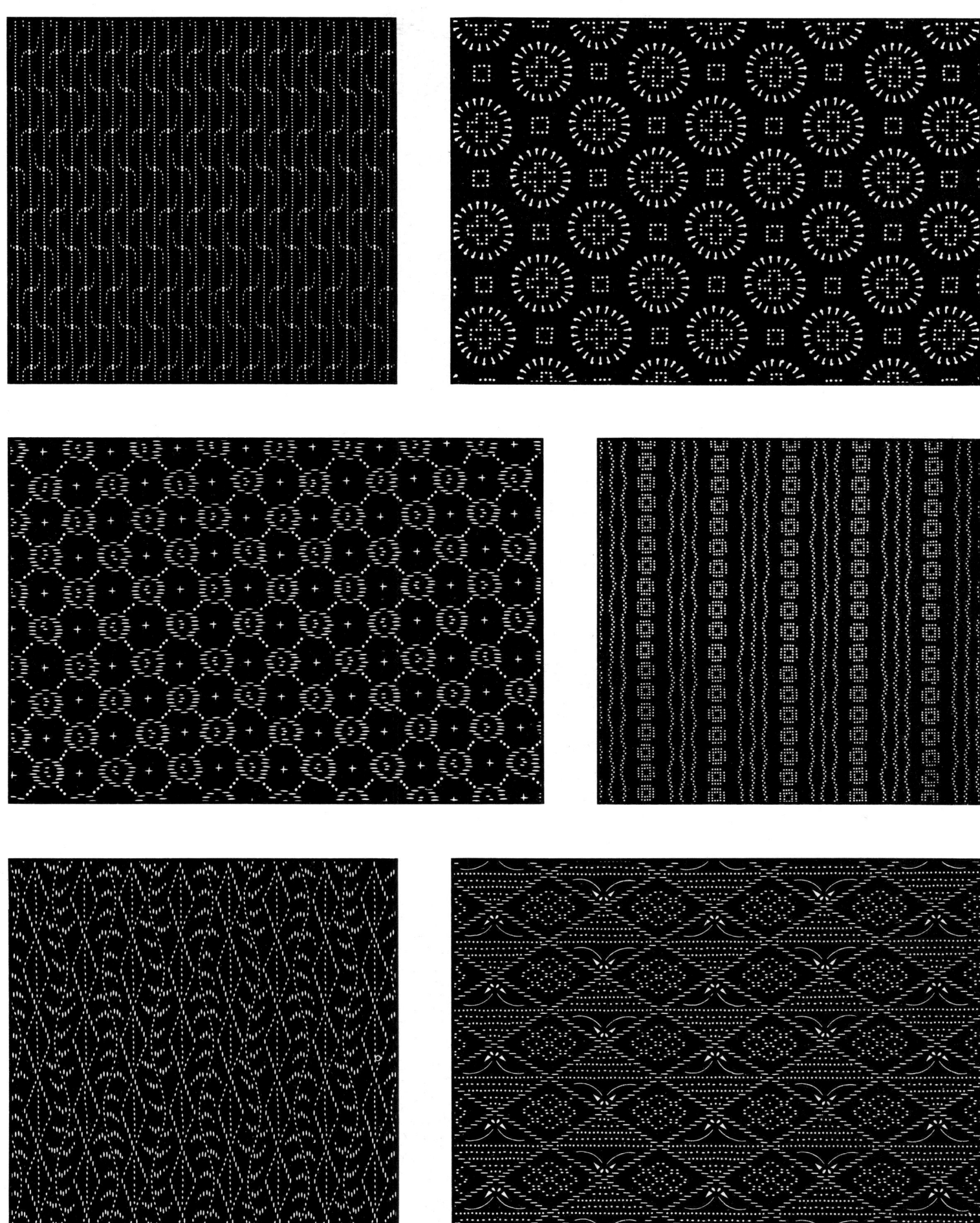

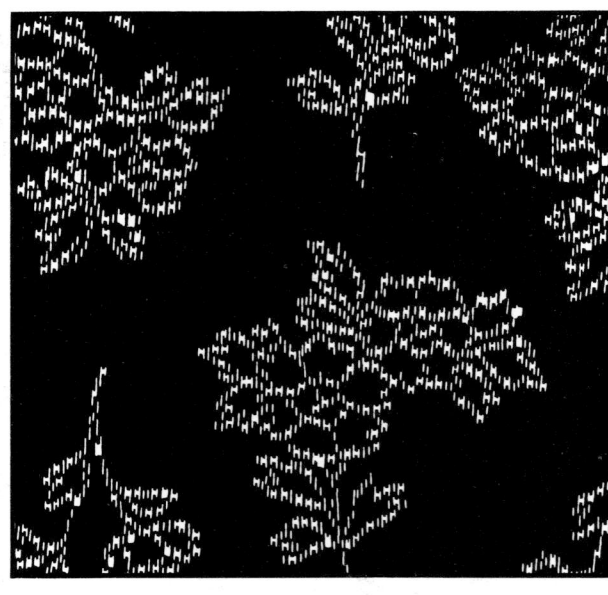

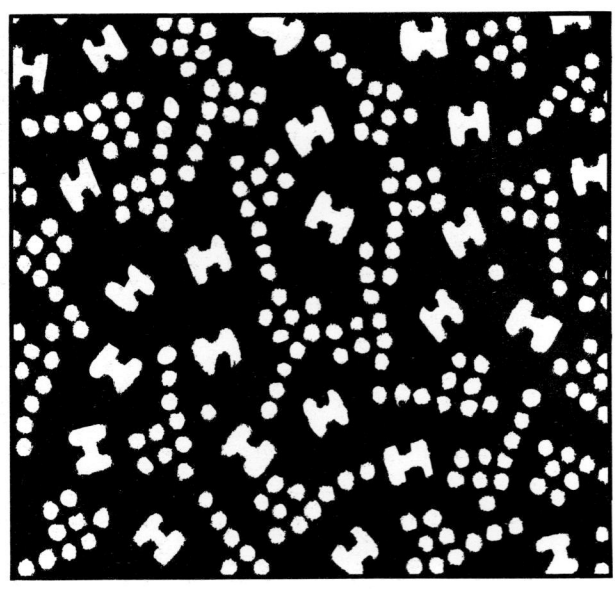

R E F E R E N C E - B O O K S

ISBN 88-7070-046-1

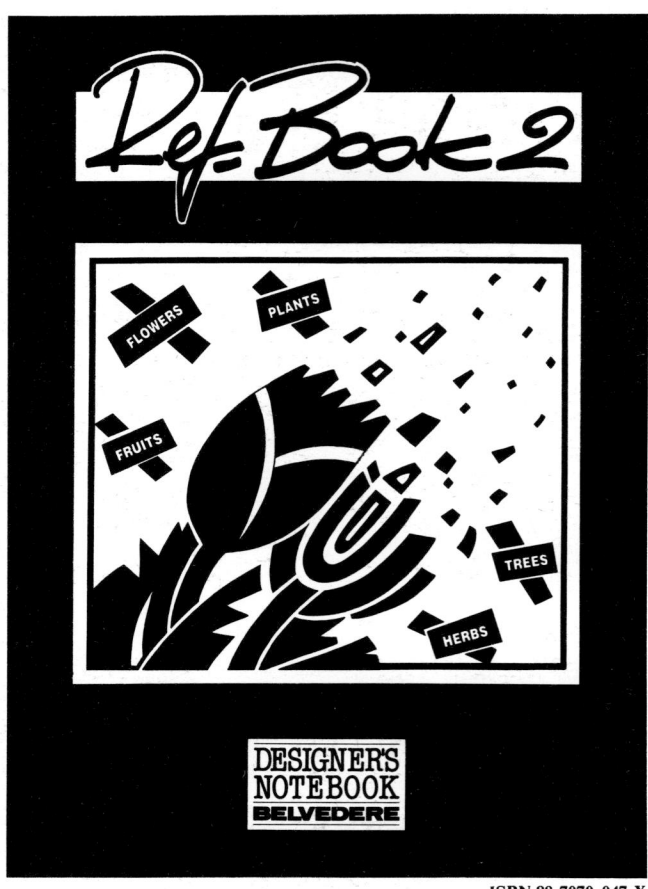

ISBN 88-7070-047-X

IN EACH VOLUME YOU FIND MORE THAN 2500 GRAPHIC MOTIFS, DESIGNS AND IDEAS
A TREASURE FOR THE "EVERY-DAY-GRAPHIC", ADVERTISING & VISUAL COMMUNICATION

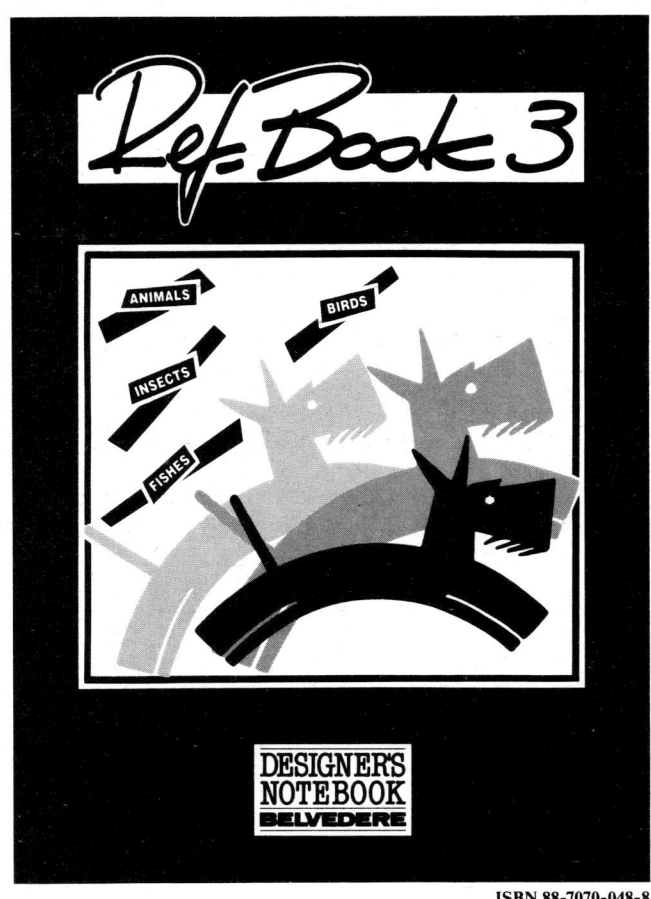

ISBN 88-7070-048-8

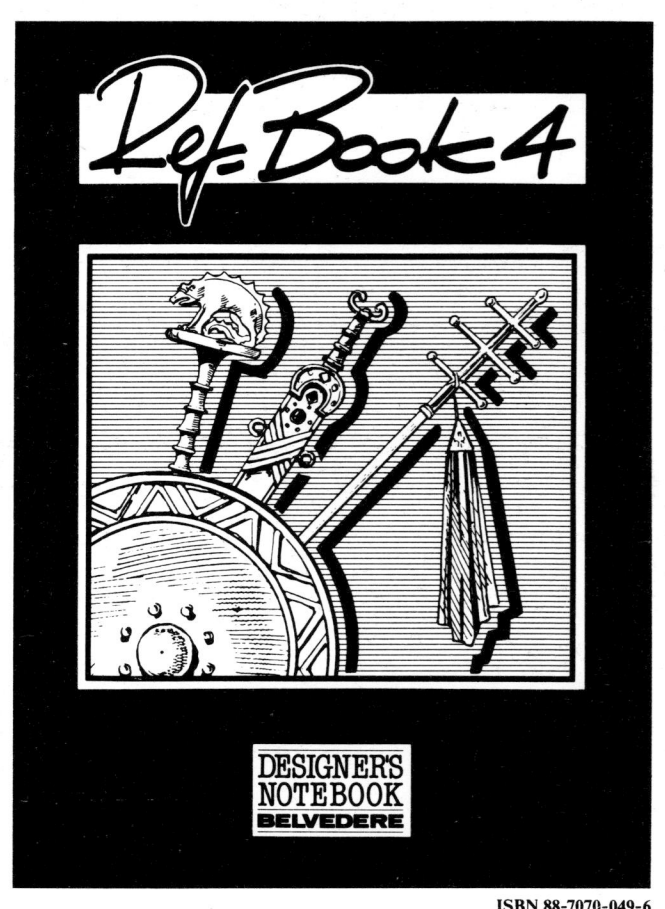

ISBN 88-7070-049-6

BEL
VEDERE

SIMPLY THE BEST

EDITION
BELVEDERE

DESIGN
BOOKS

MADE
IN
ITALY

Design Club

FASHION TEXTILES GRAPHIC DESIGN
PHOTOGRAPHY LAYOUT DECORATION
ADVERTISING STYLING ILLUSTRATION
ORNAMENTS INTERIOR ARCHITECTURE

Good Design Books are hard to find. It takes you time and money to get the right images & references you need for your work. But now you can have it all more easily. Choose simply the best in its field: Belvedere-Design-Books, "made in Italy". Go, and ask for the DESIGN CLUB, and you will get a special offer (free of charge) immediately. It will surprise you.

E' difficile trovare buoni design books. Ci vuole tempo e denaro per avere le immagini e le idee giuste. Ma adesso è tutto più facile. Scegliete solamente il meglio: i Belvedere-Design-Books, "made in·Italy". Chiedete del DESIGN-CLUB e avrete subito & gratis delle offerte eccezionali che vi sorprenderanno.

Gute Designbücher sind schwierig zu finden. Es erfordert oft viel Zeit und Geld, um an die richtigen Ideen & Vorlagen zu gelangen. Doch jetzt ist alles viel leichter. Wählen Sie einfach das Beste: Belvedere-Design-Books, "made in Italy". Erkundigen Sie sich nach dem DESIGN-CLUB und Sie werden unverzüglich & kostenlos ein Spezial-Angebot erhalten, das Sie überraschen wird.

BELVEDERE

DESIGNER'S NOTEBOOK

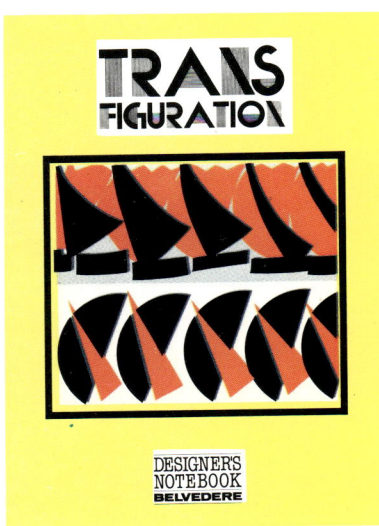

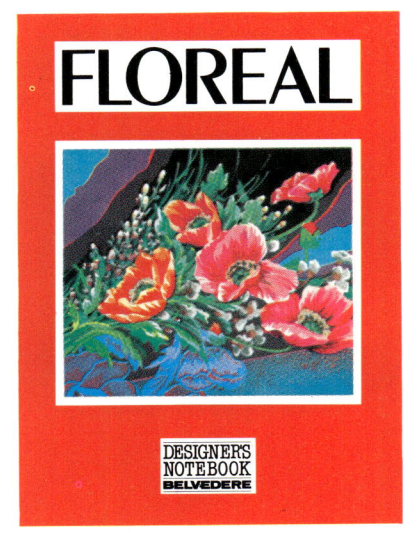

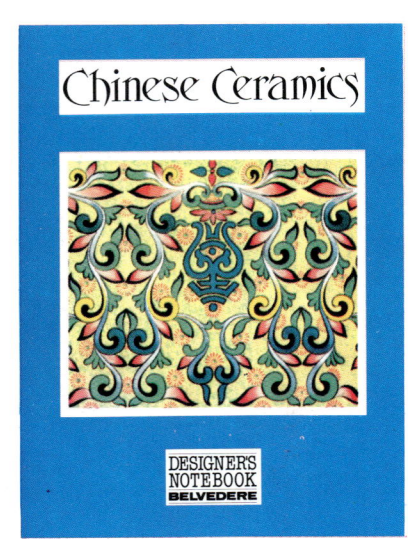

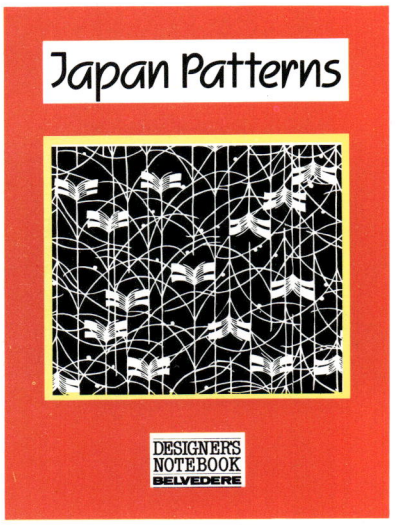

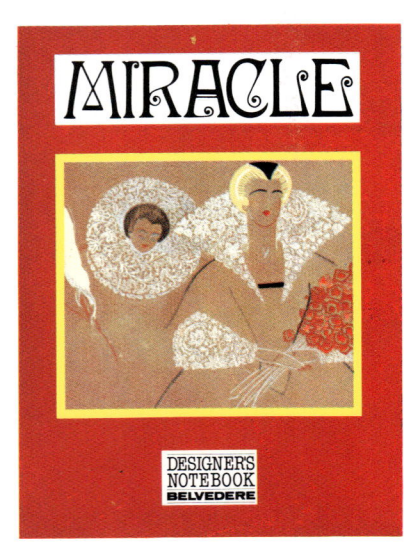

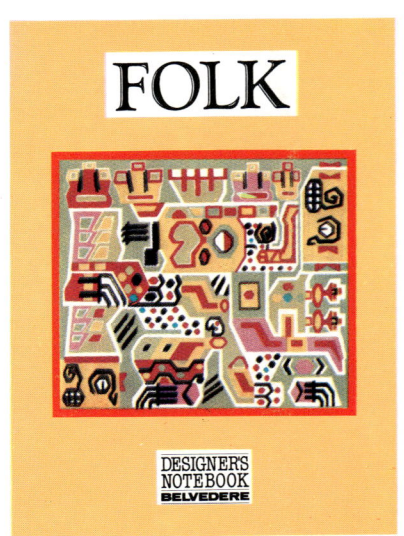

BELVEDERE